Arab Spring and Its Legacies

The essays in this edited volume seek to understand the regional and international ramifications of the wave of protest demonstrations that swept across West Asia and North Africa in the early 2010s, both on the ground and online. Dissatisfaction with political repression and corruption, economic difficulties and inequities, and a desire for freedom and democracy all played a role in the Arab Spring uprisings. It deposed long-standing dictatorships, ushering in a period of insecurity and instability that would have long-term consequences for the region's political economy and international relations. Although the protests have ended, the legacy of that turbulent era will live on, most notably in the acceleration of regional change and transformation.

Arab Spring and Its Legacies

Edited by
MUJIB ALAM and SUJATA ASHWARYA

KNOWLEDGE WORLD

KW Publishers Pvt Ltd
New Delhi

ISBN 978-93-94915-28-2 Hardback
ISBN 978-93-94915-27-5 ebook

Published in India by Kalpana Shukla

KNOWLEDGE WORLD
KW Publishers Pvt Ltd
4676/21, First Floor, Ansari Road
Daryaganj, New Delhi 110002
Phone: +91 11 43528107
Marketing: kw@kwpub.in
Editorial: production@kwpub.in
Website: www.kwpub.in

Printed and Bound in India

CONTENTS

ACKNOWLEDGEMENTS

This book arose from discussions at an online international conference hosted by us at Jamia Millia Islamia (JMI) in New Delhi on January 27-29, 2021, as part of our research project titled "Turmoil and Instability in West Asia (Middle East): Implications for India's Look West Policy," which was funded by the Indian Council of Social Science Research. We are grateful to the heads of the Centre for West Asian Studies and the Academy of International Studies, JMI, who encouraged us to keep working and organise this conference in the midst of a raging pandemic. We would like to express our heartfelt gratitude to Prof Najma Akhtar, Vice-Chancellor of JMI, for her inspiring keynote address, which sparked the idea for this edited volume. We would also like to thank everyone who gave presentations and generously shared their work with us. Finally, we would like to thank Ms Kalpana Shukla, Mr Sushanta Gayen and the editors at KW Publishers for taking the time to consider the book proposal and see it through to publication.

August 2022

Mujib Alam
Sujata Ashwarya

ABOUT THE CONTRIBUTORS

Mujib Alam is a Professor at the Academy of International Studies, Jamia Millia Islamia, New Delhi. His research and teaching areas include contemporary Turkish studies (domestic politics and foreign policy), and West Asian studies (international relations/foreign policies of West Asian countries). His authored/edited books include *The Arab Spring: Ten Years On* (co-edited; Gerlach Press, 2022); *Contemporary West Asia: Perspectives on Change and Continuity* (co-edited; Routledge, 2019), *Turkey in the Post-Cold War Period: The Regional Power Role, 1990-2002* (authored; New Century Pub, 2016), *Perspectives on Turkey's Multi-Regional Role in the 21st Century* (edited; Knowledge World Pub, 2015), *Indo-Turkish Relations: History and Current Dynamics* (edited; New Century Pub, 2012), and *Global Politics of the Iraq Crisis and India's Options* (co-edited; Aakar Pub, 2004).

Sujata Ashwarya is a Professor at the Centre for West Asian [Middle Eastern] Studies in Jamia Millia Islamia, New Delhi. She received her M.Phil. and Ph.D. degrees in West Asian Studies from Jawaharlal Nehru University, New Delhi. Her research interests include West Asian Politics and International Relations, political economy of energy, and India-West Asia relations. She has over forty research articles published and has written/edited six books, including, *The Arab Spring: Ten Years On* (co-edited; Gerlach Press, 2022) and *Israel's Mediterranean Gas: Domestic Governance, Economic Impact, and Strategic Implications* (Routledge, 2019). She has published in several top peer reviewed journals such as, *Global Discourse, Contemporary Review of the Middle East, Strategic Analysis, India Quarterly, Asian Journal of Middle Eastern and Islamic Studies, Indian Foreign Affairs Journal,* and *Perceptions: Journal of International Affairs.*

Kingshuk Chatterjee is a Professor at the Department of History, Calcutta University, and is associated with the Institute of Foreign Policy Studies, Kolkata. He has previously served as a founding professor in the Department of History, School of Humanities and Social Sciences at Shiv Nadar University and as a Fulbright Scholar-in-Residence at the United States Naval Academy in Annapolis, Maryland. Chatterjee's area of expertise is in West Asian politics and political Islam. He is the author of *Ali Shari'ati and the Shaping of Political Islam in Iran* and *A Split in the Middle: the Making of the Political Centre in Iran (1987-2004)*. Chatterjee writes and speaks extensively on Indian politics and foreign policy in academic journals, newspapers and electronic media.

Priyamvada Ankush Sawant is an Associate Professor of History at the HR College of Commerce and Economics, University of Mumbai. She has completed her PhD in International Relations from Jawaharlal Nehru University, New Delhi. Dr Sawant has done extensive archival research in India and the United Kingdom and presented research papers in various academic conferences in India and abroad. She is involved in the audio-visual media.

Mohmad Saleem Sheikh is a research scholar at the Centre for West Asian Studies, Jamia Millia Islamia, New Delhi. He completed MPhil in West Asian Studies from Jamia Millia and MA in Politics and International Relations from Pondicherry University. His research interests include sectarianism and regional security in west Asia. He has published book chapters and presented papers at several national and international conferences.

Özden Zeynep Oktav is a Professor at the Department of International Relations in Istanbul Mediniyat University (IMU), Turkey. Her areas of expertise include Middle Eastern politics and Turkish foreign policy. She was a member of the teaching faculty at Yildiz Technical University in Istanbul before joining IMU in 2016. Her publications include *Violent Non-state Actors and the Syrian Civil War* (co-edited, 2018) and *Turkey in the 21st Century Quest for a New Turkish Foreign Policy* (edited, 2011).

Sukalpa Chakrabarti is an Associate Professor (International Relations & Public Policy) & Deputy Director at the Symbiosis School of International Studies, Symbiosis International Deemed University. Dr Chakrabarti has been teaching across specialisations in International Relations (with a focus on Global Political Economy, Geopolitical Risks and International Conflict and Negotiations) and Politics & Public Policy for over two decades. Her main areas of study have been Asian geopolitics, African trade and economy, and Indian public policy and diplomacy. She has written books and chapters for edited books in foreign publications, as well as articles for prestigious journals.

Abu Zafar is a New Delhi-based researcher and journalist. Currently, he is a doctoral student at the Centre for West Asian Studies, Jamia Millia Islamia. His topic of doctoral research is "China's West Asia Policy: A Case Study of the Media Discourse on the Civil War in Syria." He has received his MPhil degree in Chinese Studies from the Department of East Asian Studies, University of Delhi. He received a Huayu Enrichment Scholarship to study Mandarin for six months in Taiwan, as well as an Inclusive Media Fellowship 2011 from the Centre for the Study of Developing Societies in New Delhi. A prolific writer, he has published in *Daily Sabah*, *Quartz India*, *IndiaTomorrow.net* and the prestigious *New York Times*.

Vrushal T. Ghoble is an Assistant Professor at the Centre for West Asian Studies, School of International Studies, Jawaharlal Nehru University, New Delhi. He has published books and articles in journals like *Strategic Analysis*, *International Studies*, *Asian Journal of Middle Eastern and Islamic Studies* and contributed chapters to edited volumes. His research interests include regional geopolitics and geoeconomics, as well as energy dynamics. He has presented papers on the region in various national and international conferences. Dr. Ghoble was a *visitor* to Brussels, Belgium under the European Union Visitors Programme in 2019.

Umar Farooq Wani is a research scholar at the Centre for West Asian Studies, Jamia Millia Islamia, New Delhi. Currently, he is working on his PhD thesis titled "Mizrahi Jews and the Politics in Israel post-1977". Previously, he worked on his MPhil dissertation on "Religion and State Legitimacy in Saudi Arabia". His research interests include sectarian conflicts in West Asia, political Islam, and Israeli Mizrahi Jews.

Priya Singh is an Associate Director at Asia in Global Affairs, Kolkata, India. She was a Fellow at the Maulana Abul Kalam Azad Institute of Asian Studies in Kolkata, an autonomous institute of the Government of India's Ministry of Culture. She worked as a researcher for the Rosa Luxemburg Stiftung's 'Asian Connectivity' project. (2017-2018). Her research focuses on nationalism/post-nationalism, identity, state formation, ethnicity, gender, migration, marginalization, indigenous and minority communities, linkages, and disconnections in West Asia, but also in a broader Asian context. She is currently working as a researcher for the Rosa Luxemburg Stiftung on a 'Handbook of Keywords on Migration and Refugee Studies.' Her research has appeared in peer-reviewed journals and as book chapters.

Md. Aftab Ahmad is an Assistant Professor at India-Arab Cultural Centre, Jamia Millia Islamia, New Delhi. His research interests include Arab-Islamic Culture, Arabic Language and Arab Literature, and Contemporary Arab Literature. He has published many research papers (both in Arabic and English) in national and international journals and presented papers in several seminars/conferences in India and abroad. Before joining Jamia, Dr Ahmad worked with the United Nations High Commissioner for Refugees and All India Radio for more than five years. He has also worked with the National Technical Research Organization, Government of India as an Arabic Linguist.

Adil Rasheed works as a Research Fellow and the Counter Terrorism Department Coordinator at the Manohar Parrikar Institute for Defence Studies and Analyses, New Delhi. Prior to joining IDSA in 2016, he worked as researcher at the United Services Institution of India as Senior Research Fellow from 2014 to 2016 and UAE-based think tank The Emirates Centre for Strategic Studies and Research as researcher between 2006 and 2014. He has authored two books: *Countering the Radical Narrative* (Knowledge World, 2020) and *ISIS: Race to Armageddon* (Vij Books, 2015). Among his other publications are a co-edited book titled *Indian Ocean Region: Emerging Strategic Cooperation, Competition and Conflict Scenarios* (USI, 2015) and a highly influential research paper titled 'Countering the Threat of Radicalization: Theories, Programme and Challenges' published in the *Journal of Defence Studies* (April-May 2016).

INTRODUCTION

Mujib Alam and Sujata Ashwarya

Beginning in mid-December 2010, the 'Middle East', or more precisely the geographically defined region of West Asia and North Africa (WANA), witnessed a series of citizen protests and face-offs against their political authorities in several countries, dubbed variously as the 'Arabellion', 'Arab Uprisings', 'Arab Awakening' and 'Arab Spring'.[1] These uprisings sparked long-lasting changes throughout WANA, fundamentally altering the region's political and socioeconomic composition. A decade after the start of these uprisings, scholars and academics from the region and beyond continue to analyse a wide variety of aspects of the uprisings, as well as their implications and the causal factors that influenced various parts of the region. The present volume is also an attempt to assess and discern protesters' expectations following the Arab Spring, as well as the realities that have emerged a decade later.

The self-immolation of a poor vegetable vendor named Mohamed Bouazizi in Sidi Bouzid, a small town far from the Tunisian capital, sparked widespread protests not only in Tunis (Tunisia's capital) and many parts of the country, but also in other areas of the WANA region. Analysts and regional experts identified a number of economic, political and social factors that contributed to the Arab uprisings, though their impact on different Arab countries was not always comparable.[2] The Jasmine Revolution protests in Tunisia began in response to the crushing economic despair faced by a large section of the population, rampant corruption in the government from local authorities to higher-ups, repression by police and general dissatisfaction with the regime. As a result, President Zein al-Abedin Ben Ali was compelled to quit the nation by the combined pressure of the Tunisian people. The call for regime change and the desire for democracy had a domino effect on Egypt and Yemen. Similar protests erupted in other WANA nations, prompting commentators in the

West and the region to enthusiastically term the situation the "Arab Spring." Despite the removal of old guards in Egypt, Yemen and Libya, in addition to Tunisia, initial optimism for democratic transition waned, prompting many to refer to the events as "Arab Winter."

Looking back more than a decade since the first uprisings of the 2010s, we can say that these popular movements influenced the political, social and economic lives of people in various countries throughout the region. At the same time, these uprisings resulted in long-term wars, more political fighting between different groups, violence, repression and a large number of people fleeing their homes in many of the region's countries. There are numerous issues, dimensions and parameters to consider when assessing the legacies of the Arab uprisings. It is neither possible nor desirable to present everything related to or resulting from the Arab Spring in a single book. Thus, certain dimensions and a few select countries have been assessed in this volume.

The subject of democracy and democratisation in the Arab world is, thus, a significant legacy of the Arab Spring. Although several issues contributed to the uprisings, the key motivators were basic human rights, dignity and corruption. Long-serving authoritarian regimes in Tunisia, Egypt, Libya and Yemen were deposed by the people's ambitions to realise these goals. In the earliest years of the upheavals, these and many other WANA nations saw a democratic upsurge. The protests that took place in the region, however, were not devoid of non-democratic elements as well, such as political Islam and sectarianism. After Hosni Mubarak was overthrown in Egypt, an elected democratic administration led by Mohammad Morsi came to power. However, the Muslim Brotherhood-affiliated government was quickly overthrown, and the military-turned-civilian rulers reclaimed control.

Even after a decade of democratic uprisings, no country, with the exception of Tunisia to some extent, has made long-term democratic progress. Even in Tunisia, recent events show a negative trend away from democratisation and democratic consolidation. Civil wars in Libya, Syria and Yemen have kept these countries from achieving democracy and popular sovereignty. Some Arab countries, particularly the energy-rich Gulf monarchies, have subverted their peoples' democratic aspirations through repression or by instituting cosmetic reforms within their borders. However, there have been some encouraging developments in one key parameter. Women's representation in many countries' political processes has improved noticeably, which can be considered an improvement in women's empowerment.[3]

Another major underlying factor in the Arab uprisings, as well as its persistence over the last decade or so, has been the people's economic conditions. Many people in the Arab world were and continue to struggle financially because of high unemployment, poverty, backwardness, together with corruption by political elite. There has been no significant improvement in the standard of living in any Arab country affected by the uprisings. Rather, in civil war-torn countries such as Syria, Yemen and Libya, the standard of living has plummeted. Moreover, the falling oil prices have had a negative impact particularly on the rentier states and their citizens. One of the primary causes of the Arab world's unrest was the high rate of youth unemployment. Moreover, the unemployment rate among people aged 15 to 24 remains the highest in the world.[4] As their populations continue to grow, the countries of the Arab world are confronted with the same grave issue. As a percentage of the population and in absolute terms, poverty has only increased in the Arab world in the last decade. The scourge of government corruption at various levels has persisted or worsened in many parts of the Arab world. The continuing conditions in this part of the world may rekindle protests like those seen over the last decade.

Prior to the Arab revolutions of the 2010s, freedom of the press and, more generally, freedom of speech had a poor track record. After the Arab upheavals, the situation in many Arab nations, including Egypt, Bahrain, Syria and Yemen, has worsened. Many governments have used all possible repressive measures against media, reporters and journalists who are critical of the regimes, both domestic and foreign. In many Arab countries, ordinary people face a slew of restrictions. Internet freedom has either stayed mainly stagnant or declined in the information age, when people aspire to and are accustomed to using social media.

The Arab uprisings of the 2010s were not entirely peaceful. The cycle of repression and violence has resulted in enormous human displacement and misery, particularly in countries ravaged by civil conflict. These protracted conflicts were exacerbated by external military interventions by the state and non-state actors. Yemen, Syria and Libya are all embroiled in civil wars. Due to the protracted hostilities, millions of people have become IDPs (internally displaced persons), refugees or asylum seekers in other nations.[5] These problems persist and will not be resolved in the foreseeable future.

The Arab Spring is far from over, as evidenced by recent uprisings in several WANA countries. However, there is no 2011 spirit. A number of Arab countries are experiencing social and political divisions. Religious, ethnic and political differences are now further dividing society in this part of the world. It may take time for Arabs to see significant changes in their social, political and economic lives.

ORGANISATION OF THE VOLUME

In Chapter 1, Kingshuk Chatterjee argues that the term "Arab Spring," coined by many western observers to refer to the uprisings and protests that swept the Arab world in the early 2010s, was premature and misplaced. As the initial successes of Arab uprisings faded and were quickly reversed, many believed that an Arab Winter would follow an Arab Spring. However, Chatterjee asserts in this chapter that even though the so-called Arab Spring occurred in this region, it was immediately followed by a scorching summer, and the fall has yet to arrive. The current state of domestic politics in many Arab states demonstrates that democracy did not flourish in the WANA region as many observers predicted. Nonetheless, the author of the chapter claims that the authoritarian regimes in the Arab world have come under tremendous pressure as a result of the popular protests of the 2010s. The "façade of authoritarianism has begun to crack in the region, and noticeable changes are occurring in the politics and discourse of politics in even the most formidable bastions of conservatism." Since 2011, various factions have been struggling for dominance. Several internal factors, combined with shifting geopolitical dynamics, have kept the region's politics competitive and conflictual. During the early years of the Arab uprisings, political Islam seemed to be a major political force and that would dominate the politics of many Arab countries. Military and secular forces are currently controlling the vigour of political Islam. For the time being, military and secular forces, and very often authoritarian political dispensations, have kept political Islam in check. However, opposition forces in various countries appear to be gaining ground against highly repressive regimes as the latter become financially vulnerable, which in turn may address the popular voice positively. Chatterjee emphasises that neither political Islam nor liberal democracy emerged as clear winners following the 2011 popular uprisings. Although the social bases of political power have widened as a result of the recent upheaval, the region's enduring dilemma of political sovereignty remains. For the time being, the region may remain in turmoil and instability. "Stability may prove elusive, as the 'Spring of 2011' was followed by a scorching summer, but this may still mellow in time for the fall."

Priyamvada A. Sawant, in Chapter 2, first describes the uprisings that swept the Arab world in 2011 as democratic upsurge and one of the important spell of democratic revolutions that took place in the post-Cold War period, such as in Eastern Europe (1989) and Sub-Saharan Africa (1990s). She further highlights and assesses India's response to these democratic movements. The Arab world's democratic upsurge was spontaneous, and many countries in the WANA region were significantly affected by it. Initially, the world was unprepared for the events that unfolded in the region, but soon a wide variety of opinions soon followed. As one of the most important democratic countries in Afro-Asia, India was expected to fully support democratic movements that were seen in its extended neighbourhood. Indian diplomacy had responded to the revolutionary events in Eastern Europe and Sub-Saharan Africa in a normal manner. It welcomed the democratic development in the Arab world in the 2010s. This chapter discusses India's stance toward the Arab world's democratic rise and its likely causes, in addition to looking at the nature of democratic advancements in the Arab world, particularly in the Gulf region.

In Chapter 3, Mohmad Saleem Sheikh discusses sectarianism as a major source of instability in WANA, particularly in the aftermath of the Arab Spring. According to the writer, the West Asian region has a natural proclivity for instability and crisis. The Arab uprisings and civil wars demonstrated that the primary sources of instability in West Asia emanate from the local political environments of the regional states. The numerous sources of instability operate both within and outside of states.

As demonstrated in this chapter, three major factors are contributing to the deepening instability in West Asia post-Arab Spring: the persistence and strengthening of authoritarianisms, as well as the struggle for regional dominance. Second, the rise of sectarianism and sectarian conflicts, which are currently taking place in various theatres such as Syria and Yemen, and previously in Iraq. Third, there is an increase in sect-based, sub-state and non-state armed entities. Conflicts and civil wars create a security vacuum and regional instability, in addition to encouraging the rise of non-state armed groups to invite external intervention (another source). The analysis also systematically investigates sectarianism, which has emerged as a dominant facet of the region's politics in particular. Sectarianism exacerbates regional insecurity and widens the security void, making the establishment of a long-overdue security order less likely or a distant reality. The chapter examines its politicisation and instrumentalisation in current conflicts from a security standpoint. According to this study, three harmful principles are exacerbating instability in post-Arab Spring West Asia: strengthening authoritarianism, the rise of sectarianism and the emergence of non-state actors.

In Chapter 4, Özden Zeynep Oktav, analyses the role of Turkey's involvement in the Syrian crisis. She argues that when the Syrian crisis began, the Turkish government sought to engage with the al-Assad government to appease the protestors and grant them the needed reforms. However, Syrian President Bashar al-Assad rejected Turkey's proposal and instead perpetrated a brutal crackdown on the protesters. Since then, Turkey has attempted to defend its borders against the PKK-affiliated PYD/YPG and ISIS, both of whom made important places for themselves during the course of the conflict. Border violations and explosions on Turkish borders, as well as the influx of approximately 3.6 million Syrian refugees, prompted Ankara to launch cross-border counter-terrorism operations along its border with Syria. Following an explanation of Turkey's actions along its borders with Syria, the author focuses on the impact of four Turkish military operations, including Euphrates Shield, Olive Branch and Spring Shield, on the country's relations with the US, EU and Russian Federation. She goes on to explicate why Turkey launched these operations after the failed coup attempt in July 2016, and makes a case for Turkey's perusal a more comprehensive grand strategy wherein it can become a decisive player in resolving the Syrian civil war.

Taking the discussion on Syria further, Sukalpa Chakrabarti entails a brief review of the Arab Spring and the Syrian crisis and the role played by extra-regional and regional powers in Chapter 5. It goes on to investigate the geopolitical context of the Syrian crisis and its implications for India. She explains how the Arab Spring was a major failure in Syria, resulting in civil war. Syria's situation has devolved into a complicated strategic mess and a theatre for proxy wars, which has been exacerbated by the role of actors with vested interests. It remained one of the most difficult foreign policy issues. As stated above, Chakrabarti's primary focus is an examination of India's foreign policy imperatives that have shaped the pragmatic approach to Syria. The current Indian government appears eager to expand its strategic presence in Syria, assist in the rebuilding process and strengthen the counterterrorism partnership. However, given Syria's failed economic development and deep-seated ethnic divisions, rebuilding and reconstruction would be a difficult task. Syria has been hard hit by the Covid-19 pandemic, as well as new sanctions imposed by the US Caesar Act, forcing the regime to rethink its strategy. India has a unique strategic leverage to engage in confidence-building measures to deescalate tensions due to its historical ties with Syria, friendly relations with regional and extra-regional players in the crisis, and the ability to use soft power and economic diplomacy tactfully. In light of this, the chapter concludes by reviewing India's current efforts to aid Syrian reconstruction and recommending actions to strengthen regional ties.

In Chapter 6, Abu Zafar examines the Syrian issue from the perspective of yet another outsider player, China. Unlike the Arab Spring developments in Egypt and Tunisia, people's protests against the Syrian regime became complicated and resulted in a protracted civil war. The crisis arose as a result of the regime's excessive use of force against civilians, the emergence of powerful militias and terrorist groups fighting each other, and, most importantly, international players using proxies to overthrow the regime. Furthermore, the rise of ISIS (Islamic State of Iraq and Syria) resulted in the direct involvement of numerous international actors. In this context, the author situates China's response to Arab uprisings in general, and the Syrian civil war in particular.

China, as a rising economic player with aspirations to become a world power, has avoided any direct involvement in the Syrian crisis. Beijing maintained the theoretical principle that state sovereignty must be maintained and that any military action taken without the approval of the UN Security Council will have serious consequences for the country and the region. Nonetheless, China remained involved in the Syrian theatre due to three key regional interests. These are primarily geostrategic, commercial and security concerns. Though relations between Beijing and Damascus were not particularly strong, and trade between the two countries was minimal, it has increased significantly in recent years. Dealing with the Syrian crisis has grown critical for China due to its diverse interests in the area in general, and growing interest in Syria in particular.

Vrushal T Ghoble evaluates Saudi Arabia's efforts to deal with the country's post-Arab uprising situations in Chapter 7. It discusses Saudi Arabia's regional dynamics and the reform process, particularly in the aftermath of Arab uprisings. Saudi Arabia, which is endowed with vast natural resources (hydrocarbons) and thus enjoys economic success, has handled the post-uprising situation admirably. The Kingdom is setting the stage with new orientation on a grand scale in the midst of changing times. The 2011 uprisings triggered a slew of issues, with the population confronted with a variety of issues. The majority of the country's concerns revolved around a lack of freedom, a demand for reforms and high unemployment. The failure to pay attention to domestic demands eventually resulted in an explosive series of events following 2011. Riyadh provided economic benefits to citizens, attempting to discourage dissent throughout the country, particularly in the Shia-dominated eastern province. Due to its massive financial reserves, the country has largely remained unaffected, allowing it to suppress any public demand. Apparently, the diversification is underway and Vision 2030 of Prince Mohammad bin Salman (MBS) reflects a clear rearrangement of the social contract and transition within the country. Furthermore, the growth of Saudi Arabia as a state and its large stature has provided some security for the rest of the Gulf countries.

In Chapter 8, Umar Farooq investigates the matter of legitimacy of the Saudi regime in the context of the Arab uprisings of 2011 and subsequent years. The central question addressed in this chapter is whether the Saudi state and/or the current regime face legitimacy, particularly in light of the Arab Spring revolts. There has been speculation that the stability of the Saudi regime is in a state of flux, especially after the Arab spring. There are two opposing viewpoints on this issue. On the one hand, there is a perception that the kingdom has previously been able to absorb challenges, such as the Ikhwan / Neo-Ikhwan uprisings or the recent Arab spring. Many people believe that the Saudi regime will survive on this basis. Despite the shock waves felt throughout the country, the kingdom was able to survive. As a result, current challenges will have little impact on the Saudi regime. Many observers, on the other hand, have observed that the kingdom has faced numerous internal challenges since the 2011 uprisings. As a result of the events of the Arab Spring, these observers predict the fall of the Saudi regime. However, Farooq claims it's impossible to predict whether Saudi Arabia will be able to cope with further upheavals, but there are more reasons to believe that the Saudi regime will be threatened in the future.

In Chapter 9, Priya Singh highlights the role of public spaces in the Arab world which acquired prominence as sites of political contestations during the popular protests and uprisings of the 2010s. The Arab uprisings are frequently portrayed as synonymous with the occupation of squares (such as Cairo's Tahrir Square) and streets (like the avenue Habib Bourguiba in Tunis). One of the main points Priya Singh makes in the chapter is that public space was central to the events of the Arab Spring. As such, the chapter further addresses the nature of the encounter between physical public space and the revolutionary process, as well as the consequences of that encounter. Although several academics recognised the importance of these spaces, the emphasis on the role of social media or social networking sites in nurturing and inciting rebellion has overshadowed their significance. The chapter is divided into three major sections, the first of which provides an overview of the concept of public spaces. The final two sections propose an account of the Arab uprising through the lens of public space, as well as reflections on this ostensibly brief episode of public articulation in Arab space.

Sujata Ashwarya and Mohmed Saleem Sheikh, in Chapter 10, analsye the role of the Islamic Resistance Movement, popularly known as Hizbullah, a dominant non-state actor that has played a significant role in defining the politics of the Levant region. The chapter examines Hizbullah's rise, growing power and increasing assertions in the context of the Arab uprisings. According to the authors, as the new 'Middle East' emerges, Hizbullah redefined its domestic position and stake, transitioning from a moderate player to an active influencer in the regional context. The chapter goes on to argue that geostrategic necessity trumped Hizbullah's ideological commitment to fighting the "oppressor" while convincing Hizbullah to rally behind regional allies in averting any threat to the "resistance axis." Furthermore, the initial praise for the Tunisian and Egyptian revolutions faded, and Hizbullah succumbed to narrow sectarian narratives as an existential threat loomed over it and the resistance block.

In Chapter 11, Md. Aftab Ahmad contextualizes the role and contribution of Arabic literature in the Arab Spring. He emphasises that, in addition to obvious factors such as poverty, unemployment and other local issues, the Arab uprisings were also fuelled and encouraged by the rich Arab literature. The Arabic literature gave ordinary Arabs the courage to express their outrage at the injustices perpetrated by various autocratic regimes. The chapter also emphasises the positive role that Arabic literature played in inspiring ordinary young Arabs and shaping their minds and hearts for these historical uprisings. Tawfiq al-Hakim, Naguib Mahfouz, and other twentieth-century Egyptian writers have written extensively about poverty, broken dreams, despair, political oppression, prison torture and suppression. During the uprising, Egypt's Tahrir Square was transformed into a literary carnival, with a number of writers, academics and artists personally participating, and others expressing their support for the uprisings. "The first days of the revolution were like an artistic or literary gathering and a cultural forum," Egyptian novelist Ibrahim Abdel Meguid said. Literary figures in the Arab world believe that while the Arab Spring did not succeed in bringing socio-political reforms to the region, it did succeed in changing the literary landscape of the Arabs, with writers and poets now feeling more free to express themselves and literature becoming more focused on socio-political issues in the region. The freedom of expression and publication of prison literatures in the post-Arab Spring period is evidence of the spring in Arab literature. The author of this chapter examines how the Arab Spring has allowed literature to flourish in terms of content and themes.

In the last chapter of the book, Adil Rasheed compares the period immediately following the Arab Spring with the period immediately following the French Revolution. He claims that the period following the Arab Spring is similar to the course of counter-revolutions and the 'Reign of Terror' that followed the fall of the Bastille in 1789. Following the initial success of the Arab uprisings in the early 2010s, which many dubbed the Arab Spring, the Arab world witnessed a counter-revolutionary upsurge and a wave of repression in many Arab countries. The author emphasises that, despite the negative trend that has temporarily overshadowed the gains of the people's revolt, the Arab Spring should not be viewed in a pessimistic light. He believes that, similar to Zhou Enlai's remark about the French Revolution, it is too early to dismiss the Arab Spring a misnomer. It is worth noting that the establishment of a stable democracy in France occurred nearly a century after the French Revolution. Similar to the spirit of the French Revolution, '*Liberté, égalité, fraternité*' (Liberty, Equality, Fraternity), which was directed against the feudal and monarchical order of France in the late eighteenth century, a vivacious anti-government slogan of the protesters during the Arab Spring, '*ash-shab yurid isqat an-nizam*' ("the people want to bring down the regime"), was directed against entrenched nepotism. The Arab people's aspirations for freedom and dignity, as well as a non-authoritarian, non-repressive, and non-corrupt government, which were reflected during the Arab Spring, may appear to have stalled now, but they are not unattainable. Looking back at the last ten years of Arab uprisings, we can see how entrenched authoritarian states in Northern Africa, the Gulf Cooperation Council and the Levant struggle to maintain the support of their restive masses while dealing with the convulsions that erupted a decade ago. Furthermore, there has been a recent resurgence of popular revolts across the region as countries such as Saudi Arabia gradually implement significant socioeconomic reforms.

NOTES

1. There have been a variety of interpretations and perspectives for each of these expressions. For the purposes of this volume, these nomenclatures have been used

loosely. When referring to the events of the early 2010s, the Arab media particularly used terms such as 'uprising' (*intifada*), 'awakening' (*sahwa*), 'revolution' (*thawrat*), and 'renaissance' (*nahda*).

2. An interesting perspective can be found in the recent book which deals withvarious micro-level dynamics at work behind the Arab Spring. For details see, Fatima El Issawi and Francesco Cavatorta, *The Unfinished Arab Spring: Micro-Dynamics of Revolts Between Change and Continuity*. Spain: Gingko Library, 2020.
3. See, Economic and Social Commission for Western Asia (ESCWA), United Nations, *Women's Political Representation in the Arab Region* (Beirut, 2017); Fatma Tawfik, "Rising in the Rankings, Arab Women Dream Of Gender Equality", *Ms Magazine,* February 18, 2022, at https://msmagazine.com/2022/02/18/arab-women-politics-gender-equality/(accessed April 15, 2022).
4. The World Bank: Data, https://data.worldbank.org/indicator/SL.UEM.TOTL.ZS (accessed April 16, 2022).
5. "North Africa and Middle East hit 10-year low in refugees as conflicts deescalate", *Arab News*, May 19, 2022, at https://www.arabnews.com/node/2085476/middle-east (accessed May 19, 2022).

1

AFTER SUMMER MAY COME THE FALL

THE ENDURING DILEMMA OF POPULAR SOVEREIGNTY IN THE MIDDLE EAST

Kingshuk Chatterjee

INTRODUCTION

When some of the Middle East's long-standing authoritarian leaders began to be overthrown in 2011, many believed it signalled the start of 'spring' in the region.[1] The 'spring' was short-lived, followed by a wave of counter-revolutionary repression in Egypt and Bahrain before devolving into a protracted civil war in Libya, Syria and Yemen, which continues even a decade later. The 'spring,' if it were so, did not last long anywhere except in Tunisia. After electing a president, the Egyptians saw him deposed shortly after. Even though Hosni Mubarak was never re-elected, power returned to the same military elite that had been in charge in Cairo since the 1950s; in Bahrain, the initial promise of spring did not even materialise for a brief moment. According to many observers, this brief and 'untimely' spring was followed by the 'Arab Winter,' in which all advances seemed to have stalled and all 'progress' towards democracy was undone.[2]

This article intends to argue that the Arab Spring was followed by a scorching summer, rather than winter, as some observers have referred to the decade since 2011, and that fall is not far away. It is true that democracy did not blossom as many observers had predicted—but was it ever meant to blossom anywhere other than in the imaginations of western observers? Additionally, this article will argue that the façade of authoritarianism has begun to crack in the region, and that noticeable changes are occurring in the politics and political discourse in even the most formidable bastions of conservatism. The struggle for dominance between those who wield the levers of power in the region and those they wield them over has continued throughout the years since 2011, and it appears to be intensifying in the near future, given the region's changing geopolitical dynamics.

2011: THE SPRING THAT WAS NOT

For the Middle East's millennial generation, 2011 was most likely the most memorable year in the region. The region's authoritarianism received its biggest shock since 1979, when the Middle East was engulfed by this magnitude of popular discontent for the first time since the Islamic Revolution in Iran, sending shockwaves through the region's capitals. Four long-serving dictators were deposed: Tunisia's Zine al-Abidine Ben Ali (1987-2011), Egypt's Hosni Mubarak (1981-2011), Yemen's Ali Abdullah Saleh (1990-2011) and Libya's Muammar Ghaddafi (1967-2011). The fabled 'Arab Street' came to life for the first time in nearly two generations, poised to usher in social revolutions unprecedented in the region. For a time, it appeared that the upheavals would not spare the region's monarchical regimes, as crowned heads from Jordan's Hashemite ruler and the House of Ibn Saud to Bahrain's Sheikhdoms all appeared vulnerable. Aside from the Arab street, Tehran—which experienced its own minor scare during the 2009 Green Movement—seemed a little less enthusiastic about watching its regional rivals struggle through the crisis.[3]

This was not the first time the Arab street asserted its independence and established itself as a formidable force. As the British and French colonial powers withdrew from the region shortly after World War II, the social coalition between traditional rulers of the countryside and educated urban elites was challenged, and almost invariably fractured, by upwardly mobile elements of society forming a new social coalition between the military and the urban underclass.[4] This social churning aided Gamal Abdal Nasser's ascension to power in Egypt (1952), Muammar Ghaddafi's ascension to power in Libya (1967) and the Ba'athists' ascension to power in Syria (1963) and Iraq (1968). However, unlike two generations ago, the 2011 upheavals lacked a military component. Indeed, the majority of the region's political churning was directed against the political regimes that the militaries of the respective countries had supported for decades. Furthermore, unlike the churning political currents of the 1950s and 1960s, the political currents generated in 2011 were quite strong, even in the monarchies and sheikhdoms of the Levant and the Persian Gulf—strong enough to threaten the regime in Manama until Riyadh intervened.[5]

While it is important to recount what happened in 2011, it is also important to remember what did not. Only Tunisia appears to have achieved some semblance of democracy, albeit shaky and weak. Egypt's hopes for a democratic regime were dashed when the military declared that it was 'reclaiming' the country from the Ikhwan, following the ouster of President Mohammed Morsi, who had been elected in the country's first popular election, and his replacement by General Abdel Fattah al-Sisi. Libya has never recovered from the Gaddafi's fall, and the country continues to make headlines whenever warlord Khalifa Haftar thwarts the Government of National Unity. Yemen has been in disarray since 2011, and Syria has nearly imploded. As a result, the road to democracy in the Middle East appears to be littered with proverbial potholes and blind alleys. Despite the removal of authoritarian rulers, the term 'democratic wave' is misleading.[6]

While the failure of democracy to establish deep roots has outraged many people (both within and outside the region), not all observers were taken aback by the turn of events. Most Middle Eastern countries' economic landscapes are not yet conducive to the development of a democratic polity. The states (mostly of the rentier variety) remain financially strong and, thus, substantially self-sufficient in terms of tax revenue. Even in states that rely on taxes paid by their subject population or citizenry (such as Egypt and Syria), the military's economic stranglehold and the sheer proportion of employment generated by such military-run outfits in the country give Middle Eastern states the power of patronage of an order that is not conducive to democracy.[7]

POLITICAL ISLAM: THE SPECTRE THAT FAILED TO APPEAR

Furthermore, it has become clear over the last decade that the strength of political Islam in the region has been overstated. Political Islam was caught off guard by the Middle East's largest popular uprising since 1979. The initial upheavals that defined 2011 occurred without the motivation or agency of political Islam. From Tunisia and Egypt to Syria and Libya, uprisings erupted spontaneously, with political Islam providing neither the ideological framework nor the leadership—even deeply entrenched organisations such as the Ikhwan al-Muslimin (Muslim Brotherhood) were caught off guard. Despite this, supporters of political Islam were successful in seizing political power in Tunisia (under the banner of al-Harkat al-Nahda or Ennahda), Egypt (albeit briefly), and, to a lesser extent, Jordan, but then began to wane in strength.[8]

However, none of the major Islamist organisations that attempted to ride the wave of popular discontent to political power had a strong economic plan capable of bringing them to power or keeping them there once they did. In such circumstances, Islamist parties had two choices: adopt a post-Islamist stance and pursue a liberal economic agenda, or continue to pursue the political Islamic agenda of political and economic renaissance. As it turns out, Rachid Ghannouchi's al-Harkat al-Nahda party in Tunisia successfully negotiated their transformation into a liberal democratic party, which included a reduction in their Islamist polemic and collaboration with secular parties.[9] By contrast, both Egypt's and Jordan's Ikhwan failed to maintain momentum, the former in retaining power and the latter in gaining it. In Egypt, the military deposed elected President Muhammad Morsi with the tacit approval of the secularist component of the movement that ousted Mubarak—the threat of Islamisation posed by Morsi's policies was deemed more undesirable by secularists than even the military staging a comeback.[10] When the uprisings began in Amman, King Abdullah was prudent enough to institute some reforms, and then capitalised on secularists' opposition to the Ikhwan agenda to neutralise them.[11]

Militant Islam faltered at first, recovered slightly, but ultimately proved largely ineffective throughout the majority of the Middle East. There were serious fears that organisations like Gama Islamiyyah, al-Jihad al-Islamiyyah, and even al-Qaeda would resurface in Egypt and elsewhere once the instruments of coercion were no longer functional—but the majority of the uprisings avoided the type of militancy that had previously been used to justify repression. Indeed, radical Islamists were relieved when Morsi's ouster demonstrated what they had been claiming all along: that the region's current regimes would not permit peaceful change.[12] However, as popular upheavals became entangled in actual violence, militant Islam demonstrated some resilience as Libya and Syria devolved into civil wars. Things began to unravel somewhat when Sunni militias allied with al-Qaeda in Iraq to establish Da'esh (*Daulat al-Islamiyah fi al-Iraq wa al-Sham*, i.e. the Islamic State in Iraq and the Levant), effectively marginalising political Islam in the process.[13]

The rapid territorial gains made by the Da'esh in Iraq and then Syria drew significant support from other militant outfits in Syria and disaffected elements in Iraq, as well as from the ranks of militant Islamists from the Middle East and Europe—by 2014, it appeared as though the Da'esh had established a foothold and even raised the prospect of redrawing the Levant's map entirely.[14] However, Daesh's territorial expansion proved to be its undoing, bringing the governments of Iran, Iraq, Jordan, Syria, Russia, the United States of America and the Kurdish Peshmerga together to put an end to its brief and disruptive presence. Indeed, the resurgence of militant Islam allowed the region's state apparatuses to use it as a smokescreen to break the back of Islamism (particularly the non-militant variety)—Ikhwan has since been banned in Egypt, Jordan, and the Gulf States,[15] despite the fact that there is scant evidence linking proponents of Islamic political ideology to Da'esh.

Another aspect of the uprisings that became immediately apparent was the number of people who preferred to revert to military rule (as in Egypt)[16] or to maintain monarchy (as in Jordan)[17] when confronted with the electoral rise of Islamists. The Islamist al-Nahda's continued existence in Tunisia, the only country where political Islam survived the scorching summer following the Arab Spring, can be explained by both its relatively moderate beginnings and its rapid transition to a post-Islamist political discourse and support for the secular-liberal economic policies.[18] All of these factors appear to indicate fairly conclusively that political Islam will not necessarily prevail in the region's public sphere, contrary to what was frequently suspected by observers both within and outside the region.

THE SUMMER THAT FOLLOWED: BUSINESS AS USUAL?

Contrary to appearances, the Middle East has not yet returned to its pre-2011 levels of stability. Nobody in the region, or anyone watching from afar, has any reason to believe that that normalcy has returned. The root causes of the upsurge—economic insecurity, political disaffection and social repression—have not abated.

The high level regional youth unemployment[19] and stagnant economic growth on the eve of 2011 have remained largely unchanged in the decade since. The prolonged downturn in the global oil market, and thus the region's oil-driven economy, appears to be a long-term occurrence. The rise of the shale oil industry, the growing popularity of alternative energy resources and the impending large-scale deployment of gas and electric vehicles all point to a trend away from fossil fuels.[20] The region's economic might has been weakened as a result of the global oil market's sluggishness. The 2011 crisis is still evident in the various capitals of the Middle East in the absence of radical structural changes in their economies.

As evidence, consider the pattern of state activity in countries that were sparked by the 2011 uprisings but did not devolve into civil war (Egypt, Bahrain, Jordan, and Saudi Arabia), as well as those that escaped with a flutter (Lebanon, UAE, Qatar, etc). These Arab countries appear to be pursuing a two-pronged policy: severe repression of all forms of political opposition and dissent, and gradual implementation of reforms to soften the sting of some opposition.

Political repression appears to have found new life. Egypt, Saudi Arabia, Jordan and Bahrain have all seen a systematic crackdown on not only political Islamist outfits, but also on any sign of dissent or disagreement within the political system. Egypt not only persecuted the Ikhwan, but also those who participated in the 2011 Tahrir Square protests,[21] and spared no one, including journalists critical of the establishment following President Mubarak's ouster.[22] In Saudi Arabia, the rise of Muhammad bin Salman has seen the execution of Islamists, such as the highly respected Shi'i cleric Nimr Baqir al-Nimr on terrorism charges,[23] as well as the assassination of figures like Jamal Khashoggi, a former adviser to the Saudi monarchy.[24]

Although Jordan's crackdown was less severe than in Egypt or Saudi Arabia, it did not prevent the Hashemite Kingdom from neutralising and then dissolving the Ikhwan; Bahrain, too, waited until after the 2011 Shi'i-led uprisings before beginning to execute their leaders.[25] Even in countries where there has been little upheaval, the Emirs of Qatar and the UAE have decided to crack down on the Ikhwan, despite the fact that, except Kuwait, the Ikhwan has not had any political agenda or aspirations in these countries.[26] The UAE is now attempting to undermine Salafism by promoting a broad and inclusive, albeit undefined, school of thought.[27] Such systematic crackdowns, however, do not convey a sense of state invincibility; rather, they indicate regime nervousness in the face of political and ideological opposition.

This is supported, in part, by the fact that regimes have begun to implement a series of gradual and consistent reforms. Regimes lacking significant reserves of wealth, such as Jordan and Kuwait, had begun gradual political reforms long before the Arab Spring; they simply continued with the reforms (accelerating them for a time after 2011) and successfully weathered the storm. Jordan's political system has been gradually reforming since 1989, with periodic setbacks in progress towards limiting the crown's power and increasing governmental accountability to an elected parliament. Following the unrest in Tunisia and Egypt, as well as street protests in Amman, King Abduallah quickly established a Royal Commission on constitutional amendments. It also began to implement long-standing people's demands for reforms, such as the right to free speech, the right to privacy (by limiting state censorship powers), and the establishment of a Constitutional Court.

While some of these reforms began to lose meaning by 2016, as reform pressure waned, the majority of them remained in place.[28] By 2009, Kuwait had implemented the majority of its political reforms, including the right of women to vote in parliamentary elections. The emirate has simply continued its pragmatic approach of gradually broadening the social basis of power and introducing the initially contentious Single-Non-Transferable-Vote (SNTV) system in place of multiple votes per person, which many believe has kept tribalism, Islamism and other forms of social affiliation alive in electoral politics.[29]

Governments in relatively wealthy states (particularly in the Gulf) continue to be capable of ignoring any significant political reforms—for example, the United Arab Emirates, Qatar and Saudi Arabia. Even so, governments appear eager to implement additional reforms requested by the public sphere—presumably to ensure that the momentum for change is not stifled by any policy of repression. Probably the most significant array of social and cultural reforms has to be seen in the Kingdom of Saudi Arabia, which has been the most conservative in terms of political reforms thus far. Since the appointment of Mohammed bin Salman as Crown Prince and heir apparent to the octogenarian King Salman, Riyadh has been gradually liberalising the arch-conservative Kingdom, albeit almost exclusively in the realms of society, culture and economy—in 2016, the Mutawwain's (religious police) powers were curtailed, easing the previously strict implementation of various social mores.

Saudi Arabia has since seen a significant relaxation of women's dress codes, the lifting of prohibitions on alcohol and public music performance, and increased public mixing of men and women. While a 35-year-old ban on cinemas was repealed in 2017, a ban on women driving cars was removed in 2018 and a ban on music playing in restaurants and sex mixing was repealed in 2019. Significantly, Riyadh announced the launch of tourist visas for foreigners, relaxed dress codes for foreign women, and allowed foreign men and women to rent hotel rooms without proving their relationship or marriage.[30] The UAE is the other Gulf state to liberalise its social code—in November 2020, the Emirates tightened its laws against domestic abuse and sexual harassment of women, reformed its laws on divorce for Emiratis and the division of assets between non-Emirati domiciles according to their countries of origin's laws, and decriminalised alcohol consumption. Another piece of legislation made it possible for unmarried couples to co-rent a home.[31]

Governments rarely reform unilaterally, and authoritarian governments even less frequently do so. Clearly, the region's strong states are no longer strong, the region's hard states are no longer as hard, and the region's deep states are no longer as deep as they once were.

WHAT AILS THE REGION?—OF TOTTERING ECONOMIES AND REPRESSIVE POLITIES

When the public enthusiasm sparked by the Arab Spring's promise was tempered by the scorching summer that followed (particularly in Egypt), many assumed 2011 was a one-time occurrence. Some observers noted that the region lacked the cultural preconditions for democracy to flourish, implying that no spring will ever fully blossom in the Middle East;[32] that authoritarianism is both historically and culturally ingrained in the region's fabric—no prizes for guessing that this was an indirect way of saying that Islam was the root cause. Other observers, on the other hand, avoided such cultural reductionist conclusions and explained 2011's failure to socio-economic and political structures that have been deeply ingrained in these societies since their national inception.[33]

Contrary to the commonly held belief that authoritarianism in the Middle East is culturally conditioned, the nature of political regimes in the region is shaped by the respective countries' historical trajectories and structural peculiarities in the twentieth century. Simply put, when the Ottoman Empire fell at the end of World War I and new nation-states were formed all over the Arab world, it completely fragmented the traditional regional polity-economy that had existed for over a millennium.

Faced with the challenge of economic modernisation, many of these new successor states (Egypt, Syria, Iraq, Jordan), as well as some older ones (Persia/Iran and Turkey), resorted to state-led development efforts in the absence of democratic participation, resulting in the rise of strong states and very weak civil society formations. The other group of entirely new states that emerged in the region as European powers withdrew gradually placed traditional social elites in positions of political authority, either through conflict or (tribal) alliances (Saudi Arabia in the 1920s, Yemen and Libya after 1945, and the UAE, Bahrain, Qatar, and Kuwait in the 1960s). Because of the near-absence of civil societies, these states began weak but appeared strong.[34]

The discovery of oil in the region in the early twentieth century, and the steady growth of oil revenues through the 1960s, when oil-rich states asserted sovereign control over their oil reserves, fundamentally altered the chessboard.

Oil-rich rentier states (Iran since the 1930s, Iraq and Saudi Arabia since the 1940s, and Libya since the 1970s) became more authoritarian as oil revenues increased several fold—by the 1970s, even the relatively new Gulf monarchies (Kuwait, Qatar, Bahrain, and the UAE) had succumbed to the temptations of blatant power, undermining the growth of civil societies in those countries. Because the majority of the Gulf's oil-rich states are sparsely populated, the rise of the oil economy drew migrant workers (skilled and unskilled) from all over the world as well as from non-oil Arab countries (Syria, Egypt, and Jordan), relieving pressure to skill and train indigenous populations and thus strengthening incumbent authoritarian regimes in both the labour sending and labour receiving countries.[35]

The rise of the oil economy, on the other hand, changed not only the region's political dynamics, but also its structural and social dynamics. Both oil-rich and oil-poor states invested heavily in social overhead capital as a result of the massive inflow of oil revenue (especially education, health, public infrastructure). The infusion of capital boosted the respective domestic economies and raised the region's material standard of living. This transformation of the structural dynamics of Middle Eastern states was nothing short of revolutionary—it altered the region's underlying principle of political legitimacy. Nobody questioned the regime's authoritarian nature as long as the oil economy continued to grow exponentially, the populace could receive heavily subsidised or nearly free public services, and economic sinecures could be generated to keep the populace happy. Concerns were likely to arise once such state-provided benefits began to dwindle. This was exacerbated by the fact that investment in public education infrastructure unintentionally produced a much larger population of educated and upwardly mobile people than even the fastest growing economies could easily absorb once oil revenues began to fall.[36]

After a few years of reflection on the 2011 upheavals, Israeli economist Paul Rivlin observed that, "the Middle Eastern economies need to run in order to stand still."[37] Little has changed in that aspect in the last decade. The region's economy, which is heavily reliant on oil prices, has taken a series of blows, with the situation worsening in 2021 than it was in 2011. This was largely due to the economic slowdown that began in 2008-09 and lasted for nearly a decade, until around 2014. This was exacerbated further by the events of 2011, as well as the civil wars that erupted in Syria, Libya and Yemen, as well as the rise of Da'esh. Even before these issues were resolved, the development of viable alternative energy technologies ensured that oil revenues would never return to pre-crisis levels. As if that were not enough, the Covid-19 pandemic caused another global economic slowdown, putting the Middle Eastern economies into overdrive. As a result, a decade after 2011, Middle Eastern regimes that rely on oil revenue are losing money. The region's economies have slowed significantly, and people are earning less money than at any other time in history. Tunisia, Egypt and, most notably, Lebanon are on the verge of collapse as a result of an increasingly dysfunctional (though not authoritarian) political system.

Proponents of some form of democracy (not necessarily liberal) are either too feeble or too severely mauled by their own failures to offer a viable economic alternative. As a result of the post-2011 crackdown, Islamists (both militant and nonviolent) have been severely weakened. In the current situation, the states are too powerful to be overthrown, but it appears that they are at least acknowledging the need for reform. Riyadh and Abu Dhabi have begun to implement a new generation of social reforms in order to address long-standing issues of public discontent in their respective kingdoms.

Constitutional reforms in Amman and Kuwait also demonstrate a willingness to reform in order to stay ahead of the curve and avoid a repeat of the 2011 popular uprising. Authoritarian regimes, on the other hand, send a clear message: rights are granted by the ruler and cannot be claimed by the subject/citizen. Thus, the most outspoken advocate for Saudi women's right to drive, Loujain al-Hathloul, was imprisoned in 2018, just as Crown Prince Mohammed Bin Salman graciously permitted Saudi women to drive. These messages are meant to obscure the irony that rights are only granted after they have been asserted.

Observers of Middle Eastern politics have long argued that, since the 1990s, the people of the Middle East have been actively negotiating with their respective governments to push the ruling regimes towards accepting popular sovereignty (albeit not necessarily electoral democracy).[38] Despite the fact that the Arab Spring of 2011 failed to achieve this goal in large part, it was successful in changing the discursive space in the region's politics by introducing two coinages—*Mosawwaliyyat al-Hokumat* (accountable government) and *al-Islah al-Dasturi* (constitutional reform)—into the Arab political lexicon.[39] These resurfaced spectacularly during the 2018-19 'Second Arab Spring,' when incumbent regimes of Omar al-Bashir (Sudan) and Abdelaziz Butteflika (Algeria) were deposed. The Saudi and Qatari *Vision 2030* programmes are essentially attempts to pre-empt similar accountability demands by almost volunteering their accountability lest they be held accountable.

As a result, while the original malady that caused 2011—repressive states presiding over stumbling economies—has not been addressed, the problem cannot be assumed to be over. One could even argue that the region's ongoing economic crisis virtually guarantees that public dissatisfaction with political repression will continue to grow until it reaches a tipping point. One factor that could amplify public discontent and give the region a boost is the region's rapidly shifting geopolitics.

THE MULTIPLE CURRENTS OF REGIONAL GEOPOLITICS

The geopolitical landscape of the Middle East is also rapidly changing. Multiple crosscurrents are now active in the region, highlighting the region's nearly endemic instability at a level not seen since the 1960s. With at least three civil wars currently raging (Libya, Syria and Yemen), and at least two states severely weakened politically and economically (Iraq and Lebanon), the region's neighbours are far more volatile than at any time since the Ottoman Empire fell at the end of World War I.

The Middle East's extended neighbourhood, which consists primarily of the three regions of the Persian Gulf, the Levant and North Africa, has been extremely volatile throughout the twentieth century. As the new states of the Arab Middle East emerged in the region in the aftermath of World War I, alongside the two older entities of Turkey and Persia, many regional actors vied for dominance over the entire region from the start. Egypt, Syria and Iraq launched the first bids for regional leadership, competing with Turkey and then Persia's existing claims.[40] Following World War II and the rise of the oil-rich states of the Persian Gulf, Saudi Arabia began to vie for a seat at the high table.[41] By 2011, the status of Iraq, Syria and Egypt had changed dramatically; they never being involved in the competition before was never even a possibility. Qatar and the UAE have redoubled their competition for regional dominance.[42]

The bid for regional dominance is reflected in the proxy wars that have come to characterise the region, as each of the leadership contenders attempts to strengthen their strategic foothold in the region. Iran operates across a wide swath of territory, from Iraq, Lebanon, Syria, and Palestine to Yemen; Saudi Arabia operates in Iraq, Lebanon, Syria, Sudan, Libya and Yemen; Turkey hovers over Iraq, Syria and Libya; the UAE operates in Syria, Libya, Sudan and Iraq today; and Qatar only operates in Syria and Iraq.

However, the treasuries of Middle Eastern countries (particularly those with significant oil reserves) are not as deep as they were in the 1970s and are unlikely to be so in the future. The most eloquent example is Lebanon's desperate situation. Despite the absence of Damascus, the single most important external factor in Lebanese politics since its inception in 1919, neither Tehran nor Riyadh have succeeded in encircling Beirut. This is largely because Iran and Saudi Arabia have very little money to spare for Lebanon's resuscitation, which is in desperate need of massive financial assistance. Compare this to the situation in the 1980s and 1990s, when Riyadh backed Hariri and his massive reconstruction of Beirut following the end of the Lebanese civil war (1975-90),[43] while Tehran backed Hizbollah both during and after the civil war.[44] Much the same explanation applies to both Iraq and Syria, where Humpty Dumpty has fallen spectacularly—none of the regional powers have been able to fund combatants on the scale that they did in the 1980s and 1990s.

As a result of the region's oil-rich countries' diminished financial capabilities, the Middle Eastern political landscape is more volatile than it has been in the last century. The axis of conflict is no longer simply Shi'i-Sunni as both the West and Arab states frequently claimed after Iraq and Yemen began to implode along sectarian lines over the last decade. Indeed, as Tehran's Arab neighbours have correctly argued, Iran has successfully expanded its sphere of influence in the region by playing significant roles in Iraq, propping up the 'Alavite Shi'i regime of Bashar al-Assad (and is now one of the regime's mainstays), Hezbollah in Lebanon, HAMAS in occupied

Palestine (particularly in Gaza), and the Houthis in Yemen. The outward projection of Tehran's power represents a pro-Tehran axis, rather than a 'Shi'i' axis, to provide Tehran with some strategic depth in a siege-like situation.[45] Similarly, while Riyadh, Doha and Abu Dhabi have supported various Sunni factions in Iraq, Yemen and Syria, this has less to do with sectarianism and more to do with the fact that such factions are engaged in (or willing to engage in) combat against Tehran's regional proxies.

Significantly, Turkey, Iran, Qatar, Saudi Arabia and the UAE have all backed different horses in Syria over the last decade; Turkey's support for Khalifa Haftar in Cyrenaica has put Turkey in the crosshairs of Saudis and the UAE, who support Libya's feeble incumbent government;[46] and even close allies Saudi Arabia and the UAE have backed various groups in Sudan.[47] Within the Persian Gulf, which has long acknowledged Riyadh's leadership, the Gulf Cooperation Council (GCC) has been torn apart by Qatar's ties with Iran and Turkey.[48] When the other GCC states imposed a crippling blockade on Qatar, Ankara and Tehran stood by Doha until the blockade was eventually lifted.

Indeed, far too many ideological regimes and political actors have demonstrated a willingness to pursue their own strategic interests in the larger neighbourhood; as a result, the search for a single ideological or political explanation is certain to prove fruitless. Iran's expansionist endeavours appear to be motivated less by a desire to spread the Islamic revolution than by a desire to rid its neighbourhood of adversarial forces (i.e., the US, UAE, and Saudi Arabia for Iraq, and Saudi Arabia and the UAE for Syria) and to maintain the possibility of a second front against the USA and Israel (hence support for the Baathist regime in Syria, Hizbollah in Lebanon and HAMAS in Palestine).[49] Saudi and Emirati policy in Syria, Iraq and Yemen appears to be motivated by a desire for regional dominance as well as a desire to keep Tehran out. Both Turkey and Iran are worried about the Kurdish regions of Syria and Iraq, fearing that they will develop an irredentist character for their own Kurdish populations. This prompted Turkey to wage war against Syrian Kurds, and Tehran to appease Kurdish irredentists by forming a strategic alliance with the Peshmerga on the condition that they refrain from courting Iranian Kurds.[50]

Israel is the elephant in the room, which has never competed for regional dominance and instead focuses on existential concerns. It has fought wars with all of its immediate neighbours (Egypt, Iraq, Jordan, Syria and Lebanon) over its occupation of what could have been Palestine, and is currently engaged in a proxy war in Syria with Iran, largely to protect itself. It has so far avoided regional issues, but it could be a deciding factor in any regional security alignment that emerges over time. Indeed, the Abraham Accords, which established Israel's ties with Bahrain, the United Arab Emirates, Morocco, and Sudan, have completely disintegrated the conventional Arab political landscape.[51] For the first time since 1967, Riyadh is getting noticeably closer to Tel Aviv.[52] With the fragmentation of Arab states' solidarity against Israel on the crucial issue of occupied Palestine, the much-touted two-state solution appears to have been buried very deeply, and Palestine appears to have been nearly forgotten. It remains to be seen whether the prospect of Iran going nuclear, or the revival of the JCPOA, can galvanise all Gulf states into an even closer security agreement with Israel. If it does, it will be a seismic shift in regional politics, similar to the establishment of the state of Israel in 1948.

The absence of a regional power strong enough to dominate the others is perhaps the most significant explanation for the region's increased geopolitical instability. For the last two centuries, the truly decisive intervention in any major conflict in the region has tended to come from the outside—first from Britain in the Persian Gulf region in the early 18th century, then from Russia in the late 18th century; Britain withdrew from both the Gulf and the Levant by the mid-20th century, leaving the United States and the Soviet Union as the region's critical external players. For the first time in at least two centuries, no single external power appears willing or able to step forward and preserve the region's peace in its own strategic interest at the start of the twenty-first century's third decade. Extraneous elements in the region today are either attempting to minimise their footprint (the United States) or are insufficiently intrusive (Russia and China) to be able to stabilise the region if the opportunity arises.

Since 9/11, the United States has been withdrawing from the region, which may be the only thread that connects the foreign policies of Bush, Obama, Trump and Biden.[53] Russia is attempting to re-enter the Middle East after a brief absence at the end of the Cold War, but it does not appear willing or able to intervene except where it has direct strategic (Syria) or economic (Iran) interests.[54] China's economic clout in the region has grown, with the country becoming the Middle East's single largest consumer of energy exports, but it has yet to demonstrate the willingness or capability to intervene directly in any conflict situation. Even ongoing talks between the People's Republic of China and the Islamic Republic of Iran about forming a strategic alliance do not imply that Beijing will automatically come to Tehran's aid in the (unlikely) event of a conflict with, say, Saudi Arabia, Israel, or (less likely) the United States.

An outbreak of conflict cannot be completely ruled out given the region's evolving geopolitical landscape. The risk of a minor blunder tipping the entire region into a larger regional conflict is quite high considering the large number of proxy wars raging behind the smokescreen of the three civil wars. Any such conflict could potentially create enough pressure to cause fissures to form among the region's various countries. Given the high degree of volatility in many of the region's internal dynamics, current political regimes risk becoming both internally and externally vulnerable. This was largely why Riyadh initiated backchannel diplomacy with Iran in the aftermath of the 2019 attack on two of its most vital oil facilities by Iran-backed Houthi militias—While starting a war would have been easy, it could have had unintended consequences in a reforming country.

CONCLUSION: COME THE FALL

All indications suggest that the Middle East is on the verge of turning a corner. As highly repressive states become financially weak (and thus politically vulnerable), opposition forces tend to consolidate. The populace in the region is demanding accountability (hence the repression, lest the order collapse entirely) and the abolition of Islamic-inspired restrictions (hence the various gestures of reform, lest the pressures go out of control). The opposition's political language accuses the ruling regime of being too narrow in scope and approach, and calls for a broadening of the social foundations of power. The next major economic downturn will exacerbate the state's vulnerability; and the one after that will exacerbate it even more. Unless the oil market miraculously recovers, the Middle East is about to undergo change. That transformation may not be to the kind of (liberal) democracy that is frequently touted as a possibility—at least not yet. Neither is political Islam a certain beneficiary of the process of change. A much more likely scenario is that chaos will reign for some time, as beneficiaries of current dispensations jostle with those who have not benefited thus far. It is extremely likely that the social basis of power would broaden, and previously excluded social groups and classes would gain access—bringing us one step closer to popular sovereignty. Stability may prove elusive, as the 'Spring of 2011' was followed by a scorching summer, but this may still mellow in time for the fall.

NOTES

1. Probably the most original of these was Hamid Dabashi, *The Arab Spring: The End of Postcolonialism* (London and New York: Zed Books, 2012).
2. See Noah Feldman, *The Arab Winter: A Tragedy* (Princeton, NJ: Princeton University Press, 2020).
3. For a very passionate and contemporary impression of that promise of change, see Dabashi, n. 1.
4. See, for instance, Reinhard Schulze, *A Modern History of the Islamic World*, translated by Azizeh Ozodi (London and New York: I.B. Tauris Publishers, 2002), 101-07, 148-53.
5. Muhammad Nuruzzaman, "Politics, Economics and Saudi Military Intervention in Bahrain," *Journal of Contemporary Asia* 43, no. 2 (2013): 363-78.
6. Karol Cerny, *Instability in the Middle East: Structural Changes and Uneven Modernisation 1950-2015* (Prague: Charles University in Prague, Karolinum Press, 2017), 78-81.
7. Ibid., 182-97.
8. Farhad Khosrokhavar, *The New Arab Revolutions that Shook the World* (Boulder, CO and London; Paradigm Publishers, 2012), 112-20.
9. Sarah J. Feuer, "From Political Islam to Muslim Democracy: Ennahda Changes Course," *Foreign Affairs* (June 8, 2016), at https://www.foreignaffairs.com/articles/tunisia/2016-06-08/political-islam-muslim-democracy (accessed on June 9, 2016).
10. Eric Tragger, *Arab Fall: How the Muslim Brotherhood Won and Lost Egypt in 891 Days* (New York: Georgetown University Press, 2016).
11. Aaron Magid, "The King and the Islamists: Jordan Cracks Down on the Muslim Brotherhood." *Foreign Affairs* (May 3, 2016), at https://www.foreignaffairs.com/articles/jordan/2016-05-03/king-and-islamists (accessed on May 4, 2016).

12. Mara Revkin, "Brotherly Love: Why Sisi's Win is Good for Al-Qaeda." *Foreign Affairs* (May 29, 2014), at https://www.foreignaffairs.com/articles/egypt/2014-05-29/brotherly-love (accessed on May 30, 2014).
13. See Patrick Cockburn, *The Rise of Islamic State: ISIS and the New Sunni Jihadism* (London: Verso, 2016).
14. Loretta Napoleoni, *The Islamist Phoenix: The Islamic State and the Redrawing of the Middle East* (New York: Seven Stories Press, 2014).
15. For a sense of the nature, influence and the crackdown on the *Ikhwan* in Qatar and UAE, see Courtney Jean Freer, *Rentier Islamism: The Influence of the Muslim Brotherhood in the Gulf Monarchies* (Oxford: Oxford University Press, 2018), 149-73.
16. Egyptian author, Ahdaf Soeif, in personal conversation with the author, Calcutta, January 2013.
17. David Schenker, "Down and Out in Amman: The Rise and Fall of the Jordanian Muslim Brotherhood," *Foreign Affairs* (October 3, 2013), at https://www.foreignaffairs.com/articles/middle-east/2013-10-03/down-and-out-amman (accessed on October 5, 2013).
18. Anne Wolf, *Political Islam in Tunisia: The History of Ennahda* (Oxford and New York: Oxford University Press, 2017).
19. Cerny, n. 6, 228-34.
20. Daniel Yergin, "The Oil Collapse: A Pandemic and a Price War Have Together Brought Energy Markets to a Crisis," *Foreign Affairs* (April 2, 2020), at https://www.foreignaffairs.com/articles/2020-04-02/oil-collapse (accessed on April 3, 2020).
21. Muhammad Mansour, "Why Sisi Fears Egypt's Liberals: Behind the Recent Crackdown on Civil Society," *Foreign Affairs* (May 18, 2016), at https://www.foreignaffairs.com/articles/egypt/2016-05-18/why-sisi-fears-egypts-liberals (accessed on May 20, 2016).
22. The most sensational was the case of the Egyptian-born al-Jazeera journalist Mahmoud Hussein, who was held for more than four years without any formal charges ever being pressed against him. Mahmoud Hussein was finally released in February 2021.
23. Sheikh Nimr al-Nimr (1959-2016) was an immensely popular Shi'i cleric who had been an extremely vocal critic of the Saudi Arabian government, and its treatment of its Shi'i population as virtually second class citizens. He was pivotal to the protests that broke out in the kingdom during 2011, for which offence he was tried and sentenced to death in 2014. His eventual execution took place in January 2016.
24. Jamal Khasoggi (1958-2018) was a Saudi journalist, serving in a number of prestigious newspapers, who was well-known for his liberal views. It is believed that at different points he even worked with Saudi intelligence, and was once even closely associated with the Saudi Ministry of the Interior (during the tenure of Turki al-Faisal). After falling out with the Saudi regime under Muhammad bin Salman, he relocated to the United States as a journalist with the *Washington Post*. He was murdered gruesomely by a team of assassins at the Saudi Consulate in Istanbul in October 2018, presumably at the order of Muhammad bin Salman.

25. "Bahrain executes three Shia men in first death sentences since 2010," *The Guardian*, January 15, 2017, at https://www.theguardian.com/world/2017/jan/15/bahrain-three-men-death-sentence-shia-muslims-gulf (accessed on January 16, 2017).
26. See Freer, n. 15.
27. A member of the Government of India's National Security Council, in personal conversation with the author on condition of anonymity, Calcutta, December 2017.
28. For a detailed and critical analysis of the political and constitutional reforms in Jordan, see Mohammed Torki Bani Salameh, "Political Reform in Jordan: Reality versus Aspirations," *World Affairs* (Winter 2017), 47-78.
29. Daniel L. Tavana, "The Evolution of Kuwaiti Opposition: Electoral Politics after the Arab Spring," issue brief 8.7.18, in A. Kadir Yildirim, *Pluralism and Inclusion in post-2011 Kuwait* (Carnegie Corporation of New York and Rice University's Baker Institute for Public Policy, Houston, Texas, 2018), at https://www.bakerinstitute.org/media/files/files/7b1a34c2/cme-pub-carnegie-kuwait-080718.pdf (accessed on September 15, 2020).
30. See Jihan Chara, "Saudi Arabia: A Prince's Revolution," *European View* 17, no. 2, (2018), at https://www.martenscentre.eu/wp-content/uploads/2018/10/14.pdf (accessed on January 21, 2020); Ebrar Sahika Kücükasci, *Saudi Arabia Under Mohammed bin Salman: Crisis, Reform or Stagnation*, Discussion Paper, TRT World Research Centre, 2019, at https://researchcentre.trtworld.com/images/files/discussion_papers/Saudi-Arabia-Crisis-Reform-Stagnation.pdf (accessed on January 1, 2019).
31. Richa Syal, "United Arab Emirates hopes easing of restrictions around alcohol, gender help boost global image and economy," *CBC News*, November 29, 2020, at https://www.cbc.ca/news/world/uae-law-expats-1.5809209#:~:text=Reforms (accessed on January 15, 2021).
32. Nader Hashemi, "The Arab Spring Two Years On: Reflections on Dignity, Democracy and Devotion," *Ethics and International Affairs* 27, issue 2 (May 2013), at https://www.ethicsandinternationalaffairs.org/2013/the-arab-spring-two-years-on-reflections-on-dignity-democracy-and-devotion-full-text/ (accessed on January 15, 2021).
33. See for instance, Cerny, n. 6.
34. Kingshuk Chatterjee, "Arab Spring: Authoritarianism in the Middle East Re-examined," in Priya Singh (ed), *Democracy in Asia: Discourses and Counter-Discourses* (New Delhi: MAKAIAS and KW Publishers, 2013), 141-44.
35. Ibid., 144-45.
36. Ibid., 146-49.
37. In personal conversation with the author, Tel Aviv, 2015.
38. See, for instance, F. Gregory Gause III, "The Gulf Conundrum: Economic Change, Population Growth and Political Stability in the Gulf States," *The Washington Quarterly* 20, no. 1 (1997), 142-65.
39. Kingshuk Chatterjee, "The Search for a New Discursive Space in the Muslim World: From the Arab Spring to the Katchi Abadis of Pakistan," in Mathew Joseph C., ed.

Pakistan and the Muslim World (New Delhi: Knowledge World Publishers, 2019), 33-61.

40. Schulze, n. 4, 123-37.
41. Ibid., 174-76.
42. See Einat Wilf, *The Battle for Hegemony in the Middle East*, ASIP Special Report, 2017 (Barton: Australian Strategic Policy Institute, 2017), at https://css.ethz.ch/content/dam/ethz/special-interest/gess/cis/center-for-securities-studies/resources/docs/ASPI-SR106_Middle-East-hegemony.pdf (accessed on January 15, 2021).
43. Hannes Baumann, *Citizen Hariri: Lebanon's Neo-Liberal Reconstruction* (Oxford: Oxford University Press, 2016), 140, 155-56, 163, 174-77.
44. Kingshuk Chatterjee, "The Tehran Factor in West Asia: Doomed to Destabilise?" in Priya Singh and Sushmita Bhattacharya, ed., *Perspectives on West Asia: The Evolving Geopolitical Discourses* (New Delhi: MAKAIAS and Shipra Publications, 2012), 120-21.
45. Ibid., 121-23.
46. Kersten Knipp, "Why Turkey"s Libya commitment angers Arab nations," *Deutschewelle*, January 18, 2020, at https://www.dw.com/en/why-turkeys-libya-commitment-angers-arab-nations/a-52052924 (accessed on January 15, 2021).
47. Justin Lynch and Robbie Gramer, "Arab States Foment Sudan Chaos While U.S. Stands By," *Foreign Policy* (June 2019), at https://foreignpolicy.com/2019/06/05/arab-states-foment-sudan-chaos-while-u-s-stands-by-sudan-khartoum-protests-violent-crackdown-saudi-arabia-united-arab-emirates-egypt-democracy-push/ (accessed on January 15, 2021).
48. Dina Esfandiary and Ariane M. Tabatabai, "The Gulf Widens: The Roots of the Regional Spat with Qatar," *Foreign Affairs* (June 6, 2017), at https://www.foreignaffairs.com/articles/middle-east/2017-06-06/gulf-widens (accessed on June 9, 2017).
49. Chatterjee, n. 44, 126-27.
50. A member of Kurdistan Regional Government in Iraq, in conversation with the author on condition of anonymity, in Antalya, Turkey, December 2014.
51. Yoel Guzansky and Zachary A. Marshall, "The Abraham Accords: Immediate Significance and Long-term Implications," *Israeli Journal of Foreign Affairs* 14, Issue 3 (2020), 379-89.
52. Felicia Schwartz and Summer Said, "Israel's Netanyahu, Saudi Crown Prince Hold First Known Meeting," *The Wall Street Journal*, November 23, 2020, at https://www.wsj.com/articles/israels-netanyahu-meets-saudi-crown-prince-hebrew-media-says-11606120497 (accessed on January 15, 2021).
53. This might seem slightly paradoxical with reference to the neo-conservative interventionism in the Middle East. However, neo-cons have always tended to justify this by arguing that America became a target in 9/11 because of its exceedingly overbearing presence in the region, and thus needed to clear out. It was argued that if Saddam could be toppled and the Islamic regime in Iran toppled or denuclearised, the rest of the Gulf could be persuaded to disarm. If, in addition, democracy could

be promoted in the region (beginning with Iraq), and the rest of the region went democratic in emulation, then the USA could pull out of the region completely. Even the Democrats, who lambast the puerile neo-con argument, contend that by denuclearising Iran through international agreements like the JCPOA of 2015 (backed by sanctions-relief) would serve to stabilise the region and thus allow Washington DC to pull out from the region in good measure.

54. H.S. Vasudevan and Kingshuk Chatterjee, "The Return of the Prodigal: The Lengthening Shadow of Russia in the Middle East," in Kingshuk Chatterjee, ed., *Political Faultlines in the Middle East* (New Delhi: Knowledge World Publishers, 2021), 173-75.

2

DEMOCRATIC UPSURGE IN THE ARAB WORLD AND INDIA

Priyamvada A. Sawant

The Arab Spring is now a decade old, a period that is close enough to remain involved in its happenings/aftermath and while still being far enough to explore its significance and ramifications for the region and beyond. In the past one decade, since 2011, the events that unfolded in the West Asia and North Africa (WANA) countries have been regularly referred to as 'unprecedented' for a region that had a history of heavy authoritarian rule and has only had rare brushed with full-fledged democratic governments. While the region buzzed with the protests and demands for participation in the governance in 2010-2011, it also caused an amused euphoria around the globe particularly in countries that were sceptical about the idea of widespread protests for political demand in the Arab world. While the public disgruntlement against the authoritarian and corrupt regimes, rising unemployment and lack of socio-cultural freedoms was a common awareness in international domain, the massive upsurge that unfolded since December 2010 was unimagined and unpredicted. It caused an immediate stir; however, no one imagined the magnanimity of that sole event, which affected more than 20 countries/ areas in the WANA region and brought down perched-on-the-roof but now elderly autocrats and sclerotic regimes which fell down like a "pack of cards" with millions of daring men and women on streets shouting slogans and raising a banner against the authorities, unemployment and corruption. As the world watched and some interfered, the rulers of the respective countries swung into action and peaceful demonstrations soon faced violent response. Different groups emerged and instead of initiating a democratic process, some countries ended up in civil strife.

Few reports did reflect upon the situation in offing. The findings of the *Arab Democracy Index* for 2010, showed "the continued presence of embryonic signs of a democratic transition in most of the Arab countries".... however, "a certain degree of regression in the transition process compared to the previous year, and that the positive signs are essentially limited to the transition's theoretical or legislative aspects. In the meantime, the practical aspect (practices) has witnessed a tangible setback."[1] As observed in one of the UN addresses in 2012, the UN Development Programme had produced a series of reports between 2001 and 2005 analysing the economic, social and demographic strains in the WANA region and accurately predicted that unless economic and social reform was accelerated, there would be political, possibly violent, upheaval.[2]

Few years later, the *Arab Democracy Index 5*, published in 2016 showed "a decline in the Arab Democracy Index and the shortcomings of the process of democratic change and its inability to transform the Arab region."[3] By the end of the decade, the Economist Intelligence Unit Democracy Index, 2019 reported, the WANA region as, "the lowest-ranked of all the regions.... with six out of the 167 countries covered in our rankings featuring in the bottom 20. The average regional score of 3.53 (was) in line with the longer-term trend of the past five years of a slow decline from an already low base."[4]

The democratic upsurge was not the first for the world though. Earlier the East European (1989) and Sub-Saharan (1990s) democratic revolutions had attained the desired outcome. India had given a normal diplomatic reaction to these two revolutions and welcomed these democratic developments. As for the happenings in the Arab world in 2011, India did not respond to the entire region but only select countries. Across the national and the international estimation India was expected to emanate a response towards the democratic process in the region. In recognition of India's growing global role and status of being an important democratic country in Afro-Asia, it was desired that it wholeheartedly supports the democratic movements in the Arab world and thus play a unique role in the process.

This raises points for discussion regarding the Indian government's response and action taken after the protests erupted in the region. In 2011, India began its seventh term as the non-permanent member of the United Nations Security Council (UNSC), a body that spent a considerable time during India's tenure there in the "most difficult debates/negotiations" on Libya, Yemen, Sudan and Syria apart from Israel/Palestine.[5] The official stand taken by India in the UNSC deliberations is significant in analysing its position towards the countries in the region during the ongoing protests and its subsequent responses. The chapter briefly reflects on the landmark events of Arab Spring and then go on to explain India's relation with the region and its significance. It attempts to understand India's response to the popular uprisings that dramatically changed the landscape of the Arab world. The chapter finally concludes with a few observations.

THE 'ARAB SPRING'

On December 17, 2010, Mohamed, a Tunisian street vendor, self-immolated in front of the Sidi Bouzid Governorate office in protest against the confiscation of his goods and public humiliation by officials. It was an act of defiance that instantly resonated with many. The first protests of the Arab Spring began in the otherwise remote Sidi Bouzid in central Tunisia. The protestors called for dignity, employment opportunities, an end to corruption and for the corrupt and authoritarian President Zine El Abidine Ben Ali to step down. As the demonstrations reached the capital city Tunis, the authorities responded with a brutal security crackdown, with controls on internet, and the police reportedly opened fire killing hundreds and imposed an internet ban. The protests were spontaneous and led by Tunisia's highly educated youth. Bouazizi died of his wounds on January 4, 2011,after the protest movement had spread in the entire country. Over the next few days it was obvious that these were not mere protests. The revolution was "rapid and characterized by a sense of unity among all Tunisians."[6]

President Zine al-Abidine Ben Ali pledged cautious reforms that did little to quell the crowd, and on January 14, 2011, Ben Ali resigned after 23 years in power and fled to Saudi Arabia with his family. The interim government was formed, and the process of framing a constitution began shortly thereafter.

For many experts, the uprisings didn't seem to be in the offing. The classical economic measures had suggested otherwise. Tunisia had gained eight points in the World Economic Forum's Global Competitiveness Index, from 40 in 2009-2010 to 32 in 2010-2011. Furthermore, Tunisia was the only north African country whose rankings in the Competitiveness Index did not decline during this time period.[7] But the reality was not sober.

The Tunisian revolts inspired other revolutions in the region. Throughout January 2011, protests erupted in Algeria, Jordan and Oman. Protests against entrenched regimes broke out simultaneously in Egypt and Yemen in late January 2011. The first Egyptian protest rally took place on January 25, 2011. The concerns were freedom, justice and human dignity, as well as the deterioration of political and social conditions during the 30-year rule of President Hosni Mubarak. The crowds stormed to Tahrir Square, in the heart of the city. The protestors challenged repression, corruption and unemployment and chanted for freedom, opportunity and fall of the regime. Egypt's revolts proved to be the high point of the Arab Spring. The Arab world's cultural and political centre remained in turmoil, and after an 18-day protest, Hosni Mubarak stepped down on February 11, 2011, ending nearly three decades of iron-fisted rule just as Yemen's revolution was getting underway.

Protestors in Yemen had alluded to similar demands. *Ash-sha'byurīdisqāṭ an-niẓām* ("people want an end to the regime") slogan rang loud on the streets as the Arab Spring engulfed Yemen. Ali Abdullah Saleh, had been in charge of Yemen since 1978 and resigned on February 25, 2012, following 33 years of rule. Placed between Tunisia and Egypt, Libya, cognizant of the revolts in the neighbourhood was moving ahead with major anti-government protests. A full-scale revolt began on February 17, 2011, in Benghazi when the protestors clashed with the militia loyal to the then leader Muhammar al-Qadhafi. Sworn to hunt those who protested his rule: "*Shebr shebr, beit beit, dar dar, zenga zenga!*" Roughly translated as "inch by inch, room by room, home by home, and alleyway by alleyway."[8] Gadhafi proved more resilient than his counterparts in the neighbourhood, believing he could continue his rule of 40 years. As the revolts reached the capital Tripoli, a violent crackdown soon escalated into an intense civil war prompting a UN action and a UN

Security Council resolution authorizing "all necessary measures" to protect the civilians of Libya. NATO launched Operation Unified Protector, with the aim of "enforcing an arms embargo, maintaining a no-fly zone and protecting civilians and civilian populated areas from attack or the threat of attack."[9] After six months of fighting and thousands of deaths, rebel forces conquered Tripoli with military backing from the West and several Arab states. Gaddafi was captured and killed outside his hometown of Sirte in August 2011.

Nearly 10,000 localised protests and riots were held in Algeria 2010 to protest poor living conditions caused by high unemployment, food inflation, a lack of housing, and widespread corruption. Protests in Syria began in March 2011, demanding the ousting of President Bashar al-Assad, and rapidly developed into a nationwide uprising. Syrian protests have faced violent repression as Bashar al-Assad maintains power.

The response of the oil rich Persian Gulf countries was equally intense, both from the demonstrators and the rulers. Protesters in Kuwait demanded resignation of the Prime Minister and end of corruption, while those in Oman urged economic reforms. Bahrain was the most turbulent country. On February 14, 2011, over 6000 people protested against the Bahraini capital Manama. They demanded political and constitutional reforms, as well as socio-economic justice and the release of political prisoners. The Pearl Roundabout in Manama, buzzed with the demands for a democratic republic as women "were among the first wave that descended on Pearl Square… to demand change."[10] Exactly a month later, forces mainly from the UAE and Saudi Arabia were dispatched to quash the protestors, as Iran sympathized with them, and the US wished to remain dispassionate with its fifth fleet of navy stationed in Bahrain. Bahrain's geopolitical importance for the GCC (Gulf Cooperation Council) countries and their allies soon made its February revolution and "inconvenient revolution for the Arab World and the international community."[11] Saudi Arabia was marked by protestors both men and women demanding political and economic changes and met with initially promised massive social welfare packets combined with brutal crushing of dissenters on the streets and mass executions. The message was loud and clear, "Don't mess with the monarchy!"

The causes for the upsurge were mostly related to issues such as a lack of democracy, human rights violations, widespread corruption, serious economic decline, rising unemployment, abject poverty, increasing food prices, and a number of other factors that contributed, such as increasing population with a large percentage of educated young people dissatisfied with the centralized systems and the marginalized population outside capital cities. Protests were often aimed at the displacement of the regime, but in some countries, demonstrations demanded the improvement of living conditions while leaving the principal foundations of the state unchallenged.[12]

THE AFTERMATH

The momentum that began in Tunisia, toppled four long serving dictators—Ben Ali of Tunisia, Hosni Mubarak of Egypt, Muammar Gaddafi of Libya and Ali Abdullah Saleh of Yemen. Tunisia had Beji Caid Essebsi as its first democratically elected head of state in 2014, a decade after being the initiator of the upsurge with no prior experience in democracy. Though the demands of people are yet to be fulfilled, Tunisia made the transition, while the other popular uprisings ended in promises, crackdown, chaos or war. Egypt's uprisings were like none other. It was the "Arab Spring's zenith." Mohammad Morsi, an Islamist, was installed as the country's first civilian president and soon deposed in 2013 in a military coup after his programme met with fierce opposition. Abdel Fattah el-Sissi, a retired general, is now in seat since 2014.

Libya and Yemen are mired in civil war. Libya is now divided between two rival camps vying for power in the oil-rich north African country, Tripolitania in the west and Cyrenaica in the east. In the west, the UN-recognised Government of National Accord (GNA) was set up in Tripoli in 2016. The east is controlled by an administration declared by the elected parliament, which does not recognise the GNA and is backed by military strongman Khalifa Haftar, with the support of the United Arab Emirates, Egypt and Russia.[13] In Yemen, Saleh's successor, Abed Rabbo Mansour Hadi fled the country after failing to find a solution to corruption, unemployment and food insecurity. The Houthi, an Islamist political and armed movement in Yemen with Shia support took charge of the North. This further altered the situation by bringing the regional Sunni and Shia dominant states such as Iran and Saudi Arabia in the picture, with the support of the US, UK and France. Yemen awaits peace, democracy and restoration of basic infrastructure.

In Algeria President Bouteflika resigned in 2019 after four successive terms following the widespread demonstrations after he announced his decision to run for a fifth term. People protesting against high-ranking officials were screaming, "*Yetnaḥāwgā*ʿ,"—"they should all go."[14] Algeria's Hirak Protest movement that began in 2019 continues to demand a transition towards more democratic governance. Those in Morocco were briefly given cosmetic reforms and the underlying legitimacy crisis of the regime persists, as do socio-economic inequalities.

In Syria, the regime's fight to the death has killed more than 380,000 people. Despite a decade of fighting and a broken country, Bashar al-Assad remains firmly in power, thanks to military support from Iran and Russia. Poverty and displacement are huge in Syria, which remains economically devastated and divided, while thousands have opted for painful migration.

The West Asian region is undergoing a change. The region is engulfed in divisive sectarian crises and continues to be impacted by the role and interference of foreign powers. The Persian Gulf monarchies are set in their seats by quashing the demonstrations. The ruling bargain has evolved but has not radically changed since the Arab Spring. While there is growing dissatisfaction with the Persian Gulf monarchies, the discontent is contained.[15]The Arab Spring has challenged the supremacy of traditional West Asian powers such as Syria and Egypt, as the Persian Gulf countries strive to position themselves as the region's new centre of activity. Some of the Gulf countries have even shifted their regional policy approaches drastically. For example, the UAE and Bahrain have established full diplomatic relations with Israel which were non-existent so far.

INDIA AND THE WANA REGION

India has had maritime contacts with the WANA region since the ancient times. Trade, commerce, religion, and culture and scientific ideas were passed down through generations. Spices were imported from India, while the Arab traders exported horses, dates, frankincense and myrrh. India's historical connection with the Persian Gulf region dates back more than 5000 years. The Magan civilization that flourished around 2300 B.C.E., is associated with parts of Oman and coastal south-eastern Iran and was a source of copper, while the Dilmun civilization that flourished in c 2100 B.C.E, is associated with the modern-day Bahrain and the adjacent coast of Arabia. Both had contacts with the Indus Valley civilization. The Persian Gulf was a key international trade route that connected the West Asian region to India, East Africa, Southern Asia and China.[16] Darius the Great, the Achaemenid emperor of the sixth century BCE, made efforts to consolidate sea power and open a cheaper route from Egypt to India and the Persian Gulf.[17] Ashoka's edicts refer to his relations with Egypt under Ptolemy-II.[18] Later in the first century B.C., the Greek navigator Hippalus developed the direct sea route from Red Sea to India taking advantage of the southwest monsoon.[19]

The Indo-Arab interaction flourished with trade that was mutually beneficial to both and remained largely uninterrupted during the mediaeval period. The Arab and the Persian merchants traded with Indian traders in expensive and exclusive items as precious stones, gold and herbal medicines. Bushire, the Persian port, was known as the *darvaza-yi Hind* or the Gateway of India, and at one time it was understood that there were more Persian speakers in India than in Persia or the Gulf.[20] The Mughals spoke Persian and patronized Persian culture.

The European presence in the Eastern trade began with the Portuguese via the Cape of Good Hope, and they soon conquered Hormuz (1507), the Persian island, gaining a complete control of the trade between India and Europe that was carried through the Persian Gulf. There was never a lull in India's historic contacts with the West Asian region, the importance of which the British recognised in the modern period. The British that saw the region as vital for India's defence particularly the Persian Gulf was considered as the outer security ring of India's defence. The Portuguese control waned as the British steadily increased their influence and conquered the strategically located ports and islands in the Persian Gulf, Red Sea and around the Cape of Good Hope, thereby making the Indian Ocean region a *mare clausum* for British trade and movement.

As trade continued to thrive under the British flag, channels of communication to Europe were kept secure on all three routes—the Persian Gulf, the Red Sea and rounding the Cape of Good Hope in the Indian Ocean.

British India's imperial interests in the Persian Gulf were determined, pursued and administered from Bombay Presidency and later the Government of India. The Indian influence remained for long in the Gulf region. Much after the British exit, the Indian rupee was widely accepted as legal tender in Kuwait, Bahrain, Qatar, Oman and the present United Arab Emirates, and even adopted as local currency in the form of the Gulf Rupee between 1959 and 1966. British colonialism in India and Egypt were established in different times and under different circumstances, but had wider ramifications on India. British colonial rule in Egypt was modelled on Indian pattern, with officers as Lord Cromer, Lord Kitchener, McMahon and others who served in both the countries.[21]

While the British Indian Government maintained a hawk's eye over the region and controlled access to its Indian empire through it, the nationalists used the contacts with people in West Asia. During the freedom movement, Indian nationalists shared notes with the Arab leaders who wholeheartedly supported India's freedom struggle. In their struggle for Indian independence, the Indian National Congress leaders had promoted the cause among the Arab national leaders and had established personal ties with them. Among them were the fiery Indian activist, Madam Bhikaji Cama, the Nightingale of India and activist Sarojini Naidu, and Maulana Abul Kalam Azad. Jawaharlal Nehru had established contacts with the national leaders of Syria, Egypt and Palestine at the Congress of Oppressed Nationalities in Brussels in 1927. India's Mahatma Gandhi and Saad Zaghloul of Egypt shared common goals on the independence of their countries. Later, an exceptionally close friendship developed between Gamal Abdel Nasser, the then President of Egypt, and Jawaharlal Nehru, independent India's first Prime Minister, culminating to the signing of a Friendship Treaty between the two countries in 1955.[22]

After independence the region scored high in India's interests. As the Cold War elicited selective affiliation to either of the two blocs for the newly independent countries, India shared a common platform of Non-aligned Movement (NAM) with the Arab countries. Given the geographical proximity, the historical past was aptly invoked to further relations between India and the Arab World. The region's stability and a boost to trade were both critical. Another aspect of India's connections with the Arabs was its support for the Palestinian cause. The region's oil and gas resources were critical to the establishment of the new India. The "oil boom" of the 1970s encouraged Indian migration to the Gulf, resulting in high remittances back home and a considerable contribution to the Gulf economy in return. The period between 1947 and 1990, before globalization, is often considered as "ideological" towards the region,[23] particularly regarding India's stand towards Iran, Israel-Palestine and Saudi Arabia.

Following the Cold War and liberalisation of India (1991) the economic development activities heightened and demand for oil and gas increased. During this time the political relations with Israel moved towards stabilisation. India had officially recognised Israel in 1950, though full diplomatic ties were established only on January 29, 1992. The two countries today share very close ties and have agreements and exchange in several fields, including defence, science, technology, agriculture and others.

Within the next decade corresponding to the call of the US after the 2001 World Trade Centre attack, India raised concern over cross-border terrorism and appealed to the West Asian countries to collaborate on combating terrorism. By the end of the same decade and the beginning of the next, India, the largest democracy in the world, witnessed a massive pro-democratic upsurge in its neighbourhood. How did India react and how soon? In case of reaction, what guided India's response? Which countries qualified for the Indian reaction? Are age-old contacts sufficient to define foreign policy in a changing situation? Do the Arabs regard India as a political player or merely a neighbour dependent on their resources? Given India's critical interests in the region, the solutions to some of these concerns are discussed briefly.

INDIA'S INTERESTS

The demonstrations in the Arab countries had held a promise then. The mass participation in street demonstrations, the busy updates on social media and call for common demands across the region had defied the stereotypical notion of inability for collective action in favour of democracy among Arabs under authoritarian regimes for long. The happenings in the region had an impact on both the protesting countries and the others that enjoyed relations with them. India had and continues to have manifold interests in WANA. Hence, India needed to secure and foster its interests in the region during the massive upsurge that rocked the region in early 2010s as well as thereafter.

Expatriates and remittances: India has a large expatriate community in the Arab world that contributes back home. Today the region is home to more than eight million Indian expatriates that account for more than 60 per cent of the inbound remittances. As of 2018 at $80 billion in money sent home, India is the world's top recipient of remittances.[24] The UAE is one of India's major sources of remittances. Indian expatriate community of approximately 3.42 million[25] is reportedly the largest ethnic community in UAE constituting roughly about 30 per cent of the country's population.[26]Expat population in UAE is followed by the US, Saudi Arabia and Kuwait. Despite the economic turmoil caused by the coronavirus, remittances to India from the Gulf region surged by the end of the decade, with many Indian banks reporting growth of up to 20 per cent by 2020.[27]

Trade and economy: In 2010, the WANA region accounted for the largest share in India's world trade. Importantly the Gulf region's share in India's world trade was 22 per cent, making it the single largest trading partner.[28] By the end of the decade, bilateral trade between India and WANA was USD 165.70 billion in 2019-20. India's exports to WANA were at USD 53.21 billion in 2019-20. India's imports from WANA were USD 112.49 billion.[29] India-Gulf trade stood around $162 billion in 2918-19, being nearly a fifth of India's global trade that was dominated by crude oil and natural gas worth nearly $75 billion, meeting nearly 65 per cent of India's total requirements.[30] The region is also a big source of Indian investment in infrastructure considering that the Gulf kingdoms wish to diversify their economy and own large foreign currency reserves. India has significantly large investments in Egypt, Syria, Libya, Jordan, Saudi Arabia and the Gulf Cooperation Council (GCC) countries, including projects, collaborations and joint ventures in petroleum, petro-chemicals, fertilizers, machinery, pharmaceutical products, consumer goods, information and communication technology and financial services.[31] Safeguarding of these interests is necessary.

Cultural connects: The religious aspect of the significant Muslim population in both the countries, and the annual pilgrimage to Hajj, adds a new dimension to the relations with countries in the West Asian region. India's has the third-largest Muslim population and the world's largest Muslim-minority population. India is home to 10.9 per cent of the world's Muslim population. Indian films are widely viewed in the Arab region, and influences of Arabic music on Indian pop music scene, apart from other cultural exchanges are common.

In short, India has political, economic and energy security interests, as well as a desire to combat terrorism with the cooperation of the countries in West Asian, Persian Gulf and North African regions. India, as the world's fastest growing economy, is an aspiring global player with increasing leverage in the international sphere and is part of the BRICS, the G20 and the G8+5. Furthermore, India has been seeking a permanent seat on the United Nations Security Council (UNSC). During the Arab Spring, India was elected as the UNSC non-permanent member (2011-2013). Its greater economic interests in the region, and given the fact that it is the largest democracy, India was seen as capable of playing a role in the democratic upsurge. Considering that the country shares a long past, has huge investment in various sectors, has growing energy demands, large workforce remitting back and better acceptability in the Arab world than most outsiders in people-to-people contact, India was expected to be more sensitised towards the massive turnout of Arabs on the streets for democratic demands.

It was left for it to demonstrate whether its interests in the region were restricted to its own economic and energy security alone, or that it could stand by its old interactions and ties built up over decades and show more political interest for the sake of the people who challenged the authoritarians in favour of increased political participation. In view of this, one may explore India's dynamics with the region during the upsurge, and the availability of a foothold for Indian opinion and action.

INDIA'S RESPONSE

The political transitions in West Asia and North Africa were neither smooth nor up to the original purpose of the demonstrators, as various rival groups claimed power in some countries, resulting in civil war. This also posed problem for the international community with strategic, economic and trade interests in the region, as they struggled to deal with the Arab Spring and tackle the challenging issues. India shared a similar concern. It was indeed a tough choice for India to balance its interests and decide on a relatively easier and appropriate policy to the ongoing crisis in the region.

India remained on the side of the progressive forces of history and the democratic forces in West Asia, and with the people, and opposed extremist non-secular aspirations. The Government of India perceived a situation and aligned it with its interests at that point in time.[32]

Indian government was cautious about its first response, even as thousands of Indians working and living in the West Asian countries witnessed the Arabs clamouring for reforms that had long been acknowledged back home. As news of the demonstrations spread, the Indian government did not react immediately but chose to "wait and watch." The expectations and criticism came quickly. India's "deafening" and "inexplicable" silence was much unacceptable to the political commentators.[33] The comments poured in stating that these events "present(ed) an opportunity to project New Delhi's soft power, which is considerable in the region...(as India) presents a working democratic model in a sociocultural environment far closer to the Gulf's than Western democracies are—and with none of the political baggage of the latter."[34] It was suggested that, "New Delhi's advice and assistance would make these countries better homes for Indian workers, better allies in stabilizing a region of great strategic importance to India's development, more reliable energy suppliers, and more prosperous trade and investment partners."[35]

India, however, followed a non-interventionist policy and avoided taking sides in the people's movement. The government of India did not respond to the early Tunisian uprisings. The first official response came on January 29, 2011, as the protest wave rose in Egypt—exactly four days after the first Egyptian protest rally—in the form of a travel advisory for Indian citizens in Egypt, followed by a crisis desk in Cairo for the safety of 3600 People of Indian Origin (PIO) living across Egypt, including Cairo and Alexandria, of which some 2200 were in Cairo.[36] Refraining from supporting either side, India's official spokesperson conveyed that India followed the developments in Egypt with concern and "hope(d) for an early and peaceful resolution of the situation without further violence and loss of lives."[37] Similar caution was exercised in reactions to other countries in Bahrain, Yemen, Syria and Libya.

EVACUATION

Evacuation of about six million Indian immigrants scattered in various small cities of different countries was a major challenge. India's early response was towards securing its political, economic and energy security interests, though safety of the Indian diaspora was the first concern. The government of India successfully evacuated its citizens from Libya within a limited time, bringing nearly 17,000 of them safely back to India.[38] Operation Safe Homecoming brought back willing Indians from Libya (Tripoli and Sebha), Egypt (Alexandria) and Malta.[39] with the assistance of Libya's neighbouring countries. The Ministry of External Affairs performed the herculean task and a combination of air and sea operation was conducted by the Indian Navy and Air India given the issues of few airports shutting down and some people stranded without passports. During the evacuation process, it was imperative to retain links with some regimes without whose support the evacuation process would have failed. The immense and sustained efforts of the MEA and government agencies were highly commendable. In April 2015, India launched Operation Raahat, a humanitarian rescue mission in Yemen. More than 4,640 Indian citizens, as well as foreign nationals, were evacuated from Yemen. In total, 1962 foreign nationals from 48 countries were evacuated as part of Operation Raahat, and the total of over 1000 Indian nationals who were in Syria at the time of the travel advisory issued by the Government in 2012.[40]

USE OF INTERNATIONAL PLATFORMS

India's reaction can also be understood on two international platforms: the BRICS and the United Nations Security Council (UNSC). In January 2011, as India assumed its non-permanent membership in the (UNSC) Libya was the first major issue to confront Indian diplomacy. India voted in favour of the UNSC resolution 1970, a measure adopted unanimously by the UN Security Council on February 26, 2011, which was about taking tough measures against the Gaddafi regime as well as referring the matter to the International Criminal Court and a comprehensive arms embargo designed to prevent the direct or indirect supply, sale or transfer of arms and military equipment to Libya.

In March 2011, however, India abstained to vote on the UN Security Council Resolution 1973 citing "very little clear information, including a lack of certainty."[41] Brazil, China, Germany and the Russian Federation also abstained. The BRICS had called for resolving the Libyan crisis through "peaceful means and dialogue," rather than using force.

In the case of Syria in 2011, when the UNSC offered to put sanctions on Syria, India abstained along with Brazil, South Africa and Lebanon, and preferred to engage in bilateral dialogue with Syria through collaborative and constructive ways, thus not getting directly involved in the conflicts and supporting stabilisation. India sent its own envoy, along with Brazil and South Africa at the Counsels Restraint, to see Syrian leaders visiting New Delhi, and it opposed Western-backed sanctions for the moment and any resolution on that subject.[42]

However, India's approach towards the Syrian conflict shifted in February 2012, when a second resolution was proposed to introduce sanctions against the Syrian regime. India voted in favour while underlining that it does not support regime change.[43] India had played a significant role in the drafting of the Security Council resolution on Syria, which advocated an inclusive, Syrian-led political solution. India condemned violence, demanded peaceful solution and stability.

Indian foreign policy makers sought to follow a non-interventionist policy. Thus, there is was no common or consistent reaction to Arab Spring, but rather a country-specific reaction.

HELP FOR HOPE

As the country prepared for presidential and legislative elections following Hosni Mubarak's fall, India organised to assist Egypt with Electronic Voting Machines (EVMs). Egypt's newly constituted government had requested assistance from the Indian Election Commission in organising the elections. Though India offered to help in conducting the elections, it refused to be part of an international team to monitor them.

In Syria, since the conflict broke out in 2011, India has provided $12 million as humanitarian assistance to the Syrian government through bilateral and multilateral channels. India has set up a biotech park and an IT Centre and extended USD 265 million in lines of credit for projects in the steel and power sectors and provided 1000 scholarships for Syrian students to study in India.[44] In January 21, 2021, during a UNSC briefing on Syria, TS Tirumurti, Indian Permanent Representative to the United Nations, reiterated, "In this regard, it is important to delink humanitarian assistance from progress on the political track. We believe that the noble and necessary cause of humanitarian assistance should always be bereft of politics" and that India is ready to play a "constructive and meaningful role" in the United Nations Security Council (UNSC) towards ending the Syrian conflict and reconstruction.[45]

India's actions were guided by caution, fundamental self-interest in the WANA region, and conventional non-interference policy. When previously stated, as the uprising gained momentum, the Indian administration had to seek help of local governments to evacuate the Indians. The government tried to balance a position that caused less harm to its interests, ensured that it did not jump to react for the sake of it and expressed its concern towards violence and sectarian strife while also proposing peace and stability in the region. With major interests in the relationships with both Saudi Arabia and Iran, two ambitious and rival regional powers, the country needed to strike a careful balance in the dealings with each for trade reasons. In the case of Syria, as the rival groups emerged with the support of international powers, the situation offered no promise for India to identify or distinguish a group that it could back. Thus, it avoided making "sharp choices". The protest in the Arab world moved away from democracy to sectarianism, much to India's disapproval, and India insisted that democratic transition cannot be impelled by external intervention.

CONCLUSION

A decade over, the region and the protestors have earned nothing they sought. With the exception of Tunisia, democracy has remained elusive to others. The problems of poverty, unemployment and authoritarianism continue to haunt the region. Added to these are the growing extremist tendencies and sectarian strife, ethnic conflicts and civil war with a complete collapse of infrastructure in some countries, which has exacerbated the snags, and yet for the world it's business as usual. While India has continued to further its trade and commercial ties with the Arab countries in the decade since the Arab Spring, the region is experiencing new dynamics with Bahrain and UAE establishing diplomatic ties with Israel. The issue of Palestine that formed the cornerstone for independent India's relations with West Asia, is no longer the defining factor. Historic relations indeed provide a strong basis to further contacts in modern times. As the West Asian and North African region unfolds, with shifting power bases such as Iran and Saudi Arabia aspiring for dominance, growing but rightful demands of educated and restless young population, overcoming the reservations of earlier diplomatic policies in case of ties with Israel, and the interests of international powers such as US, China, Russia and EU, India is expected to define its position in the public and political realm so as to be seen more than a nation dependent on West Asia's resources only for and with economic advantage.

During the British rule, Indian leaders were able to establish people-to-people contact with the Arab leaders from Egypt, Syria and Morocco, frequently against the common colonial rulers for the cause of freedom, and not without British apprehensions, who more than once attempted to prohibit the collective nationalist activities. Today as the governments carefully craft their relations, define and implement policies combined with political and diplomatic opportunities to improve trade relations and cement strategic ties with the most critical region of the world, the people-to-people contact finds rare resonance in the Arab Spring, despite the region's significant Indian population. Of course, the media, including social media, played a big role in reporting the day-to-day events and disseminating information! Media continues to remain a platform for reactions and counter reactions but given the nature of earlier people-to-people ties in both regions, the relationships now appear limited and synthetic.

India has more at stake in West Asia than any other external power in the region. While the country looks forward to taking a leap on the international front and aims to project itself as an evolving global power to play an active role in an emerging multilateral international order, it will remain engaged with the WANA for the same reasons it was when the demonstrations began. While the disgruntlement is largely targeted towards the corrupt, despotic and entrenched rulers, it must be remembered that the grievances that caused the uprisings, such as poverty, corruption, youth unemployment and lack of political representation, remain as relevant now as they were a decade ago.

The demands of the larger youth are towards education and employment, participation and dignity. The West Asia and the North African region particularly the Persian Gulf in the neighbourhood have important implications for India. Rise in extremist tendencies and violence are dangerous for security of the region and democracy. India must navigate carefully between the tensions of regional power aspirations of Saudi Arabia and Iran, sectarian turmoil and aggressive goals of China and Russia, and interests of US and Europe.

India was chosen as a non-permanent member of the UN Security Council in 2021, is the Chair of the BRICS Summit, and will chair the multilateral G-20 in 2023. As a major global actor, it may set the tone for more engaged responses in the region. People and their aspirations should be considered in interactions with governments.

NOTES

1. *The Arab Democracy Index 2011*, No. 3 (March 2012). The Index is prepared by the Arab Reform Initiative and the Palestinian Center for Policy and Survey Research, in partnership with ten research centres in the Arab world.
2. Sir Mark Lyall, "The UN's Response to the Arab Spring and the Evolving Role of the Security Council," *Address to UN APPG Grant Houses of Parliament*, May 2, 2012, at https://una.org.uk/sites/default/files/Address%20to%20the%20UN%20APPG%20by%20Sir%20Mark%20Lyall%20Grant%2C%202%20May%202012.pdf (accessed on March 30, 2021).
3. Bassma Kodmani et al, *Arab Democracy Index 5*, Arab Reform Initiative and The Palestinian Center for Policy and Survey Research, June 2017, at https://www.arab-reform.net/project/arab-democracy-index/ (accessed on March 30, 2021).

4 *Democracy Index 2019:A year of democratic setbacks and popular protest,* A report by The Economist Intelligence Unit, at http://www.eiu.com/Handlers/WhitepaperHandler.ashx?fi=Democracy-Index-2019.pdf&mode=wp&campaignid=democracyindex2019 (accessed on March 30, 2021).

5. Lyall, n. 2

6 Syrine Cherif, *Tunisian Transition Oral History Collection*, Columbia Centre for Oral History, at https://oralhistoryportal.library.columbia.edu/document.php?id=ldpd_13792036 (accessed on January 20, 2020).

7 *Tunisia: Analyzing the Dawn of the Arab Spring*, at https://news.gallup.com/poll/157049/tunisia-analyzing-dawn-arab-spring.aspx (accessed on April 4, 2021).

8. Muammar Gaddafi's Speech https://www.youtube.com/watch?v=69wBG6ULNzQ and *Profile Muammar Gaddafi*, August 22, 2011, at https://www.aljazeera.com/news/2011/8/22/profile-muammar-gaddafi (accessed on February 18, 2021).

9. Mathew Green, "To what extent was the NATO intervention in Libya a Humanitarian intervention,"*E-International Relations,* February 6, 2019, at https://www.e-ir.info/2019/02/06/to-what-extent-was-the-nato-intervention-in-libya-a-humanitarian-intervention/#_ftn4 (accessed on March 9, 2021).

10. Xan Rice, et. al., "Women have emerged as key players in the Arab Spring,"*The Guardian*, April 22, 2011, at https://www.theguardian.com/world/2011/apr/22/women-arab-spring#:~:text=From%20the%20highly%2Deducated%20Tunisian,that%20launched%20the%20Arab%20spring. (accessed on March 5, 2021).

11. Maryam Al Khawaja, Special Advisor, Gulf Centre for Human Rights, at https://www.youtube.com/watch?v=EBHUwMLT9MY (accessed on February 20, 2021).

12 Erzsébet N. Rózsa, et. al., "The Arab Spring: Its Impact on the Region and on the Middle East,"*Conference Policy Brief for the Middle East Conference* on A Wmd/Dvs Free Zone Nos. 9/10, August 2012, Academic Peace Orchestra Middle East, at https://library.fes.de/pdf-files/iez/09609.pdf (accessed on April 20, 2021).

13. "Libya mired in chaos 10 years after years 10/02/2021," France 24, at https://www.france24.com/en/live-news/20210210-libya-mired-in-chaos-10-years-after-arab-spring

14 Inès Osman, "Algeria: The Arab Spring's Late Bloomer?," *The Tahrir Institute of Middle East Policy,* February 09, 2021,at https://timep.org/commentary/analysis/algeria-the-arab-springs-late-bloomer/ (accessed on April 20, 2021).

15. Russel E. Lucas, "The Persian Gulf Monarchies and the Arab Spring," in *Beyond the Arab Spring*, ed. Mehran Kamrava (Oxford, UK: Oxford University Press, 2014), 314.

16. Gregory L. Possehl, *The Indus Civilization: A Contemporary Perspective* (Oxford: Altamira Press, 2002), 220. For reference to Magan also see, Shereen Ratnagar, *Encounters: The Westerly Trade of the Harappan Civilization* (Delhi: Oxford University Press, 1981), 80-85.

17. Roger M Savory, "The History of the Persian Gulf: 600-1800," in *The Persian Gulf States: A General Survey*, ed. Alvin J. Cottrell (Baltimore, MD: John Hopkins University Press, 1981), 20.

18. "India-Egypt Bilateral relations," Ministry of External Affairs, Government of India (updated July 2019), https://mea.gov.in/Portal/ForeignRelation/Bilateral_brief_for_website.pdf
19. Ibid.
20 Lawrance G. Potter, ed., *The Persian Gulf in History* (New York, NY: Palgrave Macmillan, 2009), 13.
21. R.L. Shukla, "British Colonialism in India and Egypt: A Comparative View," Presidential Address, Indian History Congress, *Proceedings of the Indian History Congress* 48, (1987), 603.
22. "India-Egypt Relations," Embassy of India, Cairo, Egypt, at https://www.eoicairo.gov.in/page/india-egypt/ (accessed on April 17, 2021).
23. H.V. Pant, "India and the Middle East: Before and after Arab Spring," in *The International Politics of the Arab Spring: Popular Unrest and Foreign Policy*, ed., Robert Mason (New York, NY: Palgrave Macmillan, 2014), 155-175.
24. "India remains top remittance recipient in 2018," Arab News, December 9, 2018, at https://www.arabnews.com/node/1417906/business-economy (accessed on April 15, 2021).
25 As per "International Migrant Stock 2019," UN's Department of Economic and Social Affairs (DESA), at https://www.un.org/en/development/desa/population/migration/data/estimates2/estimates19.asp (accessed on March 30, 2021).
26. "Indian Community in UAE," Embassy of India, Abu Dhabi, United Arab Emirates, at https://www.indembassyuae.gov.in/indian-com-in-uae.php (accessed on April 29, 2021).
27 "Rise in Indian remittances from the Gulf hides tales of coronavirus heartbreak," *Arabian Business*, September 9, 2020, https://www.arabianbusiness.com/banking-finance/451664-how-rise-in-indian-remittances-from-the-gulf-hide-tales-of-coronavirus-heartbreak (accessed on April 14, 2021). These are said to be propelled by the twin factors of a plunge in rupee value and expat Indians rushing to move part of their savings home in the wake of uncertainty related to the global pandemic.
28. Ministry of Commerce and Industry Database, Government of India, May 2011, at https://commerce.gov.in/about-us/divisions/foreign-trade-territorial-division/foreign-trade-wana/ (accessed on April 17, 2021).
29. "Foreign Trade (WANA)," Department of Commerce, Ministry of Commerce and Industry, Government of India, https://commerce.gov.in/about-us/divisions/foreign-trade-territorial-division/foreign-trade-wana/
30. Mahesh Sachdeva, "A Double Whammy for India-Gulf Economic Ties," *The Hindu*, April 10, 2020, at https://www.thehindu.com/opinion/lead/a-double-whammy-for-india-gulf-economic-ties/article31302542.ece (accessed on April 14, 2021).
31. See, "Indian Trade Portal" [section on GCC], Department of Commerce, Ministry of Commerce and Industry, Government of India, at https://www.indiantradeportal.in/vs.jsp?lang=0&id=0,25,45,858,912 (accessed on April 30, 2021).

32. See Suhasini Haider, "World View: Arab Spring—Should India have taken a more active line?" September 17, 2011, The Internthem-of-corruption-3716804.html (accessed on March 28, 2021).
33. Satish Chandra and Sushant Sareen, "India's Deafening Silence On The Tumult In The Arab World," *Vivekananda International Foundation*, November 25, 2011, at http://www.vifindia.org/article/2011/february/25/Indias-Deafening-Silence-On-The-Tumult-In-The-ArabWorld. (accessed on April 14, 2021).
34. "A New Engagement," *Times of India*, Feb 28, 2011, at https://timesofindia.indiatimes.com/edit-page/a-new-engagement/articleshow/7587111.cms (accessed on April 14, 2021).
35 Richard Fontaine & Daniel Twining, "India's Arab Spring Opportunity," *The Diplomat*, August 24, 2011, at https://thediplomat.com/2011/08/indias-arab-spring-opportunity/ (accessed on April 11, 2021).
36. "Indians safe in Egypt—Control room at Embassy of India," MEA, Government of India, January 29, 2011, at https://www.mea.gov.in/press-releases.htm?dtl/765/Indians+safe+in+Egypt (accessed on April 11, 2021).
37. "India concerned at developments in Egypt-hopes for peaceful resolution," Ministry of External Affairs, Government of India Media Centre, January 30, 2011, at http://www.mea.gov.in/media briefings.htm?dtl/3354/India_concerned_at_developments_in_Egypt__hopes_for_peaceful_resolution (accessed on April 5, 2021).
38. "Back on home turf after 38 years in Libya," *DNA*, March 19, 2011, at http:// www.dnaindia.com/india/report_back-on-home-turf-after-38-years-in-libya_1521896 (accessed on April 5, 2021).
39. "Operation 'Safe Homecoming' successfully drawing towards a close-Update of 10th March 2011," Ministry of External Affairs, Government of India, at https://mea.gov.in/press-releases.htm?dtl/662/Operation+Safe+Homecoming+successfully+drawing+towards+a+close++Update+of+10th+March+2011 (accessed on March 24, 2021).
40 Q. No.186 Appreciation of India's Humanitarian Rescue Operation in Yemen, February 25, 2016, at https://www.mea.gov.in/rajyasabha.htm?dtl/26411/q+no186+appreciation+of+indias+humanitarian+rescue+operation+in+yemen (accessed on April 2, 2021).
41. "UN Security Council, Security Council approves 'no-fly zone' over Libya, authorizing 'all necessary measures' to protect civilians, by vote of 10 in favor with 5 abstentions," United Nations Meetings Coverage and Press Releases, March 17, 2011, at http://www.un.org/press/ en/2011/sc10200.doc.htm. (accessedon April 10, 2021).
42 Suhasini Haider, "World View: Arab Spring—Should India have taken a more active line?" September 17, 2011, at https://www.news18.com/videos/ivideos/bjp-mp-tejasvi-surya-apologizes-to-muslim-bbmp-staffers-after-accusing-them-of-corruption-3716804.html (accessed on March 28, 2021).
43. "India votes for UN resolution on Syria," *Indian Express*, July 20, 2012, at http://archive.indianexpress.com/news/india-votes-for-un-resolution-on-syria/976819/ (accessed on March 31, 2021). UPDATED: APRIL 10, 2020 01:45 IST

44 "India ready to play 'constructive role' in UNSC to end Syrian conflict," *Business Standard*, January 21, 2021, at https://www.business-standard.com/article/current-affairs/india-ready-to-play-constructive-role-in-unsc-to-end-syrian-conflict-121012100140_1.html (accessed on April 28, 2021).

45. Ibid; #IndiainUNSC Political and humanitarian situation in Syria, at https://www.facebook.com/watch/?v=168175338418464 (accessed on April 7, 2021).

3

SECTARIANISM AND INSTABILITY IN POST-ARAB SPRING WEST ASIA

Mohmad Saleem Sheikh

INTRODUCTION

The West Asian region has recently witnessed a wide range of social, political and security challenges at both the state and regional levels. Following the 2011 civil war, one of the notable challenges that can be observed is the consolidation and articulation of sub-state identities in Syria and Yemen. In addition, the ethno-sectarian differences and deepening ideological rifts between governments have enabled non-state actors to exploit the divisions, thereby aggravating insecurity and instability in the region. Instability is not a new phenomenon in the region; it has been an integral part of the politico-security environment since the post-World War I period when the modern state system emerged. Political autocracy, weak state-society relations, multi-ethnic and multi-sectarian social groups, inter-state ideological rivalries, and the absence of a comprehensive security architecture characterise this regional system.

The instability in West Asia is evident at both the national and regional levels. This region has continuously exhibited an inherent propensity for instability and catastrophe. Numerous potential sources of instability exist both inside and outside the United States. These potential sources of regional instability and violence are interrelated and comparable. In post-Arab Spring west Asia, however, the three decisive forces responsible for escalating regional instability have crystallised: the continuation and strengthening of durable Authoritarianism and the battle for regional domination. Second, the escalation of sectarianism and sectarian conflicts in places such as Syria and

Yemen. Thirdly, the growth of substate and non-state armed entities adds to sectarianism and extremism, which have a negative impact on regional stability and collaboration. The Arab upheavals and civil wars demonstrated that the fundamental causes of regional instability in west Asia stem from the local political settings of the region's states.[1]

Although conflicts and civil wars encourage the rise of non-state armed groups, they also invite external intervention, deepening the security vacuum and increasing instability. This article contends that sectarianism has altered the dynamics of public mobilisation and provided an excuse for authoritarian rulers and their caucus to ignore reform efforts. The authorities launched a ferocious assault to put an end to the revolts. As a result, human rights violations such as torture, deaths and destruction, state failure and a fierce struggle for power and territory have exacerbated the region's instability and crisis.

RISE OF SECTARIANISM: IDEOLOGICAL AND POLITICAL DISCOURSE

The communal mobilisation began with the Lebanese civil war of 1975 and Saudi funding of Wahabism in the 1970s and 1980s.[2] The Iranian Revolution accelerated the political exposition of identity politics and ideological conflict in the regional environment. Iran sought to export revolution to other parts of West Asia, empowering minorities, mainly Shia', to assert their identity and stake in political processes. Therefore, sectarianism saw an upsurge in the post-1979 regional environment, with regional and extra-regional actors encouraging these divisions. The Iranian revolution set in tone sectarian revolutionary revivalism in the regional international relations as it kick-started the process of Islamisation of politics, trying to replace secular authoritarianism with theocratic authoritarianism. Therefore the Iranian Revolution added sectarianism (in its modern form) to the domestic political environments of the West Asian region. "Sectarian divisions became more prominent as regional populations became increasingly dissatisfied living in states without religious ideology or adequate representation across sectarian lines."[3]

The Iranian revolution exacerbated sectarianism ideologically by making regional states assertive in their foreign policies, predominantly the Sunni authoritarian governments. Furthermore, the Iranian decisiveness towards exporting the revolution alarmed these Sunni regimes, principally Saudi Arabia, who perceived it challenging to their regional dominance[4] and felt a necessity to counterbalance it. As a result, Saudi Arabia invested in Wahabism as an ideological weapon to counter Iranian revolutionary influence in Sunni Arab countries' domestic politics. Consequently, Islamist radicalism began to take root throughout the region.

However, the sectarian rivalries sharpened in the 2003 U. S.-led invasion of Iraq. The invasion not only descended Iraq into the Civil war but also triggered "a massive sectarian wave" that "has grown in size and ferocity as Syria descended into strife."[5] Therefore, Sectarianism and the Shi'atization of the Sunni Arab world resulted from these twin events—the 2003 Iraq Invasion and the Arab Spring in Syria. Although the Iranian shi'atization of the Arab world did not start suddenly in the Syrian war somewhat, the conflict in Iraq converted the simmering antagonism into a virtual Shia-Sunni civil war with the growth of Shia dominance, most notably the expansion of Shi'a dominance in what had been a Sunni political bastion, Iraq.[6] In addition, the failure of governance structures in the region both created political space and contributed to societal cleavages, which allowed intolerance, animosity and sectarian entrepreneurs to invade and compete for power.[7]

The Syrian civil war emboldened these sectarian rivalries while intensifying regional competition, setting in motion a kind of politics involving regional powers as peripheral actors, sectarian Chauvinists and non-state actors as battlefield actors. At the same time, ordinary citizens in Yemen, Syria and elsewhere naturally fell into either category. The regional powers like Iran promoted revolutions in the region except for Alawite ruled Syria, given its geostrategic importance. The civil wars strengthened the 'resistance axis' while adding Yemeni Houthis to the fold that further alarmed Sunni states of turmoil and uprisings led by Shia communities, particularly in Bahrain, Saudi Arabia and Kuwait. However, sectarian violence has been on the rise since the Iraq Civil war. In Syria, the Shia militias defending the Assad regime, trained and backed by Iran and Hezbollah, have targeted Sunni localities and their places of worship to foster sectarian war.[8]

The Arab Spring and the process of political transformation in authoritarian states like Egypt, Libya and Tunisia, followed by the uprisings in Syria, Bahrain and Yemen, triggered a counter-revolutionary response spearheaded by the region's stable authoritarian regime regimes who feared the success of democratic revolutions would unseat them. In Sunni monarchies, it was anticipated that the ascendancy of the Shi'ites in Iraq was part of a burgeoning 'Shia crescent,' which drew together Iran, Iraq and Lebanon's Hizbullah, emboldening Shia communities in Bahrain, Kuwait and Saudi Arabia. Instead, the Arab spring unleashed sectarian divisions in Syria, and Yemen and Iran's role completed the crescent into a full moon. Moreover, the sectarian armed groups deliberately attacked their opponents' worship sites to foster a sectarian war.

Following the 2011 protests against President Bashar al-Assad for social equality, democracy, and pluralism, as well as for the rights of the excluded social majority and other underrepresented minorities, sectarianism dominated the debate in Syria. People from all sections, including Alawites, joined in. The regime and its benefactors in Iran were swift to paint the opposition as a movement (radical Salafists Islamists and later terrorists) misled by foreign sponsors who wanted to destabilise Syria and the region, and this perception spread rapidly.[9] The Syrian Minorities suddenly dropped out of the opposition.

Sectarianism in the region has been further exacerbated by the relatively recent formation and growing appeal of transnational extremist groups, some with direct assistance from sectarian state players and others without. These extremist groups rely on doctrinal differences, following a reductionist interpretation of the Quran and espousing fundamentalist ideologies and policies. Another major cause pointed out by Shibley Telhami is that "sectarianism and ethnic tensions are the outcomes of declining state capacity and fraying state-society relations, not its underlining cause." Sectarianism is more resilient than it has ever been in history, thanks to a surge in popular engagement in the region's political processes and a mounting aspiration for a more direct stake in political representation. The current upheaval is the outcome of rising geostrategic rivalry and competitiveness amongst regional players, worsened by repeated extra-regional interventions and, more fundamentally, the Arab countries' failure to satisfy the needs and expectations of their populations. In nations like Iraq, Syria and Yemen, popular uprisings that culminated in the breakdown of governmental authority were not about identity politics or religious indifferences. The public was not demanding that the state be destroyed, as was the case in other nations that saw protests during the Arab upheavals. Instead, the majority of the demands were focused on socio-economic and political concerns. The Arab protest movements in Syria and Yemen were centred on demands for political restructuring and institutional change, renegotiating new social contracts, establishing democratic laws and more undeviating and genuine forms of political participation.

THE EXPONENTIAL GROWTH OF SECTARIANISM: EFFECTS OF THE ARAB SPRING AND CIVIL WARS

Before the Arab Spring, Sectarianism had little popular support. As Nasrallah, Assad and Ahmadinejad were perhaps the most popular regional leaders for denouncing the existence of Israel (Valbjrn and Bank 2011). However, sectarianism thrived as the autocratic governments crumbled to popular uprisings. The sectarianism was instrumentalised by leaders in Syria, Iraq and Bahrain as a counter-revolutionary mechanism that consolidated their support base and at the same time effectively weakened the opposition. Thus, on the one hand, sectarianism helped strengthen authoritarian powerhouses in the Gulf region, particularly in Bahrain, with the help of powers like Saudi Arabia and the UAE. On the other hand, it led to State failure in Syria, Iraq and Yemen. As civil conflicts led to state collapse, particularly in the Levant, steadily increasing border porosity enabled Islamist jihadists and a counter-coalition of Shia-driven groups to intervene. With the battle stretching in Syria, the propensity of sectarianism became transnational.

The Syrian uprising demonstrated inherent sectarian dynamics determined by the contestation over power-sharing and reconfiguration of structures of power between politically disadvantaged ethno-sectarian groups and the ruling Alawite regime. Moreover, political events on the ground enhanced the sectarian divide and the narrative in phenomenal ways. With coming in power of Bashar al-Assad in 2000, dissent and political activism began to take root. The "Damascus spring 200-2001", the "Manifesto of 99" and the "Manifesto of the thousand" formed the basis for political contestation in Syria, marking it as the 'preliminary phase of political awakening. The demands majorly included an end to martial law in force since 1963, the release of political prisoners, the permission for an independent press and the institution of political parties. However, the demand for democratic pluralism came in the famous "Damascus declaration of 2005" that called for a civilian state and an end to the Baath monopoly on power.[10]

The dissenters that underpinned the demands for change had a more comprehensive social base, including the umbrella group, the friends of civil society, the outlawed Muslim brotherhood. The coalition formally came into existence in 2006 in the name of the Syrian National Salvation Front (NSF), with Muslim brotherhood, leftists and Kurdish dissenters. The dissident leaders had realised that by working independently, they exercised little compared to the dictatorship's authority. Another factor that led to the coalition formation was the regime's allegation that if the Ba'th regime's hold on power was removed, the only feasible alternatives were even more unpalatable Islamic fundamentalism or excruciating turmoil of the type that wreaked havoc on everyday life in Iraq during the US invasion.[11] However, dissent weakened by 2009 due to increasing repression through mukhabarat (Secret service) security services and fragmentation of the coalition with Muslim brotherhood suspending support to NSF. The calls for the creation of a civil and democratic state recognising the political and cultural rights of Syria's religious minorities and Kurdish community, in other words, the creation of a pluralist society, regained pace in the wake of Arab Spring Uprisings.

As the sphere of political contestation expanded, the regimes began selective use of repression to diffuse the demands for expansion of political participation and slow down the progress of popular uprising.[12] It fragmented the political landscape and prevented the emergence of a strong political opposition that could forcefully promote an extension of political prerogatives or access to existing power structures. In Syria Assad regime was prepared to respond to the protests with full force, although with legitimate demands,[13] coupled with an alternative narrative that pushed identity (sectarian) to assume political roles and contest for political authority (Balanche 2018, xi). Despite its messages, speeches and chants of unity and camaraderie with the People of Syria, the popular movement in Syria has been accused by the authorities and specific forces either regionally or globally of being a terrorist organisation (Controlled by Islamic religious extremists supported by Saudi Arabia and Qatar). On the other hand, the Assad dictatorship has presented itself as secular and protective of religious minorities. Therefore in the tussle between the two narratives—the regime narrative and the narrative of the popular movement—the question of legitimacy and social mobilisation remained the main divers of the political contestation. The Assad regime, like other dictators, was unprepared to respond to the anti-government protests in mid-March 2011. Instead, to delegitimise these protests, Assad was quick to invoke 'external conspiracy' behind the calls for reform and economic grievance. Syria regime also used repressive force in view that demonstrators would retreat, maintaining the status quo without losing legitimacy and patrimonial loyalties. However, the use of force turned unyielding, perhaps surprising that protestors kept mobilising while rejecting temporary concessions of the regime, like lifting emergency laws in effect since 1963.

The regime and its durability rested on Alawi political elite, who were Army officers appointed excessively before 1963, the security agencies and a network of rural elite accommodating a small number of Sunni businessmen. The Alawi ascendency played a causal role in two ways—firstly, in merging sectarianism and the struggle for power in the inner circles of the Baath party over ideology and personal ambitions. This struggle culminated in Alawi domination due to internal divisions among Sunnis on a regional and class basis.[14] Secondly, this supremacy culminated in Sunni's political exclusion from the power and authority structures that earned their resentment, predominantly from urban spheres. The Sunni resentment poured out in Muslim brotherhood-led agitations throughout northern provinces, including the rebellion of 1982.[15]

The Arab Spring Uprisings allowed the excluded groups to struggle for proportional representation in governance structures. Assad clearly understood that the opposition movement against his authority was much too robust to be subdued after the first demonstrations in Syria started in January 2011. The resistance arose as a new and far stronger wave, with the people screaming "Syrians are one," challenging the sectarian alignments that had benefitted the Assad dictatorship (and, previous to that, the French mandate) for decades. Moreover, defencelessness and the prospect of political change distressed the Assad regime to weaponize sectarianism and generate fear of Sunni ascendency in Alawite and other religious minorities to renew their loyalties and earn legitimacy along with unflinching support to his authority.[16] Assad sought to exploit events, appearances and associations to portray himself as a religious Shia as part of his strategy. His public demeanour and rhetoric attempted to divide the Alawites from the opposition, transforming it from a single front against his undemocratic administration to a sectarian conflict between Sunnis and Shias. Assad soon realised that manipulating the deep-seated Alawite fear of the Sunni ascendency could still provide him with a significant amount of political influence.[17]

Regardless of how original his method was, it was effective. Shia political and military frontrunners Hezbollah and Iran decided to support Assad immediately. In a short while, Turkey and Saudi Arabia intervened, bringing their powerful Sunni ideology to bear on the situation. Iran and Hezbollah's intervention solidified Assad's security and elevated the domestic political contest into a regional security issue in the larger Sunni-Shia rivalry. By July 2011, hundreds of thousands of Syrians had taken to the streets to demonstrate against the government, with opposition supporters taking up guns in response to the security forces' brutal crackdown (BBC News 2016). However, it was not until the transformation of uprisings into a full-fledged civil war (early 2012) between the Sunnis and the Shiites that much-needed financial and military help started flowing in from regional and extra-regional players in support of their preferred groups like ISIS or the Free Syrian Army.

The militarisation of the uprisings, foreign financing and interventions brandished sectarian identity exponentially and attracted transnational militant Islamist ideologies to gain ground and fight territorial battles to establish some form of an Islamic state. Moreover, more fighters joined the Islamist militias once the conflict became transitional. The apex of this escalation was the establishment of the "Islamic State in Syria and the Levant" (ISIL) in April 2013, which evolved into the "Islamic State" (IS) in June 2014.[18] The regional governments like Saudi Arabia, Iran, Turkey and others had to respond to events unfolding in Syria and allocate resources to ensure their safekeeping and halt any spillover effect on their domestic environments.

Political contestation in Yemen and the Sectarian Divison

The post Arab Spring civil war in Yemen emanated primarily from the failure of Yemeni society to address and resolve popular anger and frustration caused by political marginalisation, economic disenfranchisement and the adverse effects of an extractive, corrupt and rentier state. Yemen has been mired in a cycle of violence, political instability and institutional disintegration since the modern state's inception in the 1960s, with the current conflict emerging as the most recent eruptive expression. Moreover, the integration of 1990 (unification of South and North Yemen) has layered the complexity with confrontational politics and deep societal divisions, allowing violence, anarchy and political upheavals to become a permanent feature of socio-political life.[19]

The political transition of 2011 generated a distinct power contestation that led the country into a civil war where sectarianism has thrived exponentially. The transition ended protests with a prospect for a breakaway from extractive and patronage-driven governance to a representative system. The genuine political and economic grievances that were pushed by the unorganised street opposition aggravated the Houthi, and the southern secessionists (*Al hirak*), were systematically marginalised in a renewed 'intra-elite struggle' for control over institutions of the state.[20]

In November 2011, the GCC negotiated a transition deal in which President Saleh agreed to a peaceful transfer of power.[21] It brought incumbent vice-president Mansur Rabu Hadi to power in February 2012, but due to the immunity provided by the transition document, it could not end Saleh's control over his party, General people's Congress (GPC), his loyalists in military and security services and patronage network, including many tribal militias.[22] The GCC strongly promoted the transition, with recognition from the United Nations, the US and the EU maintaining the status quo by mere reshuffling older elites rather than pushing genuine reforms in the decaying system. The government of Masur Rabu Hadi was tasked to build national consensus through a national dialogue (NDC established in March 2013-January 2014) incorporating marginalised Houthis and southerners in setting political and security order in Yemen.[23]

The shooting of 50 unarmed protestors by snipers on March 18, 2011, was a watershed moment that increased inter elite rivalry fundamentally. Ali Mohsin (commander of the First Armoured division) and the Ahmars ended a three-decade-old elite alliance that had maintained relative stability in Yemen by siding with the opposition. The elite defection accelerated fragmentation at the military, tribal and party levels, particularly between GPC and the Islah. The Islah-led JPM (joint meeting party, conglomeration of six opposition groups established in 2006) penetrated and hijacked street opposition while channelising a political bargain to oust Saleh and gain extensive political control. The roots of the elite contestation date back to 2000, when Saleh began to constrict the powers of dominant elites like Ali Mohsin (Sanhan Tribe) and the Hamid al Ahmar (Hashid Tribe) and their tribes in order to concentrate power in his family network to push his son Ahmad Ali for political succession to the presidency.[24] The Arab Spring Protests explicated the above faultline along with subdued political aspirations of the street protest, the Houthis and southerners.

These groups were dissatisfied with the GCC-executed transition in which the older elite retained control over the structures of state authority. On the other hand, continuous armed confrontation on the street between elite factions generated a power vacuum that provided the Armed groups like Ansarullah, the Hirak and AQAP enough space to contest militarily for political authority and control over Yemeni territories. The Houthis instrumentalised the transition period and later the NDC to diversify their agenda from mere revivalism and protectionism of Zaida identity to an expansionist agenda to expand their political influence. The Houthis were ambiguous about the GCC-initiated transition and their involvement in the NDC process. However, instead of strongly opposing the GCC idea of negotiating political power with other political parties, they engaged in the NDC while continuing to fight militarily against the regime and other opponents.[25]

Religious differences had traditionally played a minor role in the country's politics. However, there have been significant instances when sectarian differences shaped the political expressions and activism of the people. The end of the Imamate in 1962 as well as the Iranian Revolution of 1979 have been key events in Yemen's history in shaping the modern Houthi version of political Islam and sectarian narrative. The creation of the Islamic Front launched the Islamists to influence politics through ministries of education and religious endowment. The Islamic Front countered the Marxist National democratic front threat (NDF) to the Saleh regime. Meanwhile, Zaidi religious leaders were frightened by the growing Sunni Islamist presence in their territory, and they mobilised to preserve their sect. In 1982, a study group was established in Saada for learning about the Iranian revolution, which by 1986 (the Union of Believing Youth) turned into an organised core of Houthi protectionism and opposition against Salafi expansion.[26] In 1990s, following the unification, the formation of political parties formalised the sectarian opposition; and two parties were formed namely the Party of Truth (Hizb-al Haqq) and the Union of Popular Forces (UPF). Through the organisation of summer camps, the believing youth quickly expanded its social base while renovating the Zaidi religious discourse by generating collective activism from the grassroots level. The growing social activism played a significant role in the 2004 Houthi Armed opposition to the regime.[27]

When the Arab Spring started in 2011, the Houthi leaders declared their support for the street protests; it helped the rebel movement break out of its isolation in Saada, which had seen six rounds of fighting between Houthis and the Saleh regime since 2004. Between 2011 and 2014, besides participation in protests and national dialogue, Houthis made enormous territorial expansion. Which was made "possible by military coercion, astute political activism at the national level, shadowy deals, and adjustment and renegotiation of the alliance."[28] In their current struggle, Houthis have distanced themselves from a mere revival of zaidism; rather, it endeavours to create its own governance and reorganise the social structures while incorporating all other sects. In this quest, Houthis are revitalising Zaidi superiority combined with expansionist ambitions claiming the right to control all aspects of social life according to their interpolation of religious ideology. This was evidenced by their sudden occupation of Salafi strongholds in northern Yemen, even when state machinery was functional and negotiations for power transfer were in process.

Just a few months before the NDC's formal termination, Houthi and al-Islah tribesmen loyal to Sheikh Hamid al-Ahmar, an al-Islah lawmaker, battled in the province of Amran. It ignited a flurry of violence that quickly extended over Amran. The violence spread to Sadah almost immediately after the Houthis captured al-Khameri, the Ahmar family's home hamlet. When the conflict started in fights between the Houthis and Salafis in the Damaj and Qitaf regions, al-Ahmar and forces inside al-Islah mobilised tribes and Salafi militias from all across Yemen to confront the Houthis.

As the battle for political control heated up, the Houthis allied with Saleh against President Hadi's transition administration. The Houthis were displeased with the monopolisation of power in Sana, as well as their dissatisfaction with economic progress and Salafi activities in Sa'ada Region. Above all, Houthis were driven by the sectarian fears of protecting Zaidi identity and culture that they believe is in danger. During the summer of 2014, Houthi forces seized control of Yemen's capital city, Sanaa, and effectively put an end to Hadi's political authority. Houthis and Alqaeda flourished in this power vacuum to establish themselves territorially, leading to regional and extra-regional intervention.[29] A military offensive conducted by Saudi Arabia and the United Arab Emirates added a regional dimension to the conflict the following year. Religious allegiances have increased in importance as a consequence of these sectarian dynamics, and they have become critical drivers of the Yemeni conflict.

SECTARIANISM AND AUTHORITARIAN EXPLOITATION: STATUS QUO AND COUNTER-REVOLUTIONS

In the process of political transformation, a tussle between status-quoits (those who sought continuity of authoritarian rule) and the reformists (those who sought democratic transition) led to institutional failure and disintegration in Syria and Yemen. The political autocrats were quick to jump in to avert such transitions that could engulf their domestic political environments. The regional opposites—Saudi Arabia and Iran, soon jumped with their respective sectarian narratives. Saudi Arabia-led intervention in Bahrain could maintain the status quo by labelling the uprising as a sectarian plot directed from Iran to destabilise the region.

In the Syrian case, Bashar al-Assad labelled the uprising as a foreign conspiracy. The sectarian narrative that polished the coalitions that serve as the foundation of the Middle East regional system is formed for three key and interconnected reasons: 'Regime security,' 'threat balance,' and 'identity concerns.'[30]

The identity discourse has played a unique role in establishing perceptions and notions of dangers, norms of competitiveness in transnational realms, and defining the interests of nations while producing rules constraining their behaviour. When it comes to the system of the regional state, rival states compete for hegemony by employing trans-state discourses. Many regimes have had to deal with subversion, which challenges their domestic legitimacy in the name of norms derived from identity politics rather than foreign armies.

Arab revolutions challenged the region's long-established political order/status quo by mobilising popular aspiration to replace authoritarianism with participatory democracy and change the stagnant socio-economic conditions. Nevertheless, the processes of transition and change did not go as perceived. On the contrary, the outcomes were numerous, most notably the strengthening of resilient authoritarianism, the prevalence of counterrevolutions, state failure and civil wars sharpening sectarian differences and the new configurations of alliances. "While some long-standing leaders were toppled, the unleashed aspirations of the 2011 youth popular uprisings have fallen short in bringing lasting change."[31]

The democratic process began in the Middle East in the 1970s and 1980s, with some authoritarian leaders establishing a multiparty system with relatively free elections. In addition, they instituted economic and political reforms, opening up some political space with opposition. However, these limited reforms were never meant for political transformation but to expand the spheres of legitimacy. The Arab authoritarians further benefited from the "political reforms" initiated by the United States and Western allies through democratic aid in the 1990s. The process of democracy promotion in west Asia did not result in the development of democracy; rather served to stifle it. The Arab authoritarians utilised this aid to bolster their positions.[32] The first successful popular Arab revolution, which took place at the end of 2010 in Tunisia, brought the Middle East out of its long period of quiet. The Arab

Spring sparked widespread optimism about the fall of authoritarian regimes and the creation of democratic administrations in countries across the Middle East, from Tunisia to Egypt.

In the post Arab Spring, authoritarianism was first reinstated in Egypt, ousting the brotherhood's democratically elected government. In 2013, Egyptian military capitalised on the anger and distrust of the people and usurped the power through campaigns against the Muslim brotherhood. The Egyptian army staged a coup on July 3, 2013, to disrupt the democratic transition and removed the elected president Mohammed Morsi. Once regaining power, the military tightened its control via brutal repressions against those who opposed the coup, including brotherhood members. Egypt's current political situation demonstrates how the government has acquired total power over every aspect of the country, putting a stop to all independent efforts. The government has effectively concentrated power by enacting new constitutional amendments that limit political opposition while also increasing the military's participation in domestic matters. Abdel Fattah al-Sisi power grab is essentially authoritarian, though it is a semi-presidential system.[33] Since taking office in June 2014, Egyptian President Abdel Fattah al-Sisi has implemented a series of cautious but methodical legal measures to restore and strengthen the power of state institutions. He has used the constitutional vacuum left created by the absence of parliament to establish the framework for authorities to act with broad discretion and little public accountability.[34]

The rise in sectarianism having a geopolitical dimension between states has further stretched to non-state actors seeking new grounds and spheres of influence independent of regional patrons. Consider the ambitions of Hezbollah and ISIS to become regional actors. Syria, Yemen and Libya collapsed suddenly and were ravaged by brutal civil wars. In the Syrian case, authoritarianism was sustained at the cost of social disintegration, civil war and exacerbation of sectarian rivalries. The unflinching support of regional allies supplemented the weaponisation of sectarian differences in the name of regime security. The peaceful uprising is being transformed into a long-lasting civil war

Saudi Arabia has placed itself as the architect behind a counterrevolution aimed at containing, and perhaps even retrogressing, the Arab Spring to the greatest extent. The concern behind spearheading counter-revolutionary tactics has primarily been regime security and containment of sectarian strife in the domestic political system. Moreover, along with the GCC member country, Saudi Arabia bolstered regional cooperation. The second development is the GCC's attempt to strengthen its identity and mission with the inclusion of new Sunni monarchies—Morocco and Jordan—as a counterbalance, if not a substitute for the Arab League.[35]

Following the Arab Spring protests, authoritarian governments attempted to rally the support of their counterparts in order to develop counter-revolutionary rhetoric that included sectarianism. Evaluating the rise of sectarianism in recent years requires understanding the Saudi-Iranian rivalry. Saudi Arabia and Iran did not instigate the revival of sectarianism in the region. Still, as Gregory Gause pointed out, they have definitely intensified it to promote their own political agendas. Since then, sectarianism has risen to prominence in the study of conflicts, their origins and their consequences. Conflicts since 2011 have been characterised by a lot of ambiguity. These wars have geopolitical and strategic implications due to which regional players involved themselves as balancers. Besides regime security, threat balancing and identity issues became drivers for alliances formation. Identity has taken several forms, including Arab versus other, in the case of the Israeli-Palestinian conflict, pan-Arabism as uniting rhetoric and Shia-Sunni variations, which emerged primarily after the 1979 Iranian revolution and after the 2003 US-led invasion. Though the Arab Spring had revolutionary and democratic roots, it transcended sub-state characteristics such as ethnic, confessional and ideological. Nonetheless, religiously entrenched confessional identities were politicised and seized by state and non-state actors in Syria, Bahrain and Yemen.

In the wake of the Arab Spring, some observe that "every Arab regime today lives under the condition of profound perceived insecurity" (Lynch 2018, 124).[36] Authoritarian tendencies, including the use of force, can help regimes endure longer. However, they do not turn out to be a source of legitimacy. As the Arab Spring has demonstrated, they do not assure long-standing stability. As a result, using force and coercion might show a lack of legitimacy and capacity.[37]

After all, Iran is now the dominating regional force in Iraq, Syria and Lebanon. And, more than likely, Iran will exploit potential turmoil in other Arab nations, particularly if it threatens Saudi authority. While the Saudis may be worried about Iran's ambitions in the Middle East, Iran believes that Saudi Arabia is attempting to destabilise the Islamic Republic and its supporters by funding and arming them. This apprehension lies at the heart of Iran's expansion across the Arab world. Despite the fact that Iran is seen as aggressive in the Arab world, Iranians believe that their country is under attack by Sunnis and their Western sponsors, particularly the United States. From Tehran's perspective, it should come as no surprise that the United States has supported the Saudi endeavour.

EXPLOITING INSTABILITY AND IDENTITY: THE NON-STATE ACTORS

The rise of non-state actors with significant financial resources and organisational mechanisms has influenced regional politics, security relations and regional stability in certain ways. The longest-running organisations include al-Qaeda, the Muslim Brotherhood in Egypt, Hezbollah in Lebanon, the Taliban, most recently, ISIS in Iraq and Syria and the Houthis in Yemen are the most prevalent non-state players in the region. Besides these, numerous other armed groups like the Free Syrian Army, the Jabhat al Nusra, Hayat Tahrir Al-Sham (HTS) and the Kurdish-dominated Syrian Democratic force, and other Shia militias emerged in the wake of the civil war. The invasion of Iraq by the United States in 2003 is widely seen as the primary cause of the formation of al Qaeda in the Levant. A number of Sunni militias emerged in reaction to Shia proxies of Iran in Syria, including Hezbollah and other Shiite militias, fighting to save the Assad regime. ISIS (now IS) was among the most well-known of these groups.[38]

While using state brutality to quell the early waves of resistance, Assad, by late 2011, began to use sectarian sensitivities and insecurities to create the war narrative, causing the engaged groups to be characterised by their sectarian identities. His strategy was to generate political and military backing (strictly from Tehran and Hezbollah) in order to preserve his authority not as another Middle Eastern government with waning legitimacy and power but instead as a Shiite regime deeply embedded in the region against neighbouring adversarial Sunni regimes, such as Turkey, Jordan and Saudi Arabia.[39]

As a result of these actions, non-state actors have emerged who have utilised fear, threats and intimidation to achieve their objectives. In addition, failures in leadership in the countries exacerbated resentment, leading to the formation of sectarian organisations to oppose the government and demand equal participation. As a result, once these monarchs were ousted, either via foreign intervention or local uprisings, the entire state structure disintegrated, allowing sectarian and ethnic conflicts to flourish. The narrow interpretation of religious scriptures that portrays Islam negatively is a crucial element contributing to radicalisation.

One of the catastrophic effects of the US-led military operation and occupation of Iraq in 2003 was to exacerbate the Sunni/Shi'a divide, which stimulated the growth of violent jihadism in the region and promoted sectarian configurations later in Syria and Yemen that amplified the bloodshed in both countries. Regional players activated these configurations by deploying resources that spread militancy and eventually instability throughout the region. For example, Saudi Arabia has mobilised extensive financial resources in order to expand Islamic orthodoxy and militancy across West Asia, as well as Asia and Africa.[40] Likewise, since the 1980s, Iran has deployed monetary and military assets to Lebanese Hezbollah and numerous other Shia militias in the wake of State failure in Syria and Yemen following the Arab spring. In addition, Tehran has built a network of affiliates made up of numerous significant militias in the region, including several that have their own political parties. These militias contest government authority inside their own state as well as in neighbouring states.[41] In addition, armed militias and political organisations in at least six countries have received assistance from Iran's Revolutionary Guards and special Qods Force. These countries include Bahrain, Lebanon, the Palestinian Territories (Occupied Palestinian Territories), Syria, Yemen and Iraq.[42]

Hezbollah can be referred to as the first sectarian Armed group that emerged in the 1980s with Iranian and Syrian help in order to counter recurrent Israeli interventions into the Lebanese territory. Its emergence confluences with the rise of Iran's strategic outstretch as a Shia power in the region (Harik 2005, 39). Hezbollah has subsequently become an intrinsic part of the 'resistance block' banking on the sectarian narrative; the group has consolidated a stronghold on domestic politics and is also pursuing its strategic interests in the region. As Hezbollah established its dominance in the domestic arena, the Arab Uprisings wreaked havoc throughout the Middle East, providing the organisation with an opportunity to assert itself regionally. As a result, this armed group has been fighting with the Syrian Alawi (Shi'ite) government and providing logistical assistance to the Iraqi Shi'ite and Yemeni (Huthi) armed factions. At the same time, Hezbollah is publicising its moderate image as a defender of minorities, particularly Christians and Alawi's in Syria and Iraq, and is presenting itself as a moderate force. Thus, for the first time since its inception more than three decades ago, Hezbollah has begun trying to integrate its domestic goals with its broader aspirations of expanding its geopolitical ambitions in shaping a new west Asia.

Hezbollah entered the war in Syria with sectarian agenda based on the rhetoric of 'protection of holy sites,' like the Shrine of Syeda Zainab, and fighting against the 'takfiris' sponsored by foreign regimes. It vehemently instrumentalised sectarian identity as a mobilisation tool in undertaking geopolitical ambitions since the Syrian civil war.[43] One significant difference between the Hezbollah of the 1980s and that of today is that the group has shifted its ambition of merely resisting Israel to becoming a regional actor while maintaining balance at home. Syrian Civil war has emboldened its strategic importance for Iran and Syria. The decade-long Syrian war has helped Hezbollah pursue strategic ambition beyond Syrian borders. Today Hezbollah is actively involved in Yemen and Iraq, and is believed to be making inroads in Sunni ruled states.

Therefore Hezbollah's engagement in conflicts following the Arab Spring, playing sectarian card, and its unflinching commitment to strengthening the 'resistance axis' commanded by Iran has deepened the sectarian dimension of the larger geopolitical contest in the region.[44] With the events of the Arab Spring and the plunge into the Syrian Civil War, Hezbollah's methodically crafted military and political supremacy over Lebanon have received challenges, particularly from Sunni's who view it as nothing more than an expansionist actor. Although the first public protests looked to mesh nicely with its reputation of helping the vulnerable against repressive governments, it undermined that by backing Assad.[45] The military assistance to Assad and Hezbollah's sectarian justification for its intervention in Syria and beyond, explicate that the party became deeply involved in counter-revolutionary politics and supportive of the authoritarian status quo. Nasrallah admitted that Hezbollah was deviating from its historical position as a movement committed only to Lebanese resistance to Israel, in which it had been engaged since its founding in 1982. Instead, the Hezbollah of today has become a force dedicated to protecting Shi'a interests across the Arab world.[46] Besides declaring victory in Syria, Hezbollah has become vital for Iranian interests in the wake of Qassim Sulaimani's death in 2020, as it has been called upon to unite fractious militias in Iraq and elsewhere.

As early as the 1990s, a Zaydi Shiite organisation, called Ansar Allah, arose to oppose Yemen's then-regime. In 2014, the Houthis took over Yemen's capital city of Sanaa. They were instrumental in toppling the administration of President Abed Rabbo Mansour Hadi in 2015. In 2011, the Iranian Revolutionary Guards began supporting them. When the Saudi-led coalition intervened in Yemen's conflict in 2015, Iran and Lebanese Hezbollah boosted training and increased weapons supplies. As a result, Iran supported and armed Yemen's Houthi rebels. Saudi Arabia felt that it needed to intervene militarily to prevent them from becoming a Hezbollah-like force operating on its southern border, which they accomplished in 2015. The battle, however, has only helped to pull the Houthis and Iran closer together. Iran provides the Houthis with financial help in addition to missile components and training.[47] The Houthis, in partnership with former Yemeni President Ali Abdullah Saleh, controlled the highlands. Despite their mutual mistrust, they joined forces to confront Hadi and the Saudis. Over time, the Houthis were able to overpower their local rivals. Saleh was assassinated finally in December 2017 for his revocation of the alliance with Houthis. Since then, the Houthis have embarked on comprehensive administrative reform in territories under their control, with the purpose of making it difficult to remove the Houthis and consolidate Yemen.

Syria's major cities have gradually returned to government control. However, the Free Syrian Army, backed by Ankara, still controls large parts of the country, including Idlib. The last opposition stronghold is in the northwestern province of Idlib, as well as parts of northern Hama and western Aleppo. Hayat Tahrir al-Sham, a jihadist alliance, rules the region (HTS). Nonetheless, it is home to mainstream rebel factions.[48]

THE NON-STATE ACTORS AND SECTARIANISM: EROSION OF STATE AUTHORITY AND SOVEREIGNTY

Traditionally, sectarianism has not been an ordering principle in the West Asian regional order. However, there is no question about the emergence of sectarian issues in contemporary politics. This issue is deeply linked to factors like religion, history, location, class, politics and economics. Local and regional players willingly and effectively engage in sectarian manoeuvres. The present competition and proxy conflicts in the Middle East, like the one between regional rivals Saudi Arabia and Iran, have obvious political triggers driving sectarianism-induced instability in the region.[49] It is very apparent in Syria, Yemen and Bahrain. There are currently no signs of a big change in the current geopolitical situation; thus, sectarian wars are more likely to spread instability in the region. It is inaccurate to say that Sunni-Shia sectarian conflict has deep historical roots; rather, it is the outcome of the revisionist phenomena that respond to contemporary political events, power vacuums and weakening the state-society relationship. It started with the 1979 Iranian Revolution. Then, exacerbated by many successive external and internal events—the 2003 US invasion of Iraq, the 2011 Syrian uprising, the war in Yemen and their spillovers in the region.

As a result, the rise of sectarianism and non-state actors has been widely viewed as factors responsible for the erosion of governance and a challenge to sovereignty, as governments are unable to contain their proliferation. From Lebanon to Syria, Iraq and Yemen, these non-state actors have emerged as challengers to state sovereignty and governance.[50] In these territories, non-state actors are controlling significant segments of territories, resources and people.[51] In certain situations, they also assert sovereignty over these portions and numerous interrelated and transnational domains. With the loss of physical control in Syria and Yemen, other non-state entities arose and worsened instability as official authority faded and rivalry for power escalated.[52]

CONCLUSION

The regional security environment, which has been characterised by recurring cycles of instability and insecurity, has undergone significant changes during the past decade. Local, regional and international actors have been urged to participate in structural change, ranging from complex clashes to strategic realignments. The expansion of non-state actors and identity politics has generated instability that regional and global conflict resolution mechanisms have been unable to avoid. Faced with this limitation, non-state actors are boosting their ability to extend and affect events on the ground in order to assume regional security duties. It is widely acknowledged that a wave of spontaneous upheavals known as the Arab Spring launched the reconstruction of the west Asian regional order. Although the Arab Spring's central premise of democratic revolution inspired hope, the region's transition has become increasingly pessimistic in its later stages. Initial predictions of democratisation have given way to a range of emotions about the future course of regional development. The return of authoritarianism in Egypt, the ongoing conflict in Iraq, Libya, Syria and Yemen, as well as the Syrian and Yemeni civil wars, have all shifted regional and extra-regional perspectives towards regional change, with the development of new security vulnerabilities influencing all stakeholders' regional strategies.

The West Asian region is now considered riskier than it was at the start of the Arab Spring due to a slew of destabilising variables. Among the most visible manifestations of this new unsafe environment are the rise of sectarianism and the growing number of non-state actors, both of which have contributed to the region's ostensible security rapidly deteriorating.

Sectarianism promotes domestic instability by instilling in states/ regimes the fear that they will be unable to balance both power positions and domestic sources of legitimacy, such as public and civil society. As a foreign policy tool, it fuels the rhetoric of opponents, invests in intra-state conflicts and runs clandestine networks in the form of non-state armed groups. While sectarianism was a major cause of the conflict, neither Hezbollah nor the other parties were fighting for "doctrinal reasons." Instead, most state and non-state actors were motivated by their participation in a geopolitical rivalry in which they sought to gain domestic and regional influence at the expense of their competitors.[53] However, the rise of sectarianism in the aftermath of the 2011 uprisings has been exacerbated by geopolitical strategies, as power vacuums create opportunities for political ambitions and agendas. While sectarianism is real and poses significant risks, it is not the primary source of division in the region.

NOTES

1. Yannis A. Stivachtis, Political (In)Security in the Middle East (23-45) in Koch, Bettina, and Yannis A. Stivachtis, eds. *Regional Security in the Middle East.* E-International Relations Publishing, 2019. Chapter. 23
2. Toby Dodge, "Seeking to explain the rise of sectarianism in the Middle East: The case study of Iraq," In *Workshop on 'Visions of Gulf Security',* Venice, 2014, at https://pomeps.org/seeking-to-explain-the-rise-of-sectarianism-in-the-middle-east-the-case-study-of-iraq (accessed on September 05, 2020).
3. Robinson, Heather M., Ben Connable, David E. Thaler, and Ali G. Scotten. *Sectarianism in the middle east: Implications for the United States.* Rand Arroyo Center, Santa Monica, California, United States (2018): 20.
4. Harvey, Katherine, 'Iran, Iraq, and Saudi Arabia in the Late Twentieth Century,' A Self-Fulfilling Prophecy: The Saudi Struggle for Iraq (2022; online edn, Oxford Academic, 20 January 2022), https://doi.org/10.1093/oso/9780197631324.003.0002 (accessed August 26, 2022).
5. Dodge, "Seeking to explain the rise of sectarianism in the Middle East: the case study of Iraq"; Daniel Byman, "Sectarianism afflicts the new Middle East," *Survival,* vol. 56, no. 1, (Feb-March 2014): 80.
6. Geneive Abdo, *The new sectarianism: The Arab uprisings and the rebirth of the Shi'a-Sunni divide* (Oxford University Press, 2017): 59-60.
7. D. Byman, "Sectarianism Afflicts the New Middle East," *Survival* 56, no. 1, (2014): 79.
8. Naame Sham, *Silent Sectarian Cleansing: The Iranian Role in Mass Demolitions and Population Transfers in Syria,* (Naame Sham report, May 2015), at http://www.naameshaam.org/wp-content/uploads/2015/05/Silent_Ethnic_Cleansing_in_Syria_NaameShaamReport_ENGLISH_May20151.pdf (accessed on September 06, 2020).
9. David Lesch, *Syria: Fall of the House of Assad* (New Heaven: Yale University Press, 2012), p. 101.
10. Raymond Hinnebusch and Tina Zintl, *Syria from Reform to Revolt: Political Economy and International Relation*, Vol. 1 (New York: Syracuse University Press 2015): 98.

11. Ibid.
12. Steven Heydemann, Upgrading Authoritarianism in the Arab World analysis paper Number 13, The Saban Centre at the Brooking Institute, October 2007, at https://www.brookings.edu/wp-content/uploads/2016/06/10arabworld.pdf (accessed on October 10, 2021).
13. Human rights council, *Human Rights Council debates situation of human rights in Syrian Arab Republic in Special Session* 22 August 201. At https://www.ohchr.org/en/press-releases/2011/08/human-rights-council-debates-situation-human-rights-syrian-arab-republic (accessed on August 26, 2022).
14. *Raymond Hinnebusch,* "Syria: from 'authoritarian upgrading' to revolution?," *International Affairs* 88, no. 1 (2012): 95-113.
15. Ibid.
16. Vali Nasr, All Against All: the Sectarian Resurgence in the Post- American Middle East, February 2022 *Foreign Affairs* at https://www.foreignaffairs.com/articles/middle-east/2021-12-02/iran-middle-east-all-against-all (accessed on March 02, 2022).
17 Ayşe Baltacıoğlu-Brammer, "Politics of Sectarianism in the Middle East: Past and Present," Berkley Centre for Religion, Peace and World Affairs, March 24, 2021, at https://berkleycenter.georgetown.edu/responses/politics-of-sectarianism-in-the-middle-east-past-and-present (accessed on March 05, 2022).
18. Friederike Stolleis, Playing the Sectarian Card Identities and Affiliations of Local Communities in Syria; *Friedrich-Ebert-Stiftung Beirut* (2015): 9
19. Gerald M. Feierstein, Yemen: The 60-Year War, Policy Paper no. 02. *Middle East Institue* (February 2019).
20. Juneau, Thomas. "Yemen and the Arab Spring: elite struggles, state collapse and regional security," *Orbis* 57, no. 3 (2013): 408-423.
21. "Yemen's Saleh Agrees to Transfer Power," *Al Jazeera English* (24 Nov. 2011), at https://www.aljazeera.com/news/2011/11/24/yemens-saleh-agrees-to-transfer-power-2 (accessed on December 21, 2021).
22. Juneau, Thomas. "Iran's policy towards the Houthis in Yemen: a limited return on a modest investment." *International Affairs* 92, no. 3 (2016).
23. Mareike Transfeld, "Political bargaining and violent conflict: shifting elite alliances as the decisive factor in Yemen's transformation," *Mediterranean Politics* 21, no. 1 (2016): 150-169.
24. Sarah Phillips, "Chapter Five: The regime, *Adelphi Series*, 51:420 (2011): 87-104; also cited in Transfeld, n. 23, 150-169.
25. Marieke Brandt, "The Huthi Enigma: Ansar Allah and the 'Second Republic'," in Marie-Christine Heinze, ed., *Yemen and the Search for Stability Power: Politics and Society after the Arab Spring* (London, UK: I.B.Tauris & Co. Ltd, 2018): 160-183.
26. Abdullah Lux, "Yemen's last Zaydī Imām: the shabāb al-mu'min, the Malāzim, and 'ḥizb allāh' in the thought of Ḥusayn Badr al-Dīn al-Ḥūthī," *Contemporary Arab Affairs* 3 (2009): 376.

27. Marieke Brandt, *Tribes and Politics in yemen: A History of the Houthi Conflict* (London, UK: Hurst and Company, 2017): 116-117.
28. Brandt, n. 25, 337.
29. Hakan Kiyici, "Yemen in the International Security Agenda: The Context of Tribalism, Sectarianism, and Intervention." *Insight Turkey* 22, no. 1 (Winter 2020): 238-240.
30. Kamrava, Mehran. "Hierarchy and instability in the Middle East regional order." *International Studies Journal (ISJ)* 14, no. 4 (Spring 2018): 1-35.
31. Ibrahim Fraihat and Taha Yaseen, "Evolving Trends in the Post-Arab Spring Era: Implications for Peace and Stability in the MENA Region," *Journal of Peacebuilding & Development* 15, no. 3 (2020): 1.
32. Selin M. Bölme, "The Roots of Authoritarianism in the Middle East," in Jülide Karakoç, ed., *Authoritarianism in the Middle East: Before and After the Arab Uprisings* (UK: Palgrave Macmillan, 2015): 7-8.
33. Ashna Mehmood, "Egypt's Return to Authoritarianism," *Modern Diplomacy*, March 31, 2021, at https://moderndiplomacy.eu/2021/03/31/egypts-return-to-authoritarianism/
34. Nathan J. Brown, "Katie Bentivoglio, Egypt's Resurgent Authoritarianism: It's a Way of Life," October 9, 2014, at https://carnegieendowment.org/2014/10/09/egypt-s-resurgent-authoritarianism-it-s-way-of-life-pub-56877 (accessed on December 25, 2021).
35. Kamrava, Mehran. "The Arab Spring and the Saudi-led counterrevolution," *Orbis* 56, no. 1 (2012): 96-104.
36. Cited in "The State and the Problem of Legitimate Order in the Middle East," Anderson, Liam, and Vaughn Shannon. *Federal Solutions for Fragile States in the Middle East: Right-Sizing Internal Borders. World Scientific, 2021*. p. 3.
37. "The State and the Problem of Legitimate Order in the Middle East," Liam Anderson and Shannon Vaughn. *Federal Solutions for Fragile States in the Middle East: Right-Sizing Internal Borders.* (World Scientific, 2021), 4.
38. Richard Falk Rethinking the Arab Spring: uprisings, counterrevolution, chaos and global reverberations, *Third World Quarterly* (2016), 2.
39. Baltacıoğlu-Brammer, "Politics of Sectarianism in the Middle East: Past and Present," at https://berkleycenter.georgetown.edu/responses/politics-of-sectarianism-in-the-middle-east-past-and-present (accessed on January 17, 2022).
40. Richard Falk, "Rethinking the Arab Spring: uprisings, counterrevolution, chaos and global reverberations," *Third World Quarterly* (2016), 2. DOI: 10.1080/01436597.2016.1218757
41. John Dobson, "Iran's proxies are a threat to peace in Middle East," *Sunday Gaurdian Live*, July 3, 2021, at https://www.sundayguardianlive.com/world/irans-proxies-threat-peace-middle-east (accessed on December 25, 2021).
42. Ashley Lane, "Iran's Islamist Proxies in the Middle East," *Wilson Centre*, May 20, 2021, at https://www.wilsoncenter.org/article/irans-islamist-proxies (accessed on December 30, 2021).

43. Wahab, Hadi. "Syria's Sect-coded Conflict: From Hezbollah's Top-down Instrumentalization of Sectarian Identity to Its Candid Geopolitical Confrontation," *Contemporary Review of the Middle East*, 2021, 150.
44. Bassel F. Salloukh, "The Sectarian Image Reversed: The Role of Geopolitics in Hezbollah's Domestic Politics," *Sectarianism and International Relations POMEPS*, 2020, p. 37, at *https://pomeps.org/the-sectarian-image-reversed-the-role-of-geopolitics-in-hezbollahs-domestic-politics*
45. Mona Christophersen, "Split Personality: Hezbollah's Role in the New Middle East," *Global Observatory*, March 30, 2015, at https://theglobalobservatory.org/2015/03/hezbollah-syria-lebanon-israel/
46. Abdo, Geneive. *The New Sectarianism: The Arab Uprisings and the Rebirth of the Shi'a-Sunni Divide* (Oxford University Press, 2017), 93
47. Gregory D. Johnsen, "Order From Chaos: The end of Yemen," *Brookings*, March 25, 2021 at https://www.brookings.edu/blog/order-from-chaos/2021/03/25/the-end-of-yemen/
48. Durac, Vincent. "The role of non-state actors in Arab countries after the Arab uprisings." *IEMed Mediterranean Yearbook 2015*, vo. 1, 2015, pp. 37=41, at https://www.bbc.com/news/world-middle-east-35806229
49. Makdisi, Ussama. "Understanding Sectarianism in the Middle East," *The Cairo Review of Global Affairs*, 2017, at https://www.thecairoreview.com/tahrir-forum/understanding-sectarianism-in-the-middle-east/
50. Yeşiltaş, Murat, and Tuncay Kardaş, eds. *Non-state armed actors in the Middle East: Geopolitics, ideology, and strategy*, Springer, 2017, 28.
51. Vinci, A. (2008). "Anarchy, failed states, and armed groups: Reconsidering conventional analysis," *International Studies Quarterly*, vol. 52, no. 2, 2008.
52. See Charles lister, *The Syrian Jihad: Al-Qaeda, the Islamic state and the evolution of an insurgency* (Oxford, UK: Oxford University Press, 2015).
53. Wahab, Hadi. "Syria's Sect-coded Conflict: From Hezbollah's Top-down Instrumentalization of Sectarian Identity to Its Candid Geopolitical Confrontation," *Contemporary Review of the Middle East*, 2021, 150. 2347798921999191.

4

THE SYRIAN CRISIS AND TURKEY'S INVOLVEMENT

Özden Zeynep Oktav

INTRODUCTION

Enhancement of border management is a significant necessity for any country, but it is especially important for Turkey because it borders war-torn countries, primarily Syria. Turkey, as a candidate country for full membership of the EU, aimed to form 'a system of integrated border management, which includes reforms for intra-institutional, inter-institutional, and international cooperation in order to facilitate trade and traffic across its borders.'[1] However, the Syrian uprising which resulted in the influx of 4.5 million Syrian refugees to the Turkish border devastated Turkey's border management. Moreover, it led to the demographic change in northern Syria, where the two terrorist organizations—Islamic State of Iraq and the Levant (ISIL/Da'esh) and the PKK affiliated Democratic Union Party (PYD) together with its armed-wing People's Protection Units (YPG)—threatened and dominated the local people

This chapter sets out to analyse the reasons urging Turkey to become more protective of the Syrian border, focusing on the following questions: What factors influenced Turkey's transformation into a 'fortress'? What factors urged Turkey to build a wall along its south-eastern border with Syria especially after Afrin, Kobane and Jazira were invaded by the PKK-affiliated YPG terrorists in 2012 and the Turkish consulate in Mosul was occupied by ISIS terrorists in 2014? How did the regional and global actors in Syria react to Turkey's military operations such as Euphrates Shield, Olive Branch and Spring Shield? What impact did the failed coup attempt on July 15th have on Turkey's struggle to protect its border with Syria? What are the prospects for the future?

HISTORICAL BACKGROUND

The one issue that bedevilled Turkish-Syrian relations since Syria's independence in 1946 until the 1998 bilateral crisis, was their uncooperative border interactions. The illegal transfer of goods across Turkey's Syrian border in the 1950s and the PKK terrorists infiltrating from Syria to Turkey in the 1980s and 1990s were the major problem areas in bilateral relations. Ankara planted landmines along the Syrian border in order to prevent smuggling activities during the 1950s. Another reason for the mining that continued until 1969 was to prevent the spread of communism and socialism, which the then Syrian governments had adopted by following pro-Soviet policies.

The Hatay issue is a striking one with respect to understanding the continuing point of confrontation between the two states. Hatay has always been shown within Syrian territory in official maps and schoolbooks because Syria never recognized the annexation of Hatay into Turkey in 1939[2] on the ground that France had relinquished Alexandretta without the approval of the Syrian parliament. Turkey's border problem with Syria deteriorated with the issues of water and the PKK terrorism linkage during the 1990s. Turkey accused Syria of backing the Kurdistan Workers' Party (PKK), a Kurdish separatist organization aiming at the establishment of a Kurdish state in south-eastern Anatolia, and it did not agree to fix a flow quota of at least 700 cubic meters of water per second (m3/s). Syria, on the other hand, perceived Turkey as aiming for regional hegemony by aligning with Israel and controlling the water flow of the Euphrates, used the PKK as leverage on Turkey, sheltered the Kurdish guerrillas and its leader Abdullah Öcalan in its territory.[3] The two countries, which came to the brink of war in 1998, made the Adana agreement as Syria consented to stop sheltering the head of the PKK, Abdullah Öcalan in Syria. Turkey and Syria established extraordinary levels of cooperation beginning in the late 1990s. For example, 'In 2005, for the first time in history, Syria denounced a PKK attack in Turkey. Furthermore, in 2007, Turkey and Syria organized a joint operation on Syrian soil against the PKK terrorists. In that same year, Syria supported a Turkish operation in northern Iraq against the PKK terrorists.'[4]

Despite improving relations between Turkey and Syria during the first decade of the 2000s, the Assad regime never recognized Hatay as a Turkish province. The Turkey-Syria high level strategic Cooperation Council and joint ministerial meetings, removal of visas, and the signing of thirteen more agreements on trade, investment and tourism remained useless in solving the deep-rooted border issue.[5] In March 2011, the Syrian crisis spilled over into Syria, straining Turkish-Syrian relations and compromising Turkey's border security. Turkey exerted considerable effort to persuade Assad to institute political reforms, but the Syrian army continued gross human-rights violations. Turkey imposed sanctions on Syria, froze its business assets and cut off its relationship with the Syrian Central Bank. In an effort to compel the to the negotiating table, Ankara empowered Syrian opposition elements and played an important role in establishing the Free Syrian Army (FSA).[6]

THE SYRIAN CRISIS AND ESCALATING BORDER TENSION

Border violations and explosions on Turkey's borders such as Ceylanpınar, Akçakale and Reyhanl, and the appearance of the radical groups such as Jabhat al Nusra, Da'esh and the PYD/YPG along its border with Syria, ushered in a new era in Turkey's border security understanding. Put differently, the Government of Turkey had adopted the policy of open doors towards Syrian refugees and announced that people approaching Turkey's borders from the conflict in Syria would be allowed to cross the border and admitted to Turkey, as opposed to being intercepted or halted. 'However, the "open door"[7] policy became unsustainable as the number of Syrian refugees and cost of those refugees grew with each passing day. Moreover, Turkey was left alone in coping with the influx of Syrian refugees as the international community, especially the EU, remained reluctant in funding humanitarian assistance programmes and fulfil pledges made within the UN Syria regional response plan.'[8]

As Okyay argues, 'The border between Turkey and Syria displays characteristics of what are popularly regarded as "artificial" Sykes-Picot borders. First, it is, like many borders in the region, an outcome of the colonial engineering that took place after the First World War. Second, border drawing, here as elsewhere in the region, did not follow the logic of the diverse and occasionally overlapping identity markers characterizing local populations."[9] Put differently, the border areas have been home to multi-ethnic populations with trans-state affiliations in Syria and Turkey. There are small groups of Armenians, Circassians, Chechens and Arabic-speaking Christians in the areas near the Turkish border, the bigger minorities inhabiting these areas are the Kurds and—predominantly Alevi—Turkmen. Because the demarcation line, first agreed on by the French and the incipient Turkish government in 1921, was revised in 1939 when Turkey annexed the predominantly Turkish-speaking Alexandretta (now Hatay province) through another agreement signed with France, irredentist feelings still shape border policies of both Syria and Turkey as it became evident both in Hatay and Mosul.

Kurşun emphasizes that 'borders present an overarching conceptualization and understanding that involves different types of territorial and social constructions in an integrated way. In this sense, it can be argued that the term border refers to a territorial notion that is mobile, extensive and includes social realities.'[10] The border between Turkey and Syria also includes such social realities and therefore the Wall which Ankara started to build in 2016 along its border with Syria, resulted in fragmentation of tribes, families and identities.[11] The reasons why Turkey ceased to follow good neighbourhood relations with Syria and started to build the Wall are manifold and involve deeper motives: security concerns and fears of US's real intentions, nourished by Washington's piling weapons to support the PYD/YPG and suspicions nourished by the firm belief among the Turkish public opinion as well as Turkish state regarding the US covert support for Da'esh.

Turkey consistently pursued two interests over the course of the civil war in Syria. One was to prevent the formation of a US sponsored Kurdish "statelet" that consists of provinces such Afrin, Jazira, Manbij, Deir Ez-Zor, Darbasiyah, Ras Al Ain, and Hasakah, in the region called "Rojava" by the PYD/YPG. Second was to prevent the influx of a new wave of Syrian refugees to its borders and to create a buffer zone to secure territory in the south of its border largely controlled by YPG.[12] Accordingly, Turkey started to build a wall along its south-eastern border with Syria in January 2016. In addition, the Turkish Armed Forces increased border security by deploying drones and reconnaissance aircraft.[13]

The two facts, however, revealed that protecting the border per se by building a wall was not sufficient to safeguard Turkey's national security. One was the weakened Turkish army, which became evident with the failed coup attempt on July 15, 2016, organized by the Gülenists (followers of the Gülen Cemaat, now referred as FETÖ) who had infiltrated all institutions of Turkey, primarily the military. The weakened military in Turkey was mainly due to the fact that the Gulenists/FETÖ had a strong presence in the military and "they knew that their secret members in the military would be dismissed at the upcoming High Military Council, to be held from August 1 to August 4, 2016. In order to keep their establishment within the military, they attempted a coup on the 15th July night."[14] Under these conditions, it was almost impossible for Turkey to fight against the Da'esh and the YPG terrorists efficiently to protect its borders with Syria. Turkey could start cross-border counter-terrorism operations along its border with Syria only after the failed coup attempt of July 15, 2016.

The necessity of establishing a safe zone in Syria to address the high porousness at the border was the second fact, which proved that protecting the border per se by building a wall was not sufficient to safeguard Turkey's national security. The participation of other countries such as the United States, Saudi Arabia and Qatar, led to the deterioration of Turkey's image on the ground that Turkey allegedly had turned a blind eye to bidirectional border crossing by armed rebels, arms transfers. According to Yackley, although Turkish authorities vehemently and consistently denied all these allegations, Ankara's border management pattern during earlier stages of the conflict contributed unintentionally to the empowerment of extremist groups, in terms of personnel, operational networks and economic resources. This empowerment turned into a security threat to Turkey itself, and the authorities subsequently sought to reverse it.[15] It can be said that the July 15 failed coup attempt marked turning point in Turkey's inner and external politics. "Following the failed coup attempt, various groups from different ethnic, religious and political backgrounds unified against the conspirators. This included the ruling and the opposition parties cooperating in fighting against the Gulenists/FETÖ, who were subsequently classified as a terrorist group and now referred to as "FETÖ" by all factions in the country."[16]

THE FAILED COUP ATTEMPT ON JULY 15 AND CROSS-BORDER OPERATIONS

It is beyond the scope of this study to discuss the details of organizations like 'cemaat', 'tariqas' or such religious structures. It will suffice to say that the Fetullah Gülen cemaat (*the followers of the Cemaat used to call themselves as movement of service/hizmet hareketi. After the July 16, 2016, failed coup attempt, the cemaat was called as FETÖ terrorist organization by all factions in the country*) had far-reaching political and psychological/ sociological ramifications, the most important of which was FETÖ's increasing domination of the state apparatus especially from 2011 onward. Put differently, Turkey's border management policy such as the 'open door policy' and 'temporary protection regime'[17] had very negative repercussions on Turkey during the 2011-2016 period when the institutions such as NGOs, media, military were under the control of the FETÖ. The FETÖ/ 'Cemaat', thus could maximize its impact on Turkey's border management policy.[18]

For example, 'the Open-Door Policy, launched under legal responsibility of international law and from the perspective of humanitarian approach by Turkey in 2011, brought many problems with the passage of time. These varied from the attacks of terrorist organizations, financial issues and social issues that threatened the society.'[19] Most important of all, Turkey was accused of allowing passage to illegal Sunni terrorists as Ankara provided safe haven and refuge to hundreds of thousands of Syrian civilians, which resulted in a porous border. This unevenness of Turkey's 'open door' policy at the operational level led to Turkey's being labelled as a 'jihadist highway'.[20] The Open-Door Policy, which started in 2011, de facto ended in 2016.

In other words, only after the failed coup attempt on July 15, 2016, could Turkey launch anti-terrorism military operations like Euphrates Shield, Olive Branch, Peace Spring, and Spring Shield in 2016, 2018, 2019 and 2020, respectively. This was mainly due to the fact that the FETÖ 'cemaat' followers were cleared off from the military and other institutions of crucial importance in Turkey.

THE IMPACT OF CROSS-BORDER MILITARY OPERATIONS ON TURKEY'S RELATIONS WITH THE US, THE EU AND RUSSIA

Following the failed coup attempt, Turkey has taken numerous foreign policy initiatives, using both military force and an assertive legal posture. Among these initiatives, Turkey's incursions in north-eastern Syria were the most notable ones, having an intensive impact on its relations with the United States, the EU and Russia. There were three reasons for launching the first operation—Operation Euphrates Shield—in northern Syria in August 2016. One was the protection of the border, second was the elimination of the Da'esh and the third was to prevent the PKK and the PYD/YPG from establishing an autonomous entity in northern Syria. Turkey justified this operation by invoking the right of self-defence articulated in Article 51 of the UN Charter.[21]

Operation Euphrates that started in Jarablus mainly aimed to create a no-fly zone in northern Syria, which the Turkish government had insisted on for years despite opposition in Washington and limited support from NATO. Another aim of the Operation Euphrates Shield was to prevent attacks on Turkish territory by the various armed factions operating near its border, as well as to provide a safe haven for the return of the 3 million Syrian refugees who had already fled the country, if a certain degree of security could be established in northern Syria.[22]

The Operation Euphrates Shield, which lasted from August 2016 to March 2017, paved the way for the Astana process, 'wherein Russia and Turkey tried to reach a *modus vivendi* in Syria. Iran later joined this initiative and Iraq became an "observer" in October 2019.'[23]

Euphrates Shield allowed Turkey to clear the area to the west of the Euphrates of both the Da'esh and YPG, mainly Kurdish groups that are a primary component of the Syrian Democratic Forces (SDF).[24] According to many analysts, with the beginning of the Euphrates Shield operation, Turkey's further strategic decoupling from two of its allies, the EU and the United States, became more evident. This decoupling had already started on the night of the failed coup attempt as the American and EU officials remained silent whereas Russian President Vladimir Putin became the first leader who lent the unconditional support to the Turkish government on that night of July 15. Looking from a different angle, however, Russia did not hesitate to provide air support to the SDF forces in the fight against Da'esh, despite Russia's positive stance on Turkey's Euphrates Shield, and the Astana process which started in 2017. 'The PYD had already opened a representative office in Moscow in February 2016 and in contrast to the USA, the Assad regime, and Turkey, Russia was in favour of a federal Syria.'[25]

Operation Euphrates Shield was of crucial importance for several reasons. First, the operation showed how 'the institutional shock caused by the July 15 uprising, subsequent military reforms, and mass purges have affected the Turkish Armed Forces' operational efficiency and effectiveness.'[26] Second, Turkey, with this operation, achieved the two main goals: to remove Da'esh forces from towns along the Turkish-Syrian border and to prevent the terrorist PYD/YPG groups from advancing. Third, despite the fact that the removal of the former clearly helped bring the United States closer to its goal of demolishing and destroying Da'esh, the fact that Turkey's operation weakened PYD/YPG in the region clashed with the US interests in the region, as PYD/YPG were considered the most effective ground partner in combatting the Da'esh by the United States.[27] When looked at from a different angle, Operation Euphrates Shield revealed that both NATO allies, Ankara and Washington, considered PYD/YPG, which has ties to the PKK, in a different way. Turkey demanded that the United States consider the PYD/YPG in the same way as the PKK, which for decades has waged an insurgency against Turkey and is designated as a terrorist organization by the United States, Turkey and the European Union. However, the United States has not ceased to arm the PYD/YPG terrorists and has never given up considering the YPG as a very suitable leverage against Turkey.

Operation Olive Branch into Afrin, which was launched by Ankara on January 20, 2018, also aimed to repel PYD and YPG, from Turkey's immediate doorstep. The Turkish leadership's decision came right after Washington hinted at its intentions to form a 30,000-strong border guard cantered on SDF, which is largely manned by YPG militant. The arms transfer to YPG, within the framework of anti-Da'esh operations, set alarm bells in Turkey as Ankara's pleas to stop arming the YPG had fallen on deaf ears in Washington. This led to further cooperative relations between Turkey and Russia, whose military contingent in Syria controlled the country's airspace in western provinces and the capital Damascus. Thus, the Kremlin's green light for the Afrin campaign was enough for Ankara to launch Olive Branch with an overwhelming airpower along with a land incursion into the mountainous belt surrounding Afrin's urbanised centre.[28]

Turkish Foreign Minister Mr. Mevlut Çavuşoğlu explained that Operation Olive Branch mainly aimed 'to clear roadblocks to peace in Syria posed by opponents of the country's unitary future, to prevent the PKK terrorists from opening a supplementary front for PKK terrorist operations, in addition to the one in northern Iraq and from uniting them to form a continuous terrorist belt. Thus, the PKK would not be able to form a territorial beachhead for their own statelet to be built upon the carcasses of Syria and Iraq on the areas vacated by Da'esh. In Turkish Foreign Minster's words, the purpose of the Olive Branch was to open an artery toward peace.'[29] Recalling that the PKK/YPG evacuated around 400,000 Kurds from the land it gained in Syria, Turkish official circles insisted that the PKK's micro-nationalism and terrorism were a disservice to everyone including the Kurds.[30]

During Turkish President Erdoğan's visit to Washington in 2017, Turkey not only wanted the US green light on the Turkish operation in Sinjar (Iraq) but also reiterated its demand that the United States cease to host Islamic preacher Fethullah Gülen, who purportedly motivated the bloody coup attempt in Turkey.[31] However, the US had already made a choice to work with the PKK/YPG and to shelter Gülen in Pennsylvania. Turkey, hoping that a new momentum with the Trump administration could help change the US policy, spent much effort to convince the US to work with the Turkey-aligned moderate opposition groups about defeating Da'esh. Turkey's efforts, however, remained fruitless because of the Pentagon's own plans about Raqqa and beyond.[32] This policy of the US administration led to further rapprochement between Turkey and Russia and strengthened the bond between Turkey, Russia and Iran through the Astana process, which resulted in the establishment of de-escalation zones in Syria.[33]

Operation Olive Branch is noteworthy with respect to understanding the Russian-Turkish tacit agreement about cooperating in Syria. Russia withdrew its operatives from the Afrin area and also recalled workers from its 'Reconciliation Centre'[34] that had a branch in the city of Afrin. Because the YPG was left alone by Russia for their fight against the Turkish army and the Syrian opposition, YPG had no choice but to retreat from Afrin as it would be disastrous to go into a conflict with Turkish-supported Free Syrian army (FSA). It was also alleged that due to the implicit agreement between Turkey and Russia, Turkey ended its concern over Abu Duhur military airport, which had been earmarked by the Turkish forces for use as a military base in the Idlib countryside. The military airport was important to observe the areas that fall under the 'de-escalation' agreement. It was alleged that Turkey withdrew from the area allowing the regime to take control of the airport in return for Russian support for Operation Olive Branch.[35]

Operation Olive Branch had some important results. First, the argument that the only effective actor in the fight against Da'esh was the YPG was invalidated by this operation, and it was revealed that YPG was very inadequate without air support. Second, according to Orhan, the claims that 'YPG did not actually show much resistance were not true, on the contrary, the Turkish army faced significant resistance on the border line, and the outside logistic support lines of the organization were open.'[36] Third, as Afrin was one of the strongholds of YPG, the loss of this region made it quite difficult for YPG to survive in other areas where the YPG was much weaker. Most important of all, the geographical link between Idlib and Euphrates Shield was ensured, new living space was provided to the opposition and the PKK/YPG was denied an opportunity of penetration into Hatay through Afrin.

'Operation Peace Spring', launched on October 9, 2019, is the third major Turkish military operation on Syrian territory since 2016 and is of crucial importance with respect to understanding Turkey's further strategic decoupling from two of its allies, the EU and the United States. Turkey, with 'Operation Peace Spring', showed that, with the exception of British and French military forces, there were no EU troops on the ground.[37] The October 2019 operation was defined by EU officials as a 'war within a war' mainly because Russia recognised Ankara's security concerns about the YPG's military capacity for the first time, whereas the Trump administration tried to urge Turkey not to launch a military offensive against the YPG-led forces in northern Syria by sending a letter. The letter in which Trump told Erdogan: 'Don't be a tough guy. Don't be a fool!'[38] made the bilateral relations worse.

When looked at closely, 'Operation Peace Spring' was the only one which triggered strong criticism in the West on the ground that it would undermine the security of the Coalition's local partners, namely the YPG forces, and risk protracted instability in north-east Syria, providing fertile ground for the resurgence of Da'esh.

The European Parliament President, David Sassoli, characterised the Turkish military operation as an 'act of war'. In his speech to the European Council on October 17, he said: 'We must do everything in our power to stop this act of aggression and launch an initiative that can be thrashed out within NATO and submitted to the UN Security Council.'[39] Turkey, prioritizing its security concerns, realized 'Operation Peace Spring' in the east of Euphrates, which mainly aimed to push YPG fighters back from the border, and to create a 'safe zone' where up to two million Syrian refugees could be resettled. Trump was criticized vehemently in American inner politics, because he withdrew the troops and said: 'the US should not be intervening in Turkey's military operation in Syria because it is not our border', and called the former US allies the Kurds 'no angels'.[40] In sum, the Western world's immediate reaction to the 'Operation Peace Spring' was to try to convince Turkey to abandon it, while the operation certainly strengthened Turkey's strategic standing vis-à-vis American-sponsored YPG and showed the 'absence of a coherent strategic vision' that has led to 'Western marginalization in Syria'.

On October 17, 2019, eight days after the launch of Operation Peace Spring, the Turkish and American governments negotiated a ceasefire accord suspending the operation. Then, on October 22, "Russia and Turkey adopted a joint memorandum on the situation in Syria following talks between Russian President Vladimir Putin and his Turkish counterpart Recep Tayyip Erdoğan in Sochi.'[41]

In Sochi, as Köstem notes that "Russia agreed to the status quo established by Turkey's military operation covering Tal Abyad and Ras Al Ayn with a depth of 32 km (20 miles). Moscow also committed to the removal of YPG forces and their weapons from Manbij and Tal Rifat. In return, Ankara accepted the Assad regime's takeover of towns formerly controlled by the YPG."[42] Although this process served Russia's purposes of pushing the YPG to accept the Assad regime's superiority and convincing the Turkish government to consent to the regime's rule in Northern Syria,[43] when compared to previous military operations, Turkey gained more from Operation Peace Spring in northern Syria than it lost. After a quick departure, Ankara was able to undermine YPG-US military connections on the ground, resulting in the loss of the YPG's territorial claim and self-government body in northeast Syria. Another point worth mentioning here is that Turkey drew much attention to the existing refugee crisis, particularly in Europe and Ankara proved its diplomatic capacity both by persuading the Trump administration to withdraw the YPG from the east of Euphrates and convincing Russia to cooperate in stabilising the east of Euphrates.[44]

However, Turkey could not become the friend of Russians as it became evident with clashes between Turkish troops and Russia-backed Syrian regime forces in Idlib on February 8, 2020. It was the first since the beginning of the civil war in 2011. Eight Turkish officers were killed. 'Turkish President Recep Tayyip Erdogan gave an ultimatum to President Bashar Assad to withdraw his troops behind Turkey's observation post lines by the end of February or pay the price, adding that "nothing will be the same" after the attack.' Erdoğan also criticized Russia violating its commitments under the 2018 Sochi agreement (Memorandum of Understanding on Stabilization of the Situation in Idlib's De-escalation Zone) signed by Turkey and Russia.[45] The Sochi agreement had proposed the establishment of a demilitarized/de-escalation zone[46] in north-western Syria in order to protect the country's civilians against attacks by the Assad regime and to prevent the Syrian civilians, whose number was approximately three million, from fleeing to Turkey's border. In addition, radical militant groups such as Hayat Tahrir al-Sham (HTS) were expected to leave Idlib. According to the agreement, Turkey forwarded the establishment of 15 military observation points to monitor the ceasefire within the boundaries of the Sochi line. However, the conditions of the deal were never fully implemented on the ground. 'The violation of the Sochi agreement and a renewed attack on civilians have generated a severe trust issue between the Turkish and Russian sides. Turkey started its military deployment within the Sochi lines to enforce the agreement and help the moderate opposing militias—the Syrian National Army (SNA)—to take back the control of the areas that were controlled in violation of the Sochi deal. Both sides have blamed each other for breaking the deal with differing accusations, but what is clear on the ground was that the Turkish-Russian relations were deeply damaged due to the uncontrolled military exchange in the field.'[47]

That more than 30 Turkish soldiers were killed in attacks by the Syrian army in Idlib's Balyun village on February 27, 2020, came as a shock for Turkey and became a turning point in Russian-Turkish relations. The bloody conflict that resulted in the deaths of 34 Turkish soldiers showed that Turkey-Russia relations were volatile and resilient. Just a week prior to the February 27 incidents, airstrikes in Idlib, the escalating crisis and the Assad regime's attacks on civilians had already pushed almost a million Syrians toward the Turkish border. Due to European capitals› profound silence in response to Turkey›s request for EU cooperation in keeping Syrian civilians from approaching Turkey›s border, Erdoan declared on February 29 that Turkey would no longer block Syrians from attempting to enter Europe. This announcement was justified by the fact that Turkey could no longer cope with the large number of Syrians fleeing the civil war, a burden worsened by the escalating situation in Idlib.[48]

In the wake of a regime attack on Turkish troops observing the ceasefire in Idlib on February 27, which left 34 soldiers martyred, Turkey carried out Operation Spring Shield against the Syrian regime by hitting back against Syrian government forces, shooting down government jets and targeting tanks and artillery positions with drones. As previously mentioned, Erdoan, dissatisfied by the EU's reluctance to share Turkey's refugee load, simultaneously chose to open the land and maritime borders to the west. He stated categorically that "the doors are now open"[49] to migrants and refugees wanting to leave Turkey for Europe. This move aimed to show to the world that Turkey's capacity was at a breaking point and that it could no longer deal with the amount of people fleeing Russia-backed Assad regime's brutality. In other words, Ankara tried to put pressure on both European and NATO allies to come to its aid in Idlib by loosening the restrictions and allowing migrants and refugees to travel to Europe. However, Turkey's efforts remained fruitless. For example, President of the European Commission Ursula von der Leyen approved €700 million emergency aid to Greece rather than Turkey by declaring that Greek borders were also European borders.[50]

Interestingly, Turkish-American relations did not improve despite the killing of 34 Turkish soldiers bringing Turkey and Russia close to direct confrontation, and Trump called Erdoğan to reaffirm his support to Turkey in Idlib.[51] On the contrary, Ankara preferred to come to an agreement with Moscow to halt an escalation of violence in Idlib that displaced nearly a million people. The two countries reached a ceasefire agreement on March 5. In accordance with the ceasefire, 'Turkish and Russian forces would carry out joint patrols along the strategic M4 highway linking Syria's east and west and establish a security corridor either side of it.'[52]

The reasons for Ankara's and Moscow's cooperation despite their opposing interests in the region were manifold. One was the lack of mutual confidence in the United States and the European Union. Second, the sole factor that held Turkey and Russia together was their willingness to isolate the United States in the region. Both Moscow and Ankara felt threatened by Washington's further designs and ambitions in Syria that would result in the formation of an Israeli-controlled Kurdish statelet. Unlike Washington, Moscow was cautious about the presence of the YPG in north-eastern Syria. Putin wanted YPG to accept the regime's superiority in return for Assad's approval of an autonomy for north-eastern Syria under Kurdish influence.

Thirdly, from Moscow's perspective, Turkey was a key player in the region for Russia to break the transatlantic alliance. Turkey's purchase of S400 was, therefore, of crucial importance for Russia whose threat perception had already peaked with NATO leaders' decision to include Ukraine and Georgia as members at their summit in Bucharest in 2008.[53]

In a nutshell, the threefold fear was that the US military presence in Syria would enhance YPG's regional importance, threaten Syrian territorial integrity and, finally, if Israel were to be included, it would bring about a new collusion of these two against the Turks, Russians and the Syrian regime. American-sponsored YPG and the increasing Israeli influence under the guise of 'normalization with Israel' urged Moscow and Ankara to formulate some sort of solution to their diverging interests. For example, Putin stating that 'the Adana Protocol of 1998 was still in effect and should constitute the legal basis for addressing Turkey's security concerns' promoted the Adana protocol.[54] This had a twofold aim: one was to provide a rapprochement between Assad regime and Ankara, and the other was to prevent a Turkish-American cooperation on the establishment of a safe zone in north-eastern Syria. Otherwise, Assad regime forces would not be able to control the region at all. It can be said that Russia's tacit consent to Turkey's fourth military operation in Syria—Operation Spring Shield—mainly aimed to prevent a probable Turkish-American cooperation in the east of Euphrates.

Turkey's border security issue throughout the Syrian crisis and cross-border military operations proved that Turkey's ultimate preference for the Atlantic alternative over Soviet Russia and Muslim Middle Eastern one during the Cold War period has totally changed. As of today, Turkey has been following a very proactive foreign policy; she launched four military incursions, signed a maritime deal with Libya's Government of National Accord (GNA) based in Tripoli, helped Azerbaijan on the battlefield in Nagorno-Karabakh, declared a new reform package and taken some steps to have a rapprochement with the EU in order to solve the refugee problem and to find a firm solution to issues in the EastMed. Aydınlı notes that as Turkey currently needs a new grand strategy based on survival and growth, there must be a balance between capacity and desire. Today, Turkey's ideational capacity (soft power) is unlimited, and it can still embrace Westernisation, but also be open to the East. Turkey no longer requires a set Westernization philosophy in its foreign policy. Foreign policy is no longer required to have a Western or Eastern slant or any bias at all. Turkey may act Western with the West, Islamist with the Muslim world, Eurasian with the Russians. The rationalization of the foreign policy represents a freeing from ideational straitjackets.[55]

CONCLUSION

With the outburst of the Syrian crisis, Turkey's border security was endangered by the sudden appearance of the two terrorist groups along Turkey's border with Syria; one was the PKK-affiliated YPG and the other was the Da'esh. During 2014 and 2015, Turkey struggled both against these two terrorist groups and the allegations that Ankara was boosting the power of the Da'esh. Both Turkey's image as a reliable partner of the West and its economy were seriously damaged. The deteriorating relations with the West isolated Turkey and led to estrangement of Turkey from its Western allies namely, the United States and the EU for two reasons. First was the EU turning a blind eye to the influx of hundreds of thousands of Syrian civilians fleeing the brutality of the Assad regime, as well as the Da'esh and other terrorist groups. Second was the firm belief of the Turkish people that the Da'esh, just like the YPG was a proxy of the US State.

The Obama period was the worst one for Ankara during which Turkish-US relations reached their lowest point. Obama demonstrated his unreliability to the Turks in 2013 by turning a blind eye to Assad's use of chemical weapons on his own people. Although the use of chemical weapons was Obama's red line, the United States and the European Union did nothing in 2013 when hundreds of thousands of Syrian people were killed using chemical weapons (chemical agent sarin) in the east of Ghouta.

While struggling against the influx of refugees and grappling with terrorist groups, Turkey had another catastrophe in its internal politics. It was the coup attempt of a Sunni radical group, FETÖ whose patron, Gülen was sheltered by the US government in Pennsylvania since 1999. On the night of July 15, Turkey came to the edge of a civil war, was about to collapse and would be entirely controlled by a terrorist organization, FETÖ/Cemaat, which has been a puppet in the hands of Washington.

As the FETÖ terror group had taken hold of Turkish bureaucracy, intelligentsia, academia and justice system for past several years before the July 15 coup, Erdoğan, after coping with the putschists on the fateful night of the failed coup, took revolutionary steps both in inner and foreign politics to clear FETÖ off from all parts of the state apparatus. For example, he put an end to Turkey's traditional role of being a loyal gendarme of the USA in the Middle East. Soon after the failed coup attempt, Erdoğan paid his first visit to Russia and called on Putin in August 2016. Second, the Astana process was started by Iran, Turkey and Russia. Third, Turkey initiated military incursions to protect its boundary with Syria beginning with Euphrates Shield in 2016, Olive Branch in Afrin in 2018, Peace Spring offensive in 2019, Spring Shield in 2020. These operations had some major goals. One was to protect the border after pushing terrorist elements back to a safe distance. The second was to establish a safe zone of 460 km by 30-40 km along the Syrian-Turkish border, east of the Euphrates within which Turkey could resettle approximately one million Syrian refugees and transform it into a source of security in the region. The third objective was to create a demographic and geographical barrier between Turkey and the terrorist PKK-affiliated YPG militias.

As the most Syrian refugee-hosting country globally, Turkey encountered numerous challenges from its beleaguered southern neighbour and with these concerns built a wall along its boundary with Syria. Threats to internal security and territorial integrity concerns forced Turkey 'to reverse its border policy and return to the traditional concept of borders as barriers rather than places of contact. This occurred continuously in three stages—first, closure of official border crossings; second, introduction of visa requirements for Syrian citizens and third, build-up of walls along the borders with Syria, Iran and Iraq.'[56]

While securitising its border policy further, Ankara aspired to have a higher status in international relations by becoming one of the leading manufacturers of weapons system, creating a safe zone along its border with Syria, being a game changer in Libya and Nagorno-Karabakh and insisting on a two-state solution in Cyprus. Within this context, Turkey suddenly assumed a leading strategic role in the region, which was buttressed by the Turkish army's complex of power. This pushed it to have a more comprehensive grand strategy, which does not necessarily mean solely to be 'modernized' and 'Westernized'. On the contrary, Turkey broadened its relations in international relations and proved its ultimate preference for different alternatives other than the Atlantic one, as it did while protecting its border with Syria.

NOTES

1. Deniz Sert, "Turkey's Integrated Border Management Strategy," *Turkish Policy Quarterly* 12, no. 1 (2013): 1-8, at http://turkishpolicy.com/dosyalar/files/vol_12-no_1-sert.pdf (accessed on January 14, 2021).
2. Özden Zeynep Oktav, "Hatay Sorunu," *Toplum ve Ekonomi* 9 (1996): 1-23.
3. Özden Zeynep Oktav, "Water Dispute and Kurdish Seperatism in Turkish-Syrian relations," *Turkish Yearbook of International Relations* (*Milletlerarası Münasebetler Yıllığı*) 34 (2003): 91-117.
4. İdil Öztığ, "Syria and Turkey: Border Security Priorities," *Middle East Policy* 26, no. 1 (2019): 119. For further information see Özden Zeynep Oktav, "Transition from Enmity to 'Common Fate' Rhetoric: Water Issue in Turkish-Iraqi-Syrian Relations," *Turkish Yearbook of International Relations* 40 (2009): 71-90.
5. Oktav, n. 4, 71-90.
6. "The Free Syrian Army (FSA) has evolved significantly since its emergence in the summer of 2011. Initially established with the grand objective of representing a nationwide resistance organization formed to protect peaceful protesters and to initiate military operations against the Assad regime, the FSA has struggled to live up to these goals. However, despite, or perhaps because of, its subsequent decentralization, the FSA remains the cornerstone brand of Syria's moderate opposition, representing the original moderate vision of the revolution." Charles Lister, "The Free Syrian Army: A Decentralized Insurgent Brand" *Brookings*, November 7, 2016, at https://www.brookings.edu/research/the-free-syrian-army-a-decentralized-insurgent-brand/ (accessed on May 2, 2021).
7. "The open-door policy was shaped by the newly introduced "zero-problems with neighbours policy" formulated by Ahmet Davutoğlu after the Justice and Development Party (AKP)'s power takeover in 2002. According to Davutoğlu, the zero-problems approach is based on the notion that "Turkey needs to improve its relations with all its neighbours by rescuing itself from the belief that it is constantly surrounded by enemies and the defensive reflex developing thereof." Barbora Olejárová, "The Great Wall of Turkey: From "The Open-Door Policy" to Building Fortress?" *Pogranicze. Polish Borderlands Studies* 6, no. 2 (2018): 121-122.
8. Kyilah Terry, "The EU-Turkey Deal, Five Years On: A Frayed and Controversial but Enduring Blueprint," Migration Policy Institute, April 8, 2021, at https://www.migrationpolicy.org/article/eu-turkey-deal-five-years-on (accessed on April 10, 2021); also see Özden Zeynep Oktav, "The Syrian uprising and the Iran-Turkey-Syria quasi alliance: A view from Turkey," in Raymond Hinnebusch and Özlem Tür, ed. *Turkey-Syria Relations: Between Enmity and Amity* (New York: Routledge, 2013), 193-203.
9. Aslı Okyay, "Turkey's post-2011 approach to its Syrian border and its implications for domestic politics," *International Affairs* 93, no. 4 (2017): 831.
10. Ali Murat Kurşun, "Deconstructing the Sykes-Picot Myth: Frontiers, Boundaries, Borders and the Evolution of Ottoman Territoriality," *All Azimuth* 9, no. 1 (2020): 87.

11. Mukhtar of Ziyaret (who wished not to be identified by name), Village in Suruç, Urfa, Turkey in discussion with the author, June 28, 2019.
12. Ayla Jean Yackley, "Turkey, US agree to coordinate on Syrian buffer zone," *Al Monitor*, August 2019, at https://www.al-monitor.com/originals/2019/08/turkey-us-agree-syria-buffer-zone.html#ixzz6pgA2jBxk (accessed on March 29, 2021).
13. As of November 2020, Turkey had completed the construction of a 832 kilometres (517-miles) concrete wall along its border with Syria. "Suriye sınırına 832 kilometre duvar kurulumu tamamlandı," *Sabah*, November 26, 2020, at https://www.sabah.com.tr/hatay/2020/11/26/suriye-sinirina-832-kilometre-duvar-kurulumu-tamamlandi (accessed on April 2, 2021).
14. Ayşe Sözen Usluer, "The July 15 Failed Coup Attempt and Its Implications for Turkish Foreign Policy," *Bilig*, no. 79 (2016): 32.
15. Ayla Jean Yackley, "Turkey, US agree to coordinate on Syrian buffer zone," *Al Monitor*, August 2019, at https://www.al-monitor.com/originals/2019/08/turkey-us-agree-syria-buffer-zone.html#ixzz6pgA2jBxk (accessed on February 26, 2021).
16. Usluer, n. 14.
17. "This policy was based on three core principles: 1) Turkey's borders would remain open to persons seeking safety in Turkey; 2) No persons from Syria would be sent back to Syria against their will; 3) Basic humanitarian needs of the persons arriving from the conflict in Syria would be met." Zuhal Karakoç Dora, "International Migrants as a Matter of Security: Open Door Policy and Syrians in Turkey," *Güvenlik Bilimleri Dergisi* 9, no. 2 (2020): 501-524.
18. İlhami Akgül (an official and deputy head of AFAD, The Disaster and Emergency Management Presidency of the Turkish Government) in discussion with the author, August 14, 2013.
19. Zuhal Karakoç Dora, "International Migrants as a Matter of Security: Open Door Policy and Syrians in Turkey," *Güvenlik Bilimleri Dergisi* 9, no. 2 (2020): 503.
20. Kadri Gürsel, "Turkey paying price for Jihadist highway on border," *Al-Monitor*, June 12, 2014.
21. Can Kasapoğlu, "Operation Euphrates Shield: Progress and Scope," *Al Jazeera*, February 3, 2017, https://www.aljazeera.com/opinions/2017/2/3/operation-euphrates-shield-progress-and-scope (accessed on March 21, 2021).
22. *Turkish Heritage organization*, "Operation Euphrates Shield: A Brief Overview," August 2016, at https://www.turkheritage.org/en/publications/factsheets/issue-briefs/operation-euphrates-shield-a-brief-overview--2852 (accessed on January 21, 2021).
23. Branislav Stanicek, "Turkey's military operation in Syria and its impact on relations with the EU" *European Parliament*, November 2019.
24. "Syrian Democratic forces (SDF) are the *US*-backed group and SDF is mostly made up of YPG fighters which Turkey considers a 'terror group' linked to the PKK."
25. Özlem Kayhan Pusane, "How to Profile PYD/YPG as an Actor in the Syrian Civil War: Policy Implications for the Region and Beyond," in Özden Zeynep Oktav, Emel Parlar Dal and Ali Murat Kurşun, ed. *Violent Non-State Actors and Syrian Civil War the ISIS and YPG Cases* (Zürich: Springer, 2018), 85.

26. Metin Gürcan, "Assessing the Post-July 15 Turkish Military, Policy Notes," *The Washington Institute for Near East Policy*, 2019, at https://www.washingtoninstitute.org/media/1483 (accessed on January 15, 2021).
27. "The White House Approves Supply of Weapons to YPG in Syria: US Official," *Middle East Eye*, May 10, 2017, at https://www.middleeasteye.net/news/white-house-approves-supply-weapons-ypg-syria-us-official (accessed on April 30, 2021).
28. Can Kasapoğlu and Sinan Ülgen, "Operation Olive Branch: A Political Military Assessment," *EDAM*, January 30, 2018, at https://edam.org.tr/en/operation-olive-branch-a-political-military-assessment/ (accessed on January 21, 2021).
29. Foreign Minister of Turkey, H.E. Mevlüt Çavuşoğlu, "The Meaning of Operation Olive Branch," April 5, 2018, at https://www.mfa.gov.tr/article-by-h_e_-mr_-mevlut-cavusoglu_-the-minister-of-foreign-affairs-of-turkey-the-_meaning_-of-operation-olive-branch.en.mfa (accessed on April 30, 2021).
30. Ibid. Article by H.E. Mevlüt Çavuşoğlu published in *Foreign Policy* titled "The Meaning of Operation Olive Branch," *Foreign Policy*, April 5, 2018, at https://foreignpolicy.com/2018/04/05/the-meaning-of-operation-olive-branch/ (accessed on April 28, 2021).
31. "Trump and Erdogan vow friendship despite anger at US arming Kurds," *Middle East Eye*, May 17, 2017, at https://www.middleeasteye.net/fr/news/trump-and-erdogan-vow-friendship-despite-anger-us-arming-kurds-1968858854 (accessed on January 22, 2021).
32. Kadir Üstün, "The Operation Olive Branch and the US Policy in Syria," *SETA*, January 29, 2018, at https://setadc.org/operation-olive-branch-us-policy-syria/ (accessed on December 28, 2020).
33. "Final De-Escalation Zones Agreed on in Astana," *Al Jazeera English*, September 15, 2017, at http://www.aljazeera.com/news/2017/09/final-de-escalation-zones-agreed-astana-170915102811730.html (accessed on December 12, 2020).
34. "The Center for Reconciliation of Conflicting Sides in Syria (CRCSS) is one of the most active of Russia's humanitarian entities in Syria, founded in 2016," Marika Sosnowski and Jonathan Robinson, "Mapping Russia's soft power efforts in Syria through humanitarian aid," *Atlantic Council*, June 25, 2020, at https://www.atlanticcouncil.org/blogs/menasource/mapping-russias-soft-power-efforts-in-syria-through-humanitarian-aid/ (accessed on July 7, 2020).
35. Asaad Hanna, "What Turkey's campaign in Afrin means for the YPG," *Chatham House*, January 28, at 2018, https://syria.chathamhouse.org/research/what-turkeys-campaign-in-afrin-means-for-the-ypg (accessed on June 25, 2018).
36. Oytun Orhan, "Afrin in the First Year of the Operation of Olive Branch," *ORSAM*, February 12, 2019, at https://www.orsam.org.tr/en/afrin-in-the-first-year-of-the-operation-of-olive-branch-panel/ (accessed on May 15, 2019).
37. Branislav Stanicek, "Turkey's military operation in Syria and its impact on relations with the EU," EPRS Briefing, European Parliament, November 2019, 2, at https://www.europarl.europa.eu/EPRS/EPRS-Briefing-642284-Turkeys-military-operation-Syria-FINAL.pdf

38. "Donald Trump's bizarre, threatening letter to Erdoğan: 'Don't be a fool," *The Guardian*, October 17, 2019, at https://www.theguardian.com/us-news/2019/oct/16/trump-letter-erdogan-turkey-invasion (accessed on January 26, 2021).
39. Stanicek, n. 37, 2.
40. "Turkey's Erdogan 'threw Trump's Syria letter in bin," *BBC News*, October 17, 2019, at https://www.bbc.com/news/world-middle-east-50080737 (accessed on March 2, 2021).
41. "Russia, Turkey adopt memorandum on northern Syria situation after Putin-Erdogan talks," *Xinhua.net*, October 23, 2019, at http://www.xinhuanet.com/english/2019-10/23/c_138494544.htm (accessed on April 16, 2021).
42. Seçkin Köstem, "Russian-Turkish cooperation in Syria: geopolitical alignment with limits," *Cambridge Review of International Affairs* (2020): 14-15, DOI: 10.1080/09557571.2020.1719040.
43. Ibid., p.14.
44. Metin Gürcan, "A post-mortem of Turkey's Operation Peace Spring," *Al-Monitor*, October 24, 2019, at https://www.al-monitor.com/originals/2019/10/turkey-united-states-russia-syria-postmortem-of-operation.html (accessed on January 15, 2021).
45. "Turkey, Russia ties overloaded by Idlib conflict," Arab *News*, February 8, 2020, at https://www.arabnews.com/node/1624961/middle-east (accessed on August 20, 2020).
46. "The de-escalation zone had been created in Idlib on May 7, 2017, as part of the Astana process launched by Turkey and Russia."
47. Talha Köse, "From Sochi to Where? Rising Uncertainties in İdlib," *SETA*, February 27, 2020, at https://www.setav.org/en/from-sochi-to-where-rising-uncertainties-in-idlib/ (accessed on June 1, 2020).
48. David A. Wemer, "Idlib Presents Europe with Another Migration Test," *Atlantic Council*, March 10, 2020, at https://www.atlanticcouncil.org/blogs/new-atlanticist/idlib-presents-europe-with-another-migration-test/ (accessed on April 5, 2021).
49 Matina Stevis-Gridneff and Carlotta Gall, "Erdogan Says, 'We Opened the Doors,' and Clashes Erupt as Migrants Head for Europe, *The New York Times*, February 29, 2020, at https://www.nytimes.com/2020/02/29/world/europe/turkey-migrants-eu.html? (accessed on March 28, 2021).
50. Marie Menke and Stefanie Neufeld, "What's Going on at the Greek-Turkish Border?" *Current Affairs*, May 27, 2020, at https://www.thenewfederalist.eu/greek-turkish-border-what-s-going-on-there?lang=fr (accessed on September 28, 2020).
51. "Trump, in call with Erdogan, backs Turkey and urges end to violence in Syria's Idlib," *Reuters*, February 28, 2020, at https://www.reuters.com/article/us-syria-security-turkey-usa-idUSKCN20M2QL (accessed on September 21, 2020).
52. "Turkey says Idlib ceasefire details largely agreed on with Russia," *Al Jazeraa*, March 12, 2020, at https://www.aljazeera.com/news/2020/3/12/turkey-says-idlib-ceasefire-details-largely-agreed-on-with-russia (accessed on January 21, 2021).
53. Olga Stefanishyna (the deputy prime minister of Ukraine for European and Euro-Atlantic integration), "Ukraine Needs a Clear Path to NATO Membership," *Foreign Affairs*,

April 12, 2021, at https://foreignpolicy.com/2021/04/12/ukraine-nato-membership-path-russia-border-georgia/ (accessed on April 13, 2021).

54. "With the Adana Protocol (October 1998), the then President of Syria, Hafez al Assad had agreed to end Syria's military, logistical and financial support to the PKK, declared the PKK a terrorist organization and banned the PKK activities in Syrian territory." Özden Zeynep Oktav, "The October 1998 Crisis: The Change of Heart of Turkish Foreign Policy towards Syria?" *Cahiers d'études sur la Méditerranée orientale et le monde turco-iranien*, no. 31 (2001): 142-161.
55. Ersel Aydınlı, "Neither Ideological nor Geopolitical: Turkey Needs a 'Growth'-Based Grand Strategy," *Perceptions* 25, no. 2 (2020): 242.
56. Barbora Olejárová, "The Great Wall of Turkey: From "The Open-Door Policy" to Building Fortress?" *Pogranicze: Polish Borderlands Studies* 6, no. 2 (2018): 129.

5

THE SYRIAN CRISIS AND ITS IMPLICATIONS FOR INDIA

Sukalpa Chakrabarti

BACKDROP

More than a decade has passed since the turmoil began in several West Asian countries, specifically Syria in 2011. West Asia as a region has witnessed unanticipated political changes unfold through the past decade. Authoritarian regimes constructed along the lines of ethnicity have historically been a feature of the political structure of all the countries in West Asia. The politics of the region has been dominated by the irrepressible but elusive goal of an independent Palestinian state vis-à-vis Israeli mulishness on the issue of the West Bank settlements. The US invasion of Iraq in 2003, the unbridled nuclear aspirations of Iran and the reappearance of the Muslim Brotherhood added to the ongoing climate of political distrust. Violent infighting and sharpened sectarianism was the natural consequence.

The Arab Spring was an unprompted and contagious rising of the ordinary people who were disillusioned with the current state of affairs and demanded a complete overhaul of the repressive regimes. Frustrations had been building up due to bulging levels of youth unemployment, pervasive economic inequality, blatant elitism, stifled aspirations for larger freedoms and political inclusion and the absence of efficient and accountable governance institutions; it just needed a release outlet. What started as anti-government protests in December 2010 in Tunisia, found resonance among netizens who took to social media sites like Twitter, YouTube and Facebook, to express their angst against continued oppression, repression of free expression and share the aspiration for a better democratic future. This was then mirrored on the ground, with protests being organized across the Middle East. The Arab Spring or the Arab people's uprising, was the first of its kind effectively overthrowing the governments of Tunisia, Egypt, Libya and Yemen. It had all the markings of ushering in a new future that involved adoption of western democratic style of governance, and as a result, the much-awaited stability and economic growth. Soon the regional and extra regional powers decided to join the wagon and ride the wave of change to serve their own vested interests, and the uprising spiralled out of hand. There is no denying the fact that these external actors have been involved in providing covert support to the autocratic regimes through weaponisation and technological support, which were then used to overpower the people.

While the objective of the uprisings was to bring about political reforms through the establishment of democracy and overturning of governmental tyranny, they were not fully prepared to face the challenges of sustaining the political transitions. These also resulted in triggering armed civil conflicts in countries such as Syria, Iraq, Libya, and Yemen. Also the militants were quick to adopt the same technology and power of social media to further their vicious ends of planning attacks and covert recruitments. Instead of the intended future of fresh, vigorous democracies replacing the old oppressive regimes, civil wars have been spewed in the region which have provided the perfect cocoon to breed and spread Salafi jihadism. The fast spread of IS and its affiliates bears testimony to the fact that extremist movements are quick to take advantage of the power vacuums in failed states and spread their tentacles. The ripple effects of the crisis continue to rock the entire global order with major consequences for social, political and economic stability.

THE SYRIAN CIVIL WAR

Syria's strategic location in relation to Asia and Africa makes it a coveted country for all expansive powers seeking geo-economic and geo political advantage. As the Arab Spring turned into a major disappointment, the Syrian crisis became a complicated strategic mess and a theatre for proxy wars, accentuated by the role played by actors with vested interests. To quote Geraint A Hughes, the civil war has turned out to be less of a "people's revolution" and more of a "proxy war" between regional rivals, each with their own geopolitical objectives.[1] The decade-long crisis has now turned into one of the most complex foreign policy challenges.

The Syrian civil war, which began during the Arab Spring in 2011 as a non-violent uprising against the country's president, Bashar al-Assad has since intensified, shattering the lives of Syrians, unleashing destruction and horror, pressurising the global order with consequent political and economic impacts. In his commentary, Anthony H. Cordesman observes that the civil war led to serious tensions between Alawite, Shi'ite, Sunnis, and smaller religious minorities, separated Syria's Kurds from the rest of the Assad-controlled regions in the country and created large Sunni extremist elements as well as one of the most violently repressive regimes in the world.[2]

It had been nearly 50 years that Syria had been under the autocratic rule of the Ba'ath party and the youth has long been disillusioned with the future. Contrary to popular belief neither the state nor the ordinary civilian was the first to resort to violence; the first to stoke up the clash were the insurgents, i.e. the Salafi/Takfiri Islamists who crossed the border from Jordan and embarked on launching targeted provocations. Turkey and Qatar are alleged to have covertly channelized money and arms to the insurgents to start a sectarian civil war in a bid to topple the regime of Bashar al-Assad, who enjoyed greater support in the country than the other fallen dictators had in theirs. The Turkey-Syria-Iraq conflict triangle also has many causes to add to tensions—the Kurdish problem, water dispute and Shia—Sunni divide to name a few. It is no surprise that the Sunni countries seized the Syrian crisis in a bid to replace the Alawite Shia-led regime with a Sunni one. The surprisingly proactive involvement of the GCC countries in strengthening the weak opposition in Syria can be explained in the context of Syria-Iran relations. Syria has been Iran's staunchest ally in the region and had supported Iran in the war with Iraq. It is through Syria that Iran has been able project itself as the prime defender of the Palestine cause—be it the creation and sustenance of Hezbollah in Lebanon or support to Hamas in Gaza. Therefore, a death blow to Assad's regime would also cripple the Iranian influence in the sensitive Levantine region and in Arab politics. This also fitted well with the grand strategy of isolating Iran to deter it from pursuing its nuclear designs that might cause an Iran-Israel war with disastrous consequences for the world. All these complex factors combined together to heighten the regional interest in overthrowing the Assad regime, in the garb of sympathetic support for the high ideals of democracy and reform. The Arab League proposal demanded that Assad concede power to his vice president, thereby allowing for a negotiated end to the ongoing conflict and the creation of a Syrian unity government. The vetoing of the Arab League proposal in the UN Security Council by Russian and China resulted in the Syrian conflict becoming more violent and pronouncedly internationalized.

President Assad set up a drafting committee to frame a new, democratic constitution for Syria, which was to be put forth for popular referendum. He offered amnesty to all rebels and invited them to join in the voting process. The draft constitution not only required an election within three months of its passing, but also contained a clause that would bar Mr. Assad from contesting the presidential election after his term ended in 2014. For reasons best known to the opposition, they chose to boycott the elections and let the violence continue. But on February 26, 2012, a good majority of Syria's electorate turned out to endorse the new constitution. The message was clear that the Syrians were in favour of a peaceful transition to a secular democracy even if managed by President Assad. However, this was followed by unprecedented scaling up of violence. The Free Syrian Army is accused of being responsible for this since their leaders were afraid that establishment of peace would corrode most of the support they enjoyed among the people. UN reports revealed that Christians and Shias have been the main targets in a devious plan to promote sectarian aggression along religious lines. If not restrained in time, this had the potential to drown the entire region into an all-out Sunni-Shia bloodbath. In the absence of a sound alternative to the existing structures of authority, it came as no surprise that the Syrian nation plunged deeper into anarchy with violence unleashed by the radical extremist groups like the Hezbollah or the Jabhat al-Nusra (and the Syrian offshoot of Al-Qaeda,). The political unrest and the breakdown of law and order was utilized by the extremist forces to enlarge their spheres of influence. The Islamic State of Iraq and Syria (ISIS) assumed the structure and authority of a transnational proto-state when it emerged in 2013.

Assad reinforced his position by winning the election for a new presidential term, while the Islamic State made substantial territorial gains. The violence continued unmarred. The situation was further compounded by concerns about the use of chemical weapons in the ongoing fight between the rebels and the government in Syria. The opposition to Bashar al-Assad's Ba'ath regime has received Western patronage from the very beginning channelized through countries like Saudi Arabia, Qatar, and Turkey. Iran, China and Russia, on the other hand, have supported Damascus. In fact, Russia's proficient diplomatic intervention has allowed Assad's forces to gradually reclaim power over the armed opponents. As a result, the two groups were striving for domination, resulting in an ungainly stalemate.

Former UN Secretary General Kofi Annan had presided over a conference in June 2012 that produced the "Geneva communiqué". The communiqué had set forth the preconditions to stop the fighting and bring about a political transition, but failed to resolve the contentious issue of President Bashar al-Assad's role in Syria's political future. Thereafter Brahimi brought the sides together for the "Geneva 2" talks in early 2014. A successful negotiation at the Geneva 2 was taken to be the only hope for a truly participative political settlement to the ongoing crisis and a face saver for the powers involved. However, while the Assad regime had agreed to join the convention, it is the disconnect within the National Coalition of the Syrian Revolutionary and Opposition Forces that stalled any possibility of immediate resolution. In the face of a highly fragmented opposition, they were unable to arrive at a consensus on who should represent at Geneva 2 and also more fundamentally whether to participate at all. The West was wary that this inconsistency would result in favour of the Assad regime as well as Russia and Iran. At the international level, the states were divided over Iran's presence at the conference, which was then opposed by the US, France and Saudi Arabia, but backed by Russia.

The tripartite meet in Geneva on June 5, 2013, among the US, Russian and UN representatives was a clear acknowledgement of the fact that Assad's departure has to be negotiated. Post the meet it was decided that an international peace conference on Syria comprising intensive negotiations among the Syrian factions could take place in July 2013. However, the ceasefire was stalled in the face of the demand for an immediate step down of the Assad regime, as was put forward as a precondition to engage in peace talks by the opposition with support from the West. As was the case with the failure of the Geneva 1 conference, the inability to ensure the participation of all involved parties in Geneva 2 conference resulted in the failure to come up with any negotiated framework arrived at through the mediations. Three fresh recommendations were made in 2015 to resolve the Syrian conflict through consultation with various concerned political actors—including the regime, the political opposition, and the rebel groups as well as the concerned external actors. These include the "Aleppo freeze" proposal endorsed by the U.S.A and European Union, the Russian option of "Moscow-1," and the joint blueprint for transition in Syria prepared by several of the most important opposition coalitions based on a diplomatic framework involving all key external actors, including Iran. A continued theme has been that there can be no resolution to the crisis while President Bashar al-Assad retains power, a position particularly backed by the USA.

THE ONGOING CRISIS IN SYRIA

The 2011 political disturbances resulted in the bloodiest civil war in the region. It produced an Assad regime-led coalition with Iran, the Hezbollah and Russia that combatted a Sunni Arab-dominated disjointed coalition in Western and Central Iraq. The capricious associations among the local intermediaries and the local as well as central authorities have shaped the protests and consequent widespread conflict. This explains why the Syrian insurgence could not take on the character of a unified national movement. There was also the ominous formation of an ISIS "caliphate" that established control over north-eastern Syria. The presence of foreign terrorist fighters along with continued terror activities worsened the situation on the ground, and the current hostilities between military and political agencies make the attainment of the goals of peace, order and stability seem implausible.

The concern of the big powers over the political instability in Syria has been considerably eclipsed with the onset of the COVID-19 pandemic and the consequent socio-economic problems that has gripped the world at large. Syria is in fact now in a more apprehensive phase with continued socio-economic disorder during the coronavirus pandemic. The Syrian war zone is majorly embroiled in a complex web of flashpoints that mirror regional and international dissensions. In March 2020, just before the pandemic skyrocketed, Turkey and Russia were close to a face-off over Idlib, the last bastion of the Syrian opposition in the north western part of the country. The rationale for Turkey's increased engagement with the Assad regime and Russia is possibly to ensure a political solution to the Syrian crisis, which in turn would address the issue of the return of the Syrian refugees which continues to pose a major economic and security concern for Turkey. There has been a relative peace since the Idlib ceasefire that was negotiated between Russia and Turkey on March 5, 2020. The pact included the setting up of a security corridor—6 kilometres each side of Idlib's M4 motorway that links Aleppo and Latakia, a strategic space. However, it is an uneasy peace with several underlying problems that could erupt at any time. Following the withdrawal of the American forces from the border with Turkey, the condition in the north east part is also in a capricious state. With the Turkish, Syrian and Russian forces positioned alongside proxies and the Syrian Kurdish militias, the region is literally like a minefield. These crises could be caused by both external and internal factors. Rivalries between Russia and the United States, Israel and Iran and Turkey and the Kurds are potential trigger points. The dangers have been evinced by the provocative October 26, 2020, Russian airstrike close to the Turkish border. The only relief is the pause in the Assad government's offensive against the opposition, which is nearly decimated.

It is now obvious that the number of refugees and people at risk are majorly impacting the quality of conflict resolution and post-conflict stability than the number of the dead or sick, permanently injured. Destruction, displacement, injury and casualties aside, the conflict has also generated a succession of economic crises locally. To contain the spread of the coronavirus, the Syrian government closed down borders, imposed domestic travel restrictions, shut down schools and restaurants and declared a nationwide curfew. The economic impact of these measures added to the prevailing economic crisis. While the government started relaxing the restrictions towards the end of April 2021, these measures had already triggered panic-buying and severe upsurges in food prices. The prices of basic commodities such as food and fuel have doubled and the Syrian pound has devalued as well. The UN humanitarian office (OCHA) reports that more than eight in ten people are living in poverty, and the World Food Programme (WFP) has assessed that 12.4 million are food insecure. A January 2021 World Food Programme (WFP) report[3] shows that the price of standard basic food items basket in December 2020 was 236 per cent higher as compared to December 2019 in Syria; and on an average, the price of oil has increased from 1000 Syrian pounds in January 2020 to 5000 Syrian pounds in Januray 2021. This pushes the state towards major dependence on availability and effective utilization of external aid and the necessity to develop new provisions of economic development. There exists serious direct and disguised unemployment and lack of resources. Unfortunately, the current state of governance in Syria is yet to show the capability or the credibility to cope with these critical requirements. The COVID 19 pandemic aside, Syria has also been hit hard by the new sanctions in the US Caesar Act, which target the overseas sources of income for the Assad regime and its enablers. This has compelled the regime to re-strategize the finances. Given the growing uncertainties and criticisms about the impact of the sanctions on ordinary Syrian citizens and families, the new administration in the United States, led by President Joe Biden, is assessing the Caesar Act's efficacy and unintended consequences. To make matters worse, Lebanon's greatest economic breakdown resulted in a further collapse of the Syrian economy. It is not surprising that the combined impact of these events has generated yet another round of civilian protests.

The World Bank and Transparency International appraise that Syria is mired in an abysmal mesh of corrupt governance, population pressure including a "youth bulge," miscarried economic planning and deep-rooted ethnic and sectarian splits. Reform initiatives, few and far in between, have not succeeded and the country is extremely volatile. Essential building elements of social and political infrastructure have been devastated in regions hardest hit by the war such as Raqqa and Deir Ezzor Governorates. The displacements of the local population has allowed for the emergence of new power groups, which raise the risk of such places being vulnerable to volatility caused by local or regional rivalries compounded by the vested interests of the external actors.

Poor governance coupled with depleting economic reserves are a threat to the viability of any proposed reconstruction process that is disconnected from ensuring a stable political settlement.

Against this backdrop, it is of utmost priority that the government in Syria focusses not just on receiving foreign aid and bracing internal financial resources to get the economy rolling, but also undertake effective reforms of the public administration system to bring about internal stability and accountability.

FACTORS INFLUENCING INDIA'S ROLE IN SYRIA

The present government in India is keen to carve out a leading position for itself in the non-polar world of today. This is also a defining moment in India's foreign policy re-calibration with the Indian government's commitment to "shoulder greater responsibility," and "engaging the world with greater confidence and assurance".[4] We see big powers, regional powers and emerging ones jostling for space and often engaging in acts that bring about imbalance in the prevailing world order. The 2020 offensive in the Armenian region of Nagorno-Karabakh by the Turkish special forces, Syrian mercenaries and the Azerbaijani military with support from Pakistan is a recent case in point. Close on the heels of this, the 'Turkey, Pakistan and Central Asia: Partnership for Peace International Conference', emphasized that Turkey, Azerbaijan and Pakistan need to "harmonise development strategies." This effectively translates into collective support for each other's expansionist ambitions, viz. Turkey in Cyprus, Pakistan in Kashmir, East Mediterranean against Greece, Azerbaijan against Armenia. It would be pertinent to note that Turkey had raised the Kashmir issue in support of Pakistan in the UN General Assembly session of 2019. India was quick in her diplomatic strategization and a prime ministerial level meeting was held with the leaders of Cyprus, Armenia and Greece. India also criticized the offensive action launched by Turkey against the Kurds in Syria and has subsequently downsized its defence commitments with Turkey following the rising Turkey-Pakistan ties.

The politics of the Middle East are multifaceted and entwined in complex layers lending to socio-economic and geopolitical discontent in different locations. While analysing India's careful diplomatic and policy position in Syria, one has to bear in mind the key drivers of the conflict and India's own stakes in the Middle East. India's tacit support to the Assad regime is clearly underscored by her apprehensions of regional volatility and the rise of the fundamentalism as well as her staunch commitment to non-interventionism. Interestingly, notwithstanding her wide-ranging ties with the GCC countries, which have been actively working towards the eviction of Assad, India's indifference for a regime change in Syria continued. The ideological stand is one lens through which to explain this position. India has always disapproved of foreign intervention and supported state sovereignty in any nation-state, which of course concurs with her interest in preventing external involvement in Kashmir.

At the same time, India shares profound historical and civilizational connections with the wider West Asia and the Gulf region. She has significant interests in the strategic arenas of trade and investment, diaspora and its remittances, energy and security. Therefore, India would not want any sprawl from the Syrian conflict to have a negative impact on these larger interests, especially that of energy security and diaspora. Given its rising population and increased dependency on oil and gas imports, India is naturally concerned with the stability in the Middle East, especially in the Kurdish Autonomous Region and Syria. Volatility in this region is also a threat to India's 7 million migrant workers. Therefore, it is only prudent that India's foreign policy for this region follows a middle path.

Another crucial factor that influences India's position on Syria is the security need to curb the spread of terrorism. While the Islamic State has lost all control over any territory in Syria and suffered a major blow with the death of its leader, Abu Bakr al-Baghdadi, it still poses a serious security threat as long as has it continues to thrive as a movement. The IS ranks still hold the allegiance of a substantial number of fighters and supporters who can be easily mobilized to unleash insurgency and terror attacks across the region and elsewhere. Reports have revealed that a bigger presence of Indian jihadists have been witnessed in the conflict. This feeds in to the existing threat of the increasing influence of extremists in Afghanistan, Pakistan and Kashmir. Adil Rasheed has classified Jihadist terrorism in India into three types being home-grown, Pakistani inspired and transnational (reference to Al Qaida and Islamic State).[5] His research reveals that within this, transnational jihadists often have the option to conduct attacks in India or participate in conflicts abroad. While there was a fear of Indian foreign fighter presence and subsequent threat of returnees, the numbers have been very low. However, it is also a fact that many radicalized individuals still live in India. Therefore, though India has managed to prevent IS/foreign fighters, it is prudent for the Indian government to supplement internal mechanisms with counter terrorism partnerships to ensure that future waves of foreign fighters will not comprise of Indians.

The other major factor influencing India's interests in Syria is China. China has made major interventions and investments in Syria as part of its grander strategy to assimilate the Middle East into the maritime ambit of its ambitious Belt and Road Initiative (BRI). Obviously the Chinese interests go beyond the commercial prospects involved in the reconstruction of Syria, as, Syria enjoys a geostrategic location that sprints the opportunity to regulate not only the eastern zone, but the entire Mediterranean Sea.

India is therefore ardent in her efforts to widen the strategic presence in Syria and to provide assistance in the rebuilding process, and strengthen the counter-terrorism partnership.

INDIA'S DIPLOMATIC RESPONSE AND ENGAGEMENT WITH POST-CONFLICT SYRIA

India has maintained a nuanced stand on Syria which has been consistent since the tenure of former prime minister Manmohan Singh. India has been one of the few countries that has continued to have a diplomatic outpost in Syria. The Indian government had officially condemned Turkey's unilateral military offensive in north east Syria.

In India's first open meeting in the Security Council as the country began its tenure as non-permanent member for the 2021-22 term, India has told the United Nations (UN) that concerns and allegations over the use of chemical weapons in Syria should be addressed through consultation among all concerned parties, cautioning that "politicisation" of the issue is neither helpful nor productive.[6] During the recent UNSC briefings on Syria, TS Tirumurti, Indian Permanent Representative to the United Nations, has appealed to the

United Nations Security Council that the humanitarian crisis, exacerbated by the COVID-19 pandemic, calls for the relaxation of sanctions imposed on Syria, saying the international community must act with a sense of urgency to help the Syrian people.[7] He said that it is "disheartening" to note that the ongoing crisis in Syria still has no end in sight and called on the international community to provide assistance to Syria for rebuilding its infrastructure.[8] Close on the heels of the Brussels V conference, Amb. Tirumurti has also emphasized that "the politicisation of the humanitarian track does not help anyone, least of all the millions of suffering Syrians" … "What we need immediately is an engagement that is an engagement that is both consistent with Syrian independence, territorial integrity and sovereignty as well as addresses the urgency of the humanitarian issues to alleviate the suffering of the Syrian people."[9] In September 2020 the Minister of State for External Affairs V. Muraleedharan held a virtual meeting with Syrian Vice Minister of Foreign Affairs and Expatriates Dr. Faisal Mekdad to comprehensively review the bilateral relations and chart a road map for further cooperation in areas of mutual interest and reiterated that it is India's hope to see "a comprehensive and peaceful resolution of the decade-long Syrian conflict, through a Syrian-led and Syrian-owned dialogue, involving all parties to the conflict that takes into account the legitimate aspirations of the Syrian people while preserving the unity, sovereignty and territorial integrity of the country."[10] Thus we find that India has been actively espousing the Syrian case at multilateral fora and pledging her support to help the country in its uphill journey of post-conflict reconstruction.

Let us now turn to the aspect of India's active engagement in the post-conflict reconstruction. In the past decade, India has provided USD12 million as humanitarian assistance to the Syrian government through bilateral and multilateral channels.[11] India has set up a biotech park and an IT Centre and extended USD 265 million in lines of credit for projects in the steel and power sectors;[12] it has set up an artificial limb fitment camp in Damascus that benefited over 500 Syrians and have also provided 1000 scholarships for Syrian students to study in India besides the 90 slots under ITEC and 25 slots under ICCR General Scholarship Scheme given annually. India is also launching a NextGen Centre for Information Technology in Damascus. India has reached out to Syria with more than 2000 metric tonnes (MT) of food supplies in March 2021 and 10 MT of medicines. As part of its COVID-19 outreach programme, India is aiding vaccine delivery and is working closely with the UN and its agencies.[13] These outreach actions aside, India is also eyeing a wider counter-terrorism partnership and stronger information sharing mechanism given Syria's experience in fighting ISIS.

Given the failed economic development and deep-rooted ethnic fissures in Syria, rebuilding and rehabilitation will not be an easy task. The fabric of the Syrian society, which has been torn into pieces by the conflict needs to be stitched back with due care and caution. The Syrian socio-political structure exhibits a unique dimension of being centred around the locality or al-mahalla; this could be urban or rural. This structure binds the people within an association that is rooted in a sense of collective history, familial ties and identity and thereby fosters communal responsibility. In the regions worst hit with violence, these structures have dissipated due to death, destruction and mass displacement. Where they remain, the biggest domestic challenge has been to connect these different localities to the central authority. This is where India's successful experiment of embedding grass-root administration into the state and central administrative framework through urban and rural local governance setups (*Panchayati Raj*) can prove helpful in restoring political order and social cohesion. Devolution of powers to local authorities will help to address the gap between the ordinary individual and the government by allowing for greater public participation in the mobilization of resources, investment and in the design of development policies corresponding to local needs.

Syria is set to hold a presidential election this year, despite harsh US-led criticism and pressure to involve external parties to determine the political fate of the country. India however has remained un-flinched in her position that no external power should dictate the political transition and that Syria must decide its political fate as a sovereign nation.

CONCLUSION

India's current position in the world order, her historical ties with Syria, equations with the regional and extra regional powers involved in the crisis, combined with the ability for tactful use of soft power and economic diplomacy, gives India a unique strategic leverage to engage in confidence building measures and to push a global concerted effort for combating the socio-economic collapse compounded by the impact of the COVID-19 pandemic, corruption and mismanagement in Syria. To sum up, given her interests in Syria and the wider region, India should continue on the policy path of a judicious combination of economic diplomacy, humanitarian assistance, intelligence sharing and soft power assertion while keeping a close watch on the developments as the Pakistan-China-Russia and Turkey-Pakistan relations unfold. Geopolitically, India's effective engagement with the Syrian crisis stands to reinforce her role as a security partner for the Middle Eastern states, to counter the competition from China and Pakistan.

NOTES

1. Geraint Alun Hughes, "Syria and the perils of Proxy war," *Small Wars and Insurgencies* 25, No. 3, July 1, 2014, at https://doi.org/10.1080/09592318.2014.913542 (accessed on January 14, 2021).
2. Anthony H. Cordesman, "Syria: Looking Beyond the Kurdish Crisis to Long Term Instability and a Near Certain Future of Civil Violence," Commentary, October 21, 2019, Centre for Strategic and International Studies (CSIS), at https://www.csis.org/analysis/syria-looking-beyond-kurdish-crisis-long-term-instability-and-near-certain-future-civil (accessed on January 4, 2021).
3. "Twelve million Syrians now in the grip of hunger, worn down by conflict and soaring food prices," World Food Programme, United Nations, February 17, 2021, at https://www.wfp.org/news/twelve-million-syrians-now-grip-hunger-worn-down-conflict-and-soaring-food-prices (accessed on February 27, 2021).
4. "IISS Fullerton Lecture by Dr. S. Jaishankar, Foreign Secretary in Singapore," Ministry of Foreign Affairs, Government of India, July 20, 2015, at https://mea.gov.in/Speeches-Statements.htm?dtl/25493/IISS_Fullerton_Lecture_by_Foreign_Secretary_in_Singapore (accessed on January 6, 2021).
5. Adil Rasheed, "Jihadist Radicalisation in India: Internal Challenges, External Threats," *Journal of Defence Studies* 12, No. 2 (April-June 2018): 77-103; at https://idsa.in/jds/jds-12-2-2018-jihadist-radicalisation-in-india (accessed on April 7, 2021).
6. "Allegations of chemical weapons use in Syria should be addressed through consultation: India at UNSC," *Press Trust of India*, January 06, 2021, at http://ptibeta.4cplus.net/news/international/allegations-of-chemical-weapons-use-in-syria-should-be-addressed-through-consultation-india-at-unsc/209053.html (accessed on March 23, 2021).

7. Y. Singh, "India Calls for Relaxation of Sanctions Imposed on Syria at UN," *The Wire*, March 16, 2021, at https://thewire.in/external-affairs/india-calls-for-relaxation-of-sanctions-imposed-on-syria-at-un (accessed on March 18, 2021).
8. "India calls for relaxation of sanctions on Syria in light of worsening humanitarian crisis," *Economic Times*, March 16, 2021, at https://economictimes.indiatimes.com/news/politics-and-nation/india-calls-for-relaxation-of-sanctions-on-syria-in-light-of-worsening-humanitarian-crisis/articleshow/81524271.cms (accessed on March 18, 2021).
9. "UNSC needs to introspect about the cost of its 'actions and inactions' on Syria: India," *Times of India*, March 30, 2021, at https://timesofindia.indiatimes.com/india/unsc-needs-to-introspect-about-the-cost-of-its-actions-and-inactions-on-syria-india/articleshow/81754486.cms (accessed on March 31, 2021).
10. "Virtual Meeting between MOS for External Affairs and the Syrian Vice Minister of Foreign Affairs & Expatriates," Ministry of External Affairs, Government of India, September 03, 2020, at https://www.mea.gov.in/press-releases.htm?dtl/ 32928/Virtual+Meeting+between+MOS+for+External+Affairs+and+the+Syrian+Vice+Minister+of+Foreign+Affairs+amp+Expatriates (accessed on December 23, 2020).
11. "India says ready to play 'constructive, meaningful role' in UNSC to end Syrian conflict," *Asian News International (ANI)*, January 21, 2021, at https://www.aninews.in/news/world/us/india-says-ready-to-play-constructive-meaningful-role-in-unsc-to-end-syrian-conflict20210121054102/ (accessed on January 22, 2021).
12. "Virtual Meeting between MOS for External Affairs and the Syrian Vice Minister of Foreign Affairs & Expatriates," Ministry of External Affairs, Government of India, September 03, 2020, at https://www.mea.gov.in/press-releases.htm?dtl/32928/Virtual+Meeting+between+MOS+for+External+Affairs+and+the+Syrian+Vice+Minister+of+Foreign+Affairs+amp+Expatriates (accessed on February 23, 2021).
13. "India stands ready to work with UN to ensure supply of Covid-19 vaccines in Syria," *Economic Times*, March 03, 2021, at https://economictimes.indiatimes.com/news/politics-and-nation/india-stands-ready-to-work-with-un-to-ensure-supply-of-covid-19-vaccines-in-syria/articleshow/81304911.cms?from=mdr (accessed on March 10, 2021).

6

CIVIL WAR IN SYRIA
UNDERSTANDING THE CHINESE RESPONSE

Abu Zafar

INTRODUCTION

The Syrian crisis is one of the most important issues of the 21st century in West Asia and in the world, and it has become a textbook example of the failure of the international system. The crisis resulted from the excessive use of force by the regime against civilians, the use of proxies by the international players to overthrow the regime and the emergence of powerful militias and terrorist groups that fight against each other. The crisis, which started in 2011, took over half a million lives of Syrian people and displaced more than 12 million. Following the events of Arab Spring, massive protests erupted on the streets of Damascus and other major cities of the country against the Bashar al-Assad regime. The Syrian government denounced these protests and termed them as a rebellion act to overthrow the regime and push the country into a civil war that justified the military intervention. Later on, a number of local groups emerged against the government followed by the emergence of ISIS (Islamic State of Iraq and Syria), which led to the direct involvement of international players. China, which is a rising economic giant on the international stage, has to adopt some policy because being silent was never an option and that will lead to the death of its ambition as a world power. But Beijing has abstained from playing any direct role in the Syrian crisis and sticks to the theoretical principle that the sovereignty of state must be maintained and any military action bypassing United Nations Security Council (UNSC) will have a serious impact on the country and the region.

China has three core interests in the region that compelled it to engage in the Syrian. These interests are mainly geo-strategic, commercial and security. It is also related to Beijing's power projection for both domestic and international consumption.

Though relations between Beijing and Damascus were not very strong and trade between both the countries was also very negligible, it has increased significantly in the recent years. Due to China's various interests in the region in general and increasing interest in Syria, in particular, dealing with the Syrian issue has become critical for China.

CHINA'S STANCE ON THE SYRIAN CRISIS

Due to its geostrategic importance, West Asia has always been an important region for the world. The discovery of oil and gas in the mid-twentieth century has made this region more important, resulting in an economic boom in the world, and now these natural resources have become the blood of not only the industrial world but various other activities as well. Like any big power, China always gives importance to the region and since the last few decades the increasing dependency of Western countries on Chinese goods and Chinese need for the oil and gas of region are setting new milestones.

But in the strategic vocabulary of China, West Asia is the region that Mao termed as, 'an intermediate zone where hostile powers are rustling to get control'. Though the region has no border with China but since the beginning of the Communist rule apart from other factors, a kind of fear psychosis was part of China's foreign policy.[1] China was afraid that hostile forces are trying to encircle it by capturing spaces in the intermediate zone. At the same time, Beijing was struggling to get more and more recognition from foreign governments against the Republic of China (Taiwan) and trying its best to lure countries in the West Asian region too for its support. In this regard, Syria was among those few countries which have recognized PRC within a few years from its formation in 1949. Further, Syria was among those countries that supported the resolution to restore PRC's claim in the United Nations Security Council in 1971 ousting Republic of China as representative of the people of China.[2]

Beijing's passive assertiveness in the Syrian crisis can be seen in this background. Though it can be argued that the notion of encirclement is outdated now and there is no such concern in the current foreign policy of China, considering Beijing's wide range of interests in the region and the Belt and Road Initiative (BRI) project, it is easy to understand that the concern remains, but the mode has changed. Encirclement, which could take place then in terms of a direct threat, can now can be understood in terms of cutting trade routes and disrupting energy supply, etc.

Beijing has been very much concerned about the crisis in Syria, and it is one of the few major powers to appoint a special envoy to address this issue.[3] Though China didn't have much economic and strategic interest in Syria compared to in the other West Asian countries but being an emerging world power, having a strong presence in West Asia and North Africa (WANA) region and for the success of BRI, China cannot ignore such a conflict where major powers of the world are involved.

Since the beginning of the crisis, China has very idealistically adopted the non-interference policy saying that it is an internal matter of a sovereign state and all stakeholders should resolve it politically. And this was evident when Chinese Foreign Minister Wang Yi gave a five-point formula to solve the issue in an interview with Xinhua and China Central Television.

(i) The issue of Syria must be resolved through political means.
(ii) The future of Syria must be decided by its own people.
(iii) An inclusive political transition process must be promoted.
(iv) National reconciliation and unity must be achieved in Syria.
(v) Humanitarian assistance must be delivered in Syria and its neighbouring countries[4]

Similarly, China's Special envoy for Syria Xie Xiaoyan explained five steps to resolve the Syrian crisis while speaking at International Symposium on the Syrian issue in Shanghai in 2018. First, China will maintain contacts with all relevant parties to strengthen the peace process. Second, continue to advocate UN's role as central for mediation among various stakeholders. Third, support the peace process and peace talks regarding Syria, including Geneva Peace

Talks and the International Syria Support Group. Fourth, always offer support to Syrian people. Fifth, support the reconstruction of Syria.[5]

This question that why China is talking more and more about Syria and participating actively in the UN forums and peace process related to Syria is frequently raised. The simple answer could be, why not China?

China is an emerging power and one of the largest economies in the world. It is the largest oil importer from West Asia; its companies are actively involved in the region. China uses the sea route for its export to Africa and other parts of the world and that passes through West Asia. Therefore, in the larger context, Beijing's response to the Syrian crisis is critical, and it has no alternative.

Beijing holds its primary argument under the banner of non-interventionism. China believes that outside forces should not be allowed to change the status quo through force. Changing the government through military support or otherwise will not solve the problem, but it will complicate it further. China also advocated for a Syria-led and Syria-owned solution where all stakeholders should sit together and negotiate and come out with some kind of political solution. China also insisted that all of this be done in accordance with concerned guidelines and regulations of the United Nations, and that UN's role in all peace processes should be central.

In April 2018, Wang Yi explained China's Syria policy amid tensions of chemical attacks in Douma. He said that from China's perspective, "sovereignty and territorial integrity of Syria should be maintained and respected." A political settlement as the only option to solve the crisis" remains China's main policy offer.[6]

China believes that the international community's common concern is necessary to resolve the Syrian crisis. Chinese leaders have repeatedly stated that world power must respect Syria's sovereignty, independence and integrity and the future of the country should be decided by the Syrian people and the UN should act as a mediator. China also firmly stated that no other solution or military aggression bypassing UNSC is accepted. Instead, each party must be heard under the UN mediation and the solution must come out through dialogue and negotiation.[7] China believes that any military action bypassing UNSC will have a serious impact on the country and region, and be a violation of international law. Therefore, China along with Russia sucked about a dozen resolutions against Syria in the UN.[8]

In 2016, during the debate in the UNSC after the Aleppo crisis China's representative in UN ambassador WU Haitao. Said:

> "A political solution to the Syrian situation is the fundamental way out for resolving the set of issues related to Syria, including the humanitarian problem. The international community should stay the course in the general direction of moving towards a political settlement, with an intensified effort to move the political settlement forward."[9]

The US and its allies have taken shelter in the principle *Responsibility to Protect* which allows foreign intervention if there is a "risk of genocide, war crimes, ethnic cleansing and crimes against humanity."[10] Therefore, they argue that in a situation like Syria all responsible countries must protect and save common people but Chinese authorities have criticised it saying that this principle is very vague. When discussing the Syrian issue, Chinese officials and policymakers do not fail to bring up their Libyan experience. In Libya, China did not reject foreign intervention at the UN, which, according to China, resulted in more chaos and violence, and Libya became a battleground for hostile forces. China's Assistant Foreign Minister Le Yucheng while delivering a speech in China Institute of International Studies said that if they allow foreign intervention in Syria then the "Libya Model" will be repeated.[11] He criticised the *Responsibility to Protect* to justify the use of force saying that there should be some "responsible protection" in the name of *Responsibility to Protect.*[12] And it is for this reason that China has used its veto power to prevent several similar initiatives in the UN alongside Russia.

Noted Chinese foreign policy expert Yan Xuetong in his article, written in 2012, tried to justify the Chinese veto saying that China was not going to gain anything if it would have supported those resolutions. Xuetong says:

> "If China and Russia supported the resolution, rebel groups would come to power quickly in Syria. However, though those rebel groups would appreciate Western countries for their substantive military assistance, they would not think China and Russia provided valuable political support. The Arab League would also believe that the Chinese and Russian stance

was only driven by trends in the international community. The league would not thank China for its support either."[13]

He says that in the case of Libya, China didn't get any appreciation from the Arab League and Arab countries, and they only thanked Western countries and Western media didn't praise China. He also said that China has supported Arab countries in some issues including the Palestine-Israel conflict where the US supports Israel, but in case of conflict between the US and China, Arab countries always support US.[14]

It should be emphasised that the Syrian crisis started against the backdrop of the so-called Arab Spring in 2011, when decade-old governments in Tunisia and Egypt were deposed within a few months. The entire globe, particularly significant nations such as China, has been keenly monitoring events in the region. We are not going to discuss how genuine this rebellion was, but taking it at its value, one might readily conceive some new types of regimes that would be tough to deal with using traditional strategies. Because the region is highly contested due to its natural resources, the uprising may also result in a power vacuum. Therefore, when similar protests started in Syria and lingered on for months then all such powers were ready with their own understanding and calculations that how to maximise their national interests through it. Because within a few weeks it became clear that unlike in Egypt and Tunisia, protests in Syrian cities are not going to change the regime very soon. Therefore, world powers started not only monitoring the situation but also tried to become vocal, influential or critical as per their understanding and interests in the country and the region, and it continues till now. Therefore, all these powers are gathered in Syria not to resolve the issue but mostly to protect and maximise their national interests also, to some extent, to balance the global power structure. For the same reason, they favour and oppose the regime or certain opposition groups. The US and its allies started supporting the opposition groups with limited help. The Muslim world is already divided on the Shia-Sunni line and China and Russia found it more suitable to support the Assad regime and Beijing has strong reasons for that.

The main reason given by China is that it considers the Assad regime as a legitimate government of Syria and opposes any change with force and outside influence. It also says that regime change through outside force is against rule-based world and it is also against the basic UN principles. China also argues that opposition groups have no popular face and have no experience running a government, and there is no surety that if the regime will be changed and the power goes to them then there will be peace in the country. Instead, there are chances of more chaos and violence. The kind of relations China has with the region will be catastrophic if there is more violence, chaos and instability. Especially it will be dangerous for BRI. China is making every effort to maintain some peace in the region while also projecting itself as a world power concerned about these concerns in the region and eager to fix them. It is also a form of image-building exercise, as well as a test of China's capacity as an arbiter and negotiator. However, China's idealistic non-interventionist strategy has frequently devolved into another type of intervention.

CHINA'S ROLE IN THE PEACE PROCESS

In principle and in practice both, PRC followed the non-interference policy since its formation unless there is something that has any direct link to its interest.[15] Due to its complexity, Beijing considers the West Asian region as a "graveyard of great powers,"[16] and has usually avoided becoming involved or an ally of any power in any crisis of the region. But now its various economic, strategic and political needs in the region compelled it to do more and have a clear and candid policy for a crisis like the Syrian one. As a mediator and someone vocal about peace and negotiation since the beginning, Beijing's engagement includes a set of activities that gives a sense of planned and organised effort to achieve its long-term goal in the region. To show itself as a neutral and responsible power, Beijing stressed on UN-mediated effort for a meaningful result. China has participated in peace process at Astana, Geneva and Vienna which is known as the International Syria Support Group (ISSG).

Beijing's understanding about all these peace processes is to put the UN on the centre stage. It has appointed a special envoy for the issue of Syria. In 2016 representatives of opposition groups were hosted in Beijing for the same purpose. They met with Foreign Minister Wang Yi and discussed the way out of the crisis. Being a permanent member of the UNSC, Beijing also supported passing the UNSC resolution 2254 which talks about the political settlement of Syria and the immediate cease-fire.[17]

China wants to make and maintain its image as a neutral arbiter and a power that wants to play a role among conflicting parties without siding with anyone. Apart from Russia, all other major international countries are directly involved in the crisis, and China has criticised world powers for their excessive involvement in Syria. But at the one hand, China has been actively advocating, participating and, to some extent, organising mediation efforts among opposition groups but on the other hand, Beijing doesn't hesitate to defend and protect the Assad regime from any possible action that can overturn his government.

China has never played a leading mediator role in the past and its economic and geo-strategic interests compelled it to do so but still, it has a limit. On the one hand its non-interference policy faces numerous questions and on the other hand, world politics and US influence in the region may not allow it to go beyond a certain point. But these peace processes have provided a better opportunity to the diplomat community in China to enhance their crisis management capacity and help their country to expand its acceptability and soft power.[18]

Initially, Beijing expressed its uneasiness on Russia's airstrike but later on supported it saying that it is only to stabilize the country.[19] When the whole world including Russia disapproved of the use of chemical weapons by the Assad regime, it was reported that Chlorine gas which was sold by China was used in the attack, which Beijing denied.[20]

COMMERCIAL ENGAGEMENT AND RECONSTRUCTION OF SYRIA

Another factor motivating China's engagement in the Syrian conflict is the need to defend its commercial interests in the region. Because it would be problematic for China to involve in the crisis like Russia and other major powers and being silent is also not a good option. The interesting thing with the region is that due to huge oil and gas import the trade is more or less balanced between Beijing and West Asian countries, which is not the case in many developing countries. As per a report in Xinhua News, Beijing's economic ties with the region witnessed a massive surge between 2005 and 2015, which was an estimated $20 billion in 2005 and reached up to $230 billion in 2015.[21]

Another plus point with China is that it has managed relations with the rival Saudi Arabia and Iran both somehow on a same scale and it is visible in terms of economic ties as well. Saudi Arabia is the largest trading partner of China in the region and also the biggest crude oil supplier. Trade between both countries reached $63.3 billion in 2018.[22] Whereas Beijing is the largest destination of Iran's oil, export and trade between Tehran and Beijing has been recorded $50 billion in 2013.[23] The recent 25-year agreement between Iran and China is also very significant.

West Asia is also very important for China's BRI. Though most of the countries in the region are still not part of any corridor proposed and classified under the BRI but due to its geographic location and energy resources, it has significance for this project. There are several ongoing projects to build and upgrade ports, railway networks and SEZs in the region.

Geo-strategically Syria is placed as a crossroads of oil and gas pipelines as well as the sea trade connecting the Arabian Peninsula to the world. China Harbour Engineering Company has been working on an expansion plan of Port of Tripoli in Lebanon which is only 35 km from the border of Syria. This port is very important to connect BRI with the Eastern Mediterranean region. To enhance connectivity and reduce time and money, China also plans to construct a railway line between Homs in Syria to Tripoli.[24] Chinese oil company National Petroleum Corporation of China is also a shareholder of Al-Furat Petroleum and Syrian Oil Company, the two largest oil companies of Syria.[25]

RECONSTRUCTION OF SYRIA

The reconstruction of war-torn Syria is another major aspect that necessitates a broader strategy, economic diplomacy and power politics, in which Beijing is already playing a significant role and is ambitious to play a leading one. The reconstruction costs of Syria have been estimated between $260 billion to $400 billion.[26] As the US and other Western powers have hostile relations with the regime or militarily involved in the conflict and likely to play a lesser role in the reconstruction works, this gives a tremendous opportunity to counties like China to invest in the war-torn country for the betterment of the common people and secure their energy and geopolitical interest. But China's Special Envoy to Syria Xie Xiaoyan, has given green signals to work jointly with world powers including Russia in the reconstruction efforts.[27]

In 2018, Chinese Ambassador to Syria Qi Qianjin told Xinhua News Agency:

> "I think it's about time to focus all efforts on the development and reconstruction of Syria, and I think China will play a bigger role in this process by providing more aid to the Syrian people and the Syrian government."[28]

Syria is also hopeful about Chinese help for reconstruction. In 2019 President Assad told Chinese broadcaster Phoenix Television, "Now, with the liberation of most areas, we have started discussions with a number of Chinese companies experienced in reconstruction."[29]

In 2017, Beijing hosted the "First Trade Fair on Syrian Reconstruction Projects" and pledged $2 billion for the construction of industrial parks which can accommodate at least 150 companies and a year later promised an amount of US$23 billion as loans and donations for Arab counties including Syria.[30] Though it is not clear that how much amount will be going to Syria, given the need for help and growth, it appears that Damascus will receive a sizable portion of it. China has expressed interest in building steel and electricity plants in Syria in addition to producing Chinese brand cars in Homs.[31]

Apart from all this, Beijing is also active to help Syria through donations and humanitarian aid engaging through various UN and other international agencies. By 2015 Syria had received about US$36 million as humanitarian aid from China.[32] According to the Chinese Embassy in Damascus, in 2017 Beijing has donated US$1 million for various humanitarian needs along with 5400 tons of rice. To support the electrical and transportation sector and humanitarian operations, China also signed three agreements with Syria worth more than US$40 million.[33] In 2016 Foreign Minister Wang Yi in London announced that Beijing will donate 10,000 tons of food among Syrian refugees.[34] In 2017, China donated one million U.S. dollars to the

World Health Organization (WHO) to address the health issue of Syrian people and to renovate the emergency unit of the al-Muowasat University Hospital in Damascus.[35] A year later it donated some 800 electrical power generators to Syria's largest port Latakia in 2018.[36]

TERRORISM AND THREAT OF ISIS

The emergence of the Islamic State of Iraq and Syria or ISIS is no longer limited toWest Asia; it now poses a challenge to countries in South Asia and Central Asia as well and authorities in Beijing are concerned about it. The tussle and hostility between the Chinese government and its ethnic Uyghur minority are not new and several attacks took place in the last three decades. The many forms of repression used by Beijing against Muslims in Xinjiang have intensified their concern and sense of secession. Recent incidents of putting a large population of Xinjiang into camps, which Beijing terms as reformation centres, have heightened the hostility further. For many Uyghur who went to fight or to take arms training in Syria, see it is an opportunity to take 'revenge' for what happened to them in Xinjiang and is still happening to their family members and relatives. They have accepted that they had no idea about the Syria civil war and in the West Asian region.[37] Incidents of harassment and torture of Uyghurs by China, which was termed by the US as genocide,[38] have given ample room to organisations like ISIS and Turkistan Islamic Party (TIP) or East Turkestan Islamic Movement (ETIM), as referred by China, to set narratives and call for rage against China. Several threatening videos both in Mandarin and English were aired by ISIS and its allied group about targeting China or Chinese interests.[39] In 2017, a video allegedly made by ISIS surfaced in which Uyghur militants threatened bloodshed in China.[40]

Wang Yi at the Ninth Ministerial Conference of the Heart of Asia-Istanbul Process in March this year said:

> "All parties need to join forces and double down on fighting terrorist organizations like Al-Qaida, ISIS and the ETIM until they are completely eliminated."[41]

During the discussion on ISIS and other extremist groups in UN Security Council in 2014, China supported the resolution. China's permanent representative to the UN Liu Jieyi demanded to the international community an enhanced support to neutralise such groups.

> "China is also a victim of terrorism. We strongly oppose all forms of terrorism and will continue to actively participate in international counter-terrorism cooperation and to combat the threat of terrorism together."[42]

He said that such groups have become dangerous threats to the West Asian region and to the world.

"Recently, ISIL[43] and the ANF[44] have become rampant in deliberately attacking civilians, persecuting people of other religions and ethnic groups, resulting in large casualties among innocent civilians and displacement of millions."[45] Liu also appealed to the international community for 'concrete measures' to stop funds, arms and personnel supply to such groups.

The concern for China is the growing number of Uyghur militants fighting in Syria, who will pose a major challenge after returning home. It is reported that Turkistan Islamic Party or TIP created a new front in Syria with the help of ISIS and Al Qaida, known as Turkistan Islamic Party in Syria.[46]

In 2014, after travelling to several of countries in West Asia, Wu Sike, China's then special envoy on West Asian affairs, said that about 100 Chinese militants were fighting in the region.[47] There are still conflicting claims about the actual number of Uyghur militants fighting in Syria, but the Syrian ambassador to China stated in 2017 that there are about 5000 militants of Uyghur ethnicity fighting in Syria.[48]

As a result, it is also one of the major factors that drove the Chinese to back the Assad regime and prevent power from passing to shattered opposition groups. Beijing is Beijing is concerned that following Assad, Syria will be more open and supportive of extremist groups such as the ETIM of Xinjiang, which will be disastrous for its energy security, commerce supplies, and the BRI. The presence of such groups in Syria can have an impact on Beijing's interests in the broader West Asian and African region, and if they come home, they will pose a threat to China's internal security and sovereignty too.[49]

CONCLUSION

China follows the principle of non-intervention in the Syrian crisis, which gives it an opportunity to work on various fronts including securing its supply route, fighting terrorism and reconstruction works in Syria. The threat of non-state actors, particularly ISIS, spreading over to South Asia and Central Asia is something that China is taking seriously. Beijing believes that its national interest including economy, security and oil supply are best served only in a stable West Asia and conflicts like Syria pose major challenges.

China always plays its card between Syrian people's right to self-determination and sovereignty of the Syrian state, and in all these years of war and instability in Syria, Beijing may be considered the biggest winner because it didn't lose anything and only gained perhaps more than any other major power. It has established itself as a serious power committed to resolving the situation through dialogue and negotiations. It has the confidence of the government and opposition groups. Also, such a crisis in the region in general, and the Syrian crisis, in particular, has given a golden opportunity to Beijing to test its diplomatic competency and convert it into long-term political and economic influence.

China aims to convey a strong message to the world, particularly the developing world, about its sincerity and commitment to peace and conflict resolution through dialogue and negotiations, as well as strengthened its diplomacy and arbitration.

NOTES

1. Yitzhak Shichor, *The Middle East in China's Foreign Policy, 1949-1977* (London: Cambridge University Press, 1979), 1-2.
2. Mohamed Hamchi, "The Political Economy of China-Arab Relations: Challenges and Opportunities," *Contemporary Arab Affairs* 10, no. 4 (2017): 577-595.
3. "China Appoints First Special Envoy for Syria Crisis," *Reuters*, March 29, 2016, at https://www.reuters.com/article/us-mideast-crisis-syria-china-idUSKCN0WV0RG (accessed January 19, 2021).
4. "Wang Yi Proposes Five Principles to Facilitate a Political Settlement of Syrian Issue," Ministry of Foreign Affairs, People's Republic of China, January 20, 2014, at https://www.fmprc.gov.cn/mfa_eng/wjb_663304/zzjg_663340/xybfs_663590/xwlb_663592/t1124573.shtml (accessed February 20, 2020).

5. "Special Envoy of the Chinese Government on the Syrian Issue Xie Xiaoyan Attends International Symposium on the Syrian Issue," Ministry of Foreign Affairs, People's Republic of China, May 14, 2018, at http://www.fmprc.gov.cn/mfa_eng/wjbxw/t1559820.shtml (accessed February 20, 2020).
6. "Wang Yi Expounds China's Stance on Syrian Issue," Ministry of Foreign Affairs, People's Republic of China, April 13, 2017, at http://www.fmprc.gov.cn/mfa_eng/zxxx_662805/t1454104.shtml (accessed February 20, 2020).
7. "Special Envoy of the Chinese Government on the Syrian Issue Xie Xiaoyan Attends International Symposium on the Syrian Issue," Ministry of Foreign Affairs, People's Republic of China, May 14, 2018, at http://www.fmprc.gov.cn/mfa_eng/wjbxw/t1559820.shtml (accessed February 20, 2020).
8. "The Security Council Veto," *Security Council Report*, at https://www.securitycouncilreport.org/atf/cf/%7B65BFCF9B-6D27-4E9C-8CD3-CF6E4FF96FF9%7D/working_methods_veto.pdf (accessed January 25, 2021).
9. "Statement by Ambassador WU Haitao at the Security Council Debate on Syria," Ministry of Foreign Affairs, People's Republic of China, August 22, 2016, at http://www.fmprc.gov.cn/mfa_eng/wjb_663304/zwjg_665342/zwbd_665378/t1392228.shtml (accessed June 20, 2020).
10. Ivan Šimonović, "The Responsibility to Protect," *The UN Chronicle*, at https://www.un.org/en/chronicle/article/responsibility-protect (accessed April 30, 2021).
11. "China's Relations with the World at a New Starting Point--Speech by Assistant Foreign Minister Le Yucheng at the CIIS Forum, Ministry of Foreign Affairs of the People's Republic of China, April 10, 2012, at https://www.fmprc.gov.cn/mfa_eng/wjdt_665385/zyjh_665391/t925181.shtml (accessed on June 24, 2020).
12. Ibid.
13. Yan Xuetong, "China's Veto on Syria: A View from China," *Carnegie-Tsinghua Centre for Global Policy*, February 8, 2012, at *https://carnegietsinghua.org/2012/02/08/china-s-veto-on-syria-view-from-china-pub-4721* (accessed May 15, 2018).
14. Ibid.
15. Mashallah Heidarpour, "Syria Crisis and a New Political Agenda for China: Changes or Continuity?" *Middle East Political Review* 4, no. 1-2 (2015): 32.
16. Jon B. Alterman and John W. Garver, *The Vital Triangle: China, the United States, and the Middle East* (Washington DC: The CSIS Press, 2008), 17.
17. "Security Council Unanimously Adopts Resolution 2254 (2015), Endorsing Road Map for Peace Process in Syria, Setting Timetable for Talks," United Nations, December 18, 2015, at https://www.un.org/press/en/2015/sc12171.doc.htm (accessed December 10, 2019).
18. Heidarpour, "Syria Crisis and a New Political Agenda for China," 29.
19. Ibid., 27.
20. *China Arms Giant Says Never Exported Chlorine Gas to Syria,* Reuters, May 16, 2014, at https://www.reuters.com/article/us-syria-crisis-china-idUSBREA4F08A20140516 (accessed January 19, 2021).
21. Heidarpour, "Syria Crisis and a New Political Agenda for China," 32.

22. Michael Standaert, "Saudi Arabia Strikes $10bn China Deal," *Aljazeera.com*, February 22, 2019, at https://www.aljazeera.com/news/2019/02/saudi-arabia-strikes-10bn-china-deal-190222151639392.html (accessed December 10, 2020); Mordechai Chaziza, "China's Economic Diplomacy Approach in the Middle East Conflicts," *China Report* 55, no. 1 (2019): pp. 24-39, 7.
23. Gordon Houlden and Noureddin M. Zaamout, *A New Great Power Engages with the Middle East: China's Middle East Balancing Approach* (Canada: China Institute, University of Alberta, 2019), 33.
24. "The BRI Needs Syria Just As Syria Needs It," *China Daily*, December 12, 2019, at https://global.chinadaily.com.cn/a/201912/19/WS5dfae54aa310cf3e3557f382.html (accessed January 22, 2021).
25. Ibid.
26. Joseph Daher, "Beyond Physical Reconstruction: Planning a Stable and Prosperous Post-War Syria" in *Rebuilding Syria: The Middle East's Next Power Game?* edited by Eugenio Dacrema and Valeria Talbot (Milano: ISPI, 2019), 37.
27. "China Ready to Work With Russia On Post-War Reconstruction in Syria," Syrian Arab News Agency, April 29, 2016, at http://sana.sy/en/?p=75985 (accessed November 25, 2019).
28. "China to Play Bigger Role in Syria's Reconstruction, Development Process: Ambassador," Xinhua News Agency, February 12, 2018, at http://www.xinhuanet.com/english/2018-02/12/c_136967861.htm (accessed March 8, 2020).
29. "Syria Reaches out to China for Post-War Reconstruction," *Middle East Eye*, December 16, 2019, at https://www.middleeasteye.net/news/syria-reaches-out-china-post-war-reconstruction (accessed July 20, 2020).
30. Nicholas Lyall, "China in Postwar Syria," *The Diplomat*, March 11, 2019, at https://thediplomat.com/2019/03/china-in-postwar-syria/ (accessed August 17, 2020).
31. Logan Pauley, "China Stakes Out A Role for Itself in Post-War Syria," *Asia Times*, October 3, 2018, at https://asiatimes.com/2018/10/china-stakes-out-a-role-for-itself-in-post-war-syria/ (accessed on November 20, 2020).
32. Haifa Said, "China's Humanitarian Contribution to Syria Adds to Its Int'l Profile," *China.org.cn*, January 18, 2018, at http://www.china.org.cn/opinion/2018-01/18/content_50239714.htm (accessed February 20, 2021).
33. Ibid.
34. "China to Deliver Committed Humanitarian Aids to Syria Soon: Diplomat," *China Daily*, March 31, 2016, at https://www.chinadaily.com.cn/world/2016-03/31/content_24197809.htm (accessed February 20, 2020).
35. "China to Play Bigger Role in Syria's Reconstruction, Development Process: Ambassador," Xinhua News Agency, February 12, 2018, at http://www.xinhuanet.com/english/2018-02/12/c_136967861.htm (accessed March 8, 2020).
36. "800 Electrical Power Transformers Arrived In Latakia As A Grant From China," Syrian Arab News Agency, October 10, 2018, at https://www.sana.sy/en/?p=148524 (accessed July 20, 2019).

37. Gerry Shih, "AP Exclusive: Uighurs Fighting in Syria Take Aim at China," Associated Press, December 23, 2017, at https://apnews.com/article/79d6a427b26f4eeab226571956dd256e (accessed September 7, 2020).
38. "US: China 'Committed Genocide Against Uighurs'," *BBC News*, January 20, 2021, at https://www.bbc.com/news/world-us-canada-55723522 (accessed February 20, 2021).
39. Marcin Adamczyk, "The Islamic State as a Potential Threat to the National Security of the People's Republic of China." *Historia i Polityka 37*, no. 30 (2019): 139.
40. Kabir Taneja, "Decoding China's New Threat from ISIS," Observer Research Foundation (ORF), March 8, 2017, at https://www.orfonline.org/expert-speak/decoding-chinas-new-threat-from-isis/ (accessed June 15, 2020).
41. "Remarks by State Councillor and Foreign Minister Wang Yi At the Ninth Ministerial Conference of The Heart of Asia-Istanbul Process," Ministry of Foreign Affairs, People's Republic of China, March 30, 2021, at https://www.fmprc.gov.cn/mfa_eng/zxxx_662805/t1865443.shtml (accessed April 20, 2021).
42. "China Calls for Enhanced Efforts to Combat ISIL Through UNSC Resolution," *Global Times*, August 16, 2014, at https://www.globaltimes.cn/content/876532.shtml (accessed April 20, 2021).
43. The Islamic State of Iraq and the Levant, another name of ISIS.
44. Al-Nusra Front of Syria.
45. Ibid.
46. Heidarpour, "Syria Crisis and a New Political Agenda for China," 28.
47. Teddy Ng, "Xinjiang Militants Being Trained in Syria and Iraq, Says Special Chinese Envoy," *South China Morning Post*, July 28, 2014, at http://www.scmp.com/news/china/article/1561136/china-says-xinjiang-extremists-may-be-fighting-middle-east (accessed June 15, 2018).
48. Ben Blanchard, "China Envoy Says No Accurate Figure on Uighurs Fighting in Syria," *Reuters*, August 20, 2018, at https://www.reuters.com/article/us-mideast-crisis-syria-china-idUSKCN1L508G (accessed April 20, 2021).
49. Heidarpour, "Syria Crisis and a New Political Agenda for China," 36.

7

SAUDI ARABIA AFTER THE ARAB SPRING

THE OIL ERA AND REFORMS

Vrushal T. Ghoble

Modern Arab political formations are based on primordial affiliations, and their economies are rentier, though both of these features are changing. On the one hand, the rentier state structure met people's needs and subsidised commodities, raising their expectations; on the other hand, their voices of dissent could be heard time and again. As a result, the oil rents could no longer quell the unrest, and the regime could no longer turn a deaf ear to the people's demands. Dissatisfaction could be seen in the region's most powerful state. Nonetheless, the changing Kingdom will usher in a new Saudi Arabia in the coming years.

KINGDOM OF SAUDI ARABIA: AN OIL STATE

What limits the growth of a state is a question that must be answered in order to investigate its inherently tribal growth pattern. The twenty-first century saw an important pattern for many countries where modes of development differed; for Asians, agriculture was a primary means of development, whereas industry was for the West. "The agricultural sector (including forestry and fishing) can refer to a history of continuous growth......, the agricultural sector went into a period of strong growth despite the decline in oil revenues. The explanation is the government's effort to pursue a policy of greater self-sufficiency in agriculture, particularly in wheat and dairy products. This was achieved by means of large subsidies."[1] West Asia has traditionally relied on agriculture, date farming, fishing and other subsistence activities. The Five-Year Plans in modern Saudi Arabia, as in many other countries in the region, discuss and formulate the foundation of education, economy, health and other structures. In addition to his many accomplishments, such as promoting education, King Faisal bin Abdul Aziz abolished slavery. The coming of the oil age reoriented the simple social life into a complex political economy of the region. Saudi Arabia, the only country in the world named after its founder ruler—Abd al-Aziz Ibn Saud (Ibn Saud), that unified tribes having an alliance with religious cleric—Muhammad bin Adb-al-Wahhab, came to be known as an oil economy. The discovery of oil in Saudi Arabia in 1938 ushered in a social revolution, resulting in a social contract between the people and the ruler. Since the oil boom, economic development has increased income and created a new class of wealthy Saudis. Crude oil production has only increased since its discovery. After years of high oil revenues, the 2014 crisis forced regimes to take drastic measures to maintain revenues and meet expenditures. Prior to the 2014 drop in oil prices, oil revenues accounted for 90 per cent of export earnings, 87 per cent of budget revenues and 42 per cent of GDP.[2] The US used to import more oil than it exported before the shale oil revolution. This not only made people question how close Saudi Arabia and the US were, but it also pushed Saudi Arabia to make changes to its economy, like putting taxes in place to keep its budgets in order. Low oil prices caused by other sources of energy also force Riyadh to take other steps that will eventually lead to diversification, since oil revenues were vulnerable to changes in geopolitical situations around the world.

The social contract between the ruler, the Al-Saud Royal family, and the people is bound by oil revenues used for country development and subsidies provided to the people. In the case of Saudi Arabia, the concept of social contract is solely dependent on the concept of rent, oil revenue in this case, which facilitated the people's lavish lifestyle while depriving them of freedom. The proceeds from oil sales were distributed in the form of subsidies, allowing the Al-Saud family to accommodate and collaborate with any opposition, resulting in a more secure rule. People's rights have been in control since 2014, thanks to low oil prices. Saudi foreign policy is always focused on ensuring security and finding a stable market for its oil. The massive revenue generated ned not only benefited the government but also helped the Gulf state create vast infrastructure. It increased the economic credibility of the governing Al-Saud dynasty. By co-opting and dispersing oil resources and supplying people with social packages, the Saudi monarchy established itself as a credible power, earning the support of the kingdom.

In contrast to other monarchs, Saudi Arabia invested these billions in infrastructure and an inclusive society. The provision of all utilities to its populace remains a crucial aspect of Saudi domestic policy. Wahhabism, which was created by an alliance between the Al-Sauds and the Al-Wahhabis, was the source of political and religious legitimacy. A state founded on expansion, safeguarded by its cultural and tribal ties, and endowed with economic legitimacy by oil revenues. Apparently, the instability of oil prices, which questioned the regime's viability and its capacity to meet the expectations of the people, prompted Saudi Crown Prince MBS to create *Vision 2030*. The concept of Vision is to look beyond oil and its profits. Riyadh has often presented new proposals that favour a government with a non-oil foundation. Many inside and outside the kingdom believed that the country's social and economic structure must alter; this was contrary to Vision 2030. Under the *Vision 2030* programme, Riyadh is attempting an unprecedented transition, one that is more western and also resembles some of its neighbours, such as the UAE.

MBS introduced the Saudi Aramco IPO, as well as social reforms such as the abolition of women's segregation, economically, in order to finance Vision 2030. A significant portion of the Saudi populace would vacation in neighbouring nations such as Bahrain or the United Arab Emirates. With the development of malls, the reopening of cinemas that were outlawed decades ago and efforts to make Saudi Arabia a popular tourist destination, Saudis can now invest in their own country for recreation. The religious authority held a contrary view. A previous Imam of the Grand Mosque of Mecca stated in an article published by *The New Arab* (2019) that singing and musical instruments existed during the time of the Prophet Muhammad. To discourage criticism of his social changes, the crown prince maintained government control over the issuance of religious edicts and had the grand mufti constantly remind Saudis of their religious need to show allegiance to the king.[3]

People sought the release of activists jailed without trial, the right to vote for women, equal driving privileges for women, etc. Vision 2030 will give rise to an entirely new Saudi Arabia. It will improve the Saudi royal family's popularity. Fewer Saudis are employed in the private sector. The Saudi government implemented Saudization to address the problem of foreign expatriate labour. The Saudization programme or Nitaqat policy aims to employ more Saudi citizens, hence decreasing dependency on foreign labour. The 2011 Saudi "*Nitaqat*" policy also refers to the Saudization initiative. The policy encouraged the creation of more low-paying jobs for locals, with an emphasis on women entering the workforce. The participation rate of Saudi women in the country's economic development is rising, resulting in a significant shift in the growth narrative. Saudi Arabia has a significant role in the global economy, since its oil reserves have supplied the world with a crucial resource. The Vision Paper represents the Prince's vision for a more accountable administration. Reductions in gasoline and other commodity subsidies, which have an impact on the populace, will alter the population's perception of the regime. "Vision 2030 is different insofar as it has the clear backing of a very powerful prince. Some real changes have occurred: subsidies for utilities (electricity, water) and gasoline at the pump have been reduced, resulting in increased costs for Saudis."[4] Riyadh's new economic course under the guise of Vision 2030, is a preparation for a new age that will seek to develop the Kingdom's economy, threatening the old contract between the Saudi people and the monarch, which supplied the cradle-to-grave facility.

SAUDI VISION AND DOMESTIC / REGIONAL DYNAMICS POST ARAB UPRISINGS

A relatively young state rose to prominence due to its vast oil reserves Its significance grew as a result of its dominance in organisations such as OPEC, GCC, OIC, and others. Its oil power in OPEC was unrivalled, culminating in its control of the organisation; its position as a swing producer in international markets is well known. A founding member of the GCC also praised its status as an important country capable of assisting its neighbours, which increased its accountability in the region. Saudi assistance is provided both bilaterally and multilaterally. Bilaterally, it is provided through institutions such as the Saudi Fund for Development (SFD) and the newly created King Salman Humanitarian Aid and Relief Centre. Multilaterally, it is provided through regional bodies such as the Islamic Development Bank, the Arab Fund for Economic and Social Development, the African Development Bank, and the Arab Bank for Economic Development for Africa (BADEA). Globally, it is provided through organisations such as the International Monetary Fund, World Bank, OPEC Fund for International Development (OFID), and the United Nations. "Driven by the needs of recipient countries, there has been a sharp increase in the volume and country coverage of Saudi assistance. Total assistance went up dramatically in 2014 from the previous year by 230%, from US $4.3 billion to US $14.5 billion (SAR 16 billion to SAR 54 billion)."[5] However, supplying help provided the Kingdom access to the borrowed country, allowing it to exert some control over it.

After 2011, Saudi Arabia assisted nations such as Egypt and Yemen. In this regard, the Egyptian instance is unique; in 2017, Cairo ceded the Sanafir and Tiran Islands to Saudi Arabia. Since the Iranian Revolution, the aid factor was created primarily to contain the expanding Iranian influence. Through its assistance diplomacy, Saudi Arabia has also been effective in securing regional partners that may aid in alignment; this would bring together donor-recipient nations and aid Riyadh's cause. The Yemeni offensive that commenced in March 2015 exemplifies Egypt's partnership. In the words of Matthiesen, "Generally, Saudi Islamists did not agree with the government's policies in Egypt and Tunisia, but they largely supported the crackdown on the Shiite-led protests in the Eastern Province and Bahrain, and the war against the Houthis. In addition, the Saudi government and the Islamists are equally hostile to Iran, which they see as being behind all these problems".[6] The regional crisis is also significant in terms of security and stability, as the region has been a hotbed of conflicts, including the Iran-Iraq war, the 2003 Iraqi invasion, the Yemen war in 2015, unstable Syria and Libya, and the Saudi-Iranian rivalry, among others. Aside from the sectarian divide, the regional security structure has weakened. The security architecture that had been built around the US was now seen to be vacant. The United States' approach to the region is waning.

Several major upheavals occurred in the region over the last decade, resulting in a massive humanitarian crisis and threatening the region's and the world's energy trade, resulting in lower revenues. The 2011 uprisings that shook the region also reached Riyadh. While the people's demands grew stronger, many marched against authoritarian rule and discrimination against Shias. Among those executed in 2016 was Shia cleric Nimr al-Nimr. The deterioration of relations between Riyadh and Tehran accelerated as the Uprisings reached their climax, culminating in further deterioration of relations. There were also immediate payouts: a one-time bonus equivalent to two months' salary for government employees, military personnel, and retirees, with the largest private-sector employers following suit; the introduction of unemployment benefits; an increase in the minimum wage for the vast majority of Saudis in the workforce who are employed by state or parastatal enterprises; the continuation of the 5 per cent (approximate) inflation allowance to state salaries; and the introduction of the minimum wage for the vast majority of Saudis in the workforce who are.[7] The Arab Uprisings (2010-2011) witnessed additional instability that confused regional hegemons, resulting in sectarian civil wars and the employment of proxy armies that undermined regional stability. In the current crisis, the area anticipates utilising external sources, namely the United States and its European allies. The United States was observed to be withdrawing from the regional graph, creating favourable space for other actors like China and, most significantly, Russia.

The Arab Uprisings were stifled by public spending and financial incentives. According to *Arab News*, "Inflation in Saudi Arabia dropped back to 5.3 per cent year-on-year in the final month of 2020. .....inflation rate eased from 5.8 per cent year-on-year in November to 5.3 per cent in December, the slowest monthly change since value-added tax (VAT) was increased from 5 per cent to 15 per cent. Bucking the trend, health inflation hit a two-year peak on the back of higher inflation of pharmaceutical products, as well as increased demand on outpatient and hospital services."[8] As part of its response to the volatile oil prices, the Saudi government is collecting tax from expatriates. "The new fee will be 100 Saudi riyals (SAR) per dependant per month, approximately £21 or $27," according to expatnetwork. The amount is expected to increase gradually every year until 2020. .....the figure will double to SAR200 and increase to SAR300 in 2019 and SAR400 in 2020."[9] "Meanwhile in January 2018, the kingdom began charging companies a monthly fee of SAR400 for each foreign worker they hire. Firms that employ an equal or greater number of Saudis than expats paid SAR300."[10] Following the May 2020 issuance of a Royal Decree, Riyadh opted to increase the value-added tax (VAT). In addition, because there is a yearning for reform in Saudi Arabia, King Salman issued a historic Royal Decree. In June of 2018, the decree allowing women to drive went into force. This shift in Saudi Arabian policy mirrors its Vision 2030 modernisation strategy. In addition, the kingdom has undergone a number of modifications. "The Kingdom of Saudi Arabia has announced a series of sweeping legal changes to enhance the role of women in society, including an end to restrictions on travel and far-reaching labour provisions that guarantee women equal pay in the workplace and protection against dismissal during pregnancy. Beyond travel documents, the Kingdom has also lifted restrictions on the mobility of women, granting them the right to independently open and run a business."[11] The neighbouring Bahraini Uprising was subdued by security troops from Saudi Arabia, the United Arab Emirates, and Kuwait, preventing the Al-Khalifa dynasty from collapsing and coming under Iranian authority.

The accession to power of Crown Prince Mohammad Bin Salman, also known as MBS, launched a crackdown on corruption. As a result, he ordered the house imprisonment of his wealthy relatives and kin, which has not gone over well with everyone. As no shift in a political system is caused by a single factor, the Saudi Arabian Uprising is also the consequence of a confluence of circumstances. "Four events or challenges, as Wurm states, can be identified as root causes of the reform process. Firstly, September 11 and subsequent criticism from Washington with respect to the contacts between the Saudis and terrorist groups became a foreign policy issue. Secondly, terrorist attacks inside the Kingdom, on the one hand, and growing participatory aspirations of the public, on the other hand, increased domestic political pressure. Moreover, familiar old problems became even more explosive. The persistent population growth and resulting high unemployment, as well as the aging of the leadership circle pose obvious dangers to the stability of the country."[12] The attack on the Twin Trade Towers remains a significant thorn in Saudi-American ties, which has given rise to considerable criticism. There were parts of the people that were dissatisfied with the government and Saudi Arabia's proximity to its Western friends, therefore the state was not secure on the inside. Several terrorist attacks have happened on Saudi territory: in 2003 (March, May, June and November); in 2004 (April, May, June, and December); in 2005 (June); in 2006 (February and May); in 2009; in 2012 (November); in 2014 (July and November); and in 2015 (January, March, April, May and November).[13]

The Arab Uprisings of 2010-11, which brought down Egypt's Hosni Mubarak, Libya's Muammar Gadhafi and Syria's Assad, were the catalysts for the regional crisis. The vacuum created an opportunity for Daesh or ISIS to carry out its vision. When Bashar al-Assad took office as Syrian President in July 2000, Saudi Arabia pledged its full support. However, Damascus was blamed for the 2005 assassination of Lebanese Prime Minister Late Rafiq Hariri, a staunch ally of Riyadh, which strained relations between the Saudis and Syria. Syrian support for Hezbollah and its proximity to Iran are also seen as impediments in Saudi-Syrian relations. The Saudi-Iran rivalry, a geopolitical conflict, and sectarianism have all influenced the political transitions in Libya and Yemen. Apart from being sectarian, the Saudi approach to Yemen is also strategic.

FROM RENTIER STATE TO A POST—OIL OUTLOOK

The 9/11 incident shattered mutual trust between Saudi Arabia and its strategic ally, the United States. To add to the unease, Saudi Arabia has expressed its displeasure with the US invasion of Iraq in 2003 and, more recently, with the Shale revolution. Between 1998 and 2009, Saudi foreign policy shifted, eventually leading Riyadh to look eastward. Among these events, Vision 2030 was a critical decision and a springboard for resuming the Kingdom in a new direction and path forward. Many of the Vision's goals align with and respond to the people's concerns. One of the Vision's most important goals is to diversify the country's revenue pattern, which is currently heavily reliant on oil. Some of the goals of Vision 2030 are To lower the rate of unemployment from 11.6 per cent to 7 per cent; To increase SME contribution to GDP from 20 per cent to 35 per cent; To increase the average life expectancy from 74 years to 80 years; To rise from our current position of 25 to the top 10 countries on the Global Competitiveness Index; To raise the share of non-oil exports in non-oil GDP from 16 per cent to 50 per cent; To increase women's participation in the workforce from 22 per cent to 30 per cent;[14] among others. Due to the limited industries in which the local labour force is employed, the majority of expatriates working in Saudi Arabia send the majority of their earnings back home as remittances. The Millennium Development Goals (MDGs) were implemented in the year 2000, implying a higher level of governmental commitment to achieving the development goals. Qiddiya, a park similar to Disneyland, is being built as part of Vision 2030. In addition, Saudi Arabia hosted its first public film screening in April 2018 and granted women the right to drive in 2018, as well as more opportunities for women in professional careers, and women can now attend sporting events. However, male guardianship of women in the kingdom has been reduced, and non-Muslims are prohibited from constructing houses of worship.

Due to its economic expansion, Saudi Arabia has outpaced many of its neighbouring governments, transforming from a tribal economic framework to a well-designed powerhouse in West Asia. Throughout the history of contemporary Saudi Arabia, various kings strove to modernise the kingdom. The goods were subsidised by the royal family, a comprehensive welfare system, business contracts, and oil income. A state's rentier character has both beneficial and negative effects on its economy. Oil projects and their discovery, which on the one hand provided luxury and prosperity to the country, also had its flaws. Prior to its creation, the tribes fought one another for scant resources. In addition to generating billions of dollars in revenue, it was also responsible for concentrating cash in a few hands. Evidently, the age of oil has always been affected by global oil prices, which are tied to the economic life of people. The financial and economic benefits granted to the populace and the royal prince or princes were, after all, funded by the billions of dollars generated from oil sales.

When Prince MBS came to power, he effectively took over the state's preparations for the post-oil period. An external player's attempt to seize a portion of the oil market will inevitably reduce the other firms' stake, resulting in decreased income. The majority of the revenue used to fund the budget comes from oil exports. Oil market fluctuations also result in lower prices and income for the country. This has implications for the overall growth and diversification strategy. The Kingdom's oil income exceeds 90 per cent, and it is effective in promoting development outside of oil and gas exports. MBS accounted for a post-oil scenario in order to prepare its Kingdom for oil, which was a critical source of revenue for the stated. Saudi Arabia's post-oil outlook called for the Vision 2030 to be implemented in 2016. The process of diversification is central to the Vision document, which aims to create more jobs, particularly for Saudi youth. There is emphasis on non-oil fuel sources and diversification to other production patterns.

The Arab rebellion of 2010-2011 ushered in a new regional political order that challenged tyrants. The movement was quite successful in a way that would affect the country, while some monarchs stayed in power. Friends and neighbours such as Saudi Arabia assisted in managing the crisis in neighbouring countries like Bahrain, which also had difficulties. In a way, this also forced countries whose economies were based on one source of money or income, like oil, to take a second look at them. They were forced to move beyond oil and look at the dynamics of a world without oil. In addition to the fact that religious clerics in the Kingdom are naturally against the reform process, the geopolitical problems the country is facing also raise questions about the security of the country and the region. The MBS's reforms, which are part of Vision 2030 as a whole, are unique in that they change the religious system of the Wahhabs and the Saud family, which has been in place for centuries, so that the clergy class has no choice but to change and lose power. Wahhab and his teachings had a huge impact on Saudi politics and society. But as the new age way of thinking spreads, changes are being made and a path has been chosen that could lead to a modern Saudi state. Also, the way Shia people are treated in the eastern part of the Kingdom makes the country look bad. In many of the Gulf countries, the uprisings ended in a way that no one expected. At the same time, many of the governments made changes that gave the people new ways to hope and live.

NOTES

1. Adne Cappelen and Robin Choudhury, "The Future of the Saudi Arabian Economy Possible Effects on the World Oil Market," *Reports 2000/7* (April 2000):13, at https://www.ssb.no/a/english/publikasjoner/pdf/rapp_200007_en/rapp_200007_en.pdf (accessed December 27, 2019).
2. Stephen Grand and Katherine Wolff, *Assessing Saudi Vision 2030: A 2020 Review*, Atlantic Council Report, June 2020: 4, Rafik Hariri Center for the Middle East, at https://www.atlanticcouncil.org/wp-content/uploads/2020/06/Assessing-Saudi-Vision-2030-A-2020-review.pdf (accessed March 5, 2021).
3. David B. Ottaway, "Will Saudi Arabia's Social Revolution Provoke a Wahhabi Backlash", May 2018, Viewpoint No. 126, p. 3, Middle East Fellow, Wilson Center, at https://www.wilsoncenter.org/sites/default/files/media/documents/publication/126_mep_viewpoint_david_ottaway.pdf (accessed December 30, 2021)
4. Joshua Teitelbaum (eds.), "Saudi Arabia, the Gulf, and the New Regional Landscape," *Mideast Security and Policy Studies, The Begin-Sadat Center for Strategic Studies and The National Security Studies Center*, May 2017, No. 133, p. 28, at https://besacenter.org/wp-content/uploads/2017/06/MSPS133.pdf (accessed on February 13, 2020).
5. "Partnership in Development and South-South Cooperation," Official Development Assistance of the Kingdom of Saudi Arabia, *King Salman Humanitarian Aid and Relief Centre And United Nation's Development Programme*, Kingdom of Saudi Arabia, 2016, p. 2, at https://www.sa.undp.org/content/dam/saudi_arabia/docs/Publications/ODA%20English%20Report%20Full.pdf (accessed December 30, 2021)
6. Toby Matthiesen, "The domestic sources of Saudi foreign policy: Islamists and the state in the wake of the Arab Uprisings," *Rethinking Political Islam Series, Working Paper, Project on U.S. Relations with the Islamic World at Brookings*, August 2015, p. 11, at https://www.academia.edu/15259726/The_domestic_sources_of_Saudi_foreign_policy_Islamists_and_the_state_in_the_wake_of_the_Arab_Uprisings?email_work_card=view-paper (accessed on April 6, 2021).
7. F. Gregory Gause III, "Saudi Arabia in the New Middle East", Council Special Report No. 63, *Council on Foreign Relations*, December 2011, p. 6, at https://cdn.cfr.org/sites/default/files/pdf/2011/12/Saudi_Arabia_CSR63.pdf (accessed on March 7, 2021).
8. Saudi inflation eases, but impact of VAT hike to remain into 2021: Economics report, *Arab News*, January 14, 2021, at https://www.arabnews.com/node/1792741/business-economy (accessed on March 5, 2021).
9. *Saudi Arabia Collects New Tax on Expats*, at https://www.expatnetwork.com/saudi-arabia-collects-new-tax-expats/#:~:text=The%20new%20fee%20will%20be,2019%20and%20SAR400%20in%202020 (accessed on March 3, 2021).
10. *Expat fees will continue to increase in 2020 as planned—Saudi finance ministry*, Gulf Business, November 4, 2019, at https://gulfbusiness.com/expat-fees-will-continue-increase-2020-planned-saudi-finance-ministry/ (accessed on March 3, 2021).

11. *Saudi Arabia Issues Sweeping Changes to Enhance Role of Women in Society*, The Embassy of the Kingdom of Saudi Arabia, August 02, 2019, Washington DC, at https://www.saudiembassy.net/news/saudi-arabia-issues-sweeping-changes-enhance-role-women-society (accessed on March 3, 2021).
12. Iris Wurm, "Operation: Reforming the Kingdom, External and Internal Triggers of the Reform Process in Saudi-Arabia", *Peace Research Institute Frankfurt*, March 2008, p. 4, at https://www.academia.edu/5082302/Operation_Reforming_the_Kingdom_External_and_Internal_Triggers_of_the_Reform_Process_in_Saudi_Arabia?email_work_card=view-paper (accessed on February 20, 2021).
13. *Timeline: Al-Qaeda and ISIS attacks in Saudi Arabia*, Al Arabiya News, May 20, 2020, at https://english.alarabiya.net/News/middle-east/2015/08/06/Timeline-Al-Qaeda-and-ISIS-attacks-in-Saudi-Arabia (accessed on February 20, 2021)
14. *Vision 2030*, The Kingdom of Saudi Arabia, p. 39, at https://www.vision2030.gov.sa/sites/default/files/report/Saudi_Vision2030_EN_2017.pdf (accessed on February 7, 2020)

8

SAUDI STATE AND THE CRISIS OF LEGITIMACY

Umar Farooq

The stability of the Saudi Arabian regime has been at crossroads, especially after the era of Arab Spring. On the one hand, there is a perception that the kingdom has been able to absorb the challenges in the past, be it the Ikhwan/Neo-Ikhwan uprisings or the latest Arab Spring. Using this argument, many believe that the Saudi regime will continue to survive. The fact has to be reiterated that the kingdom was actually able to survive despite the shock waves caused by the aforementioned incidents. Hence, the contemporary challenges will have little impact on the Saudi regime. On the other hand, there are many who speculate the downfall of the Saudi regime citing several reasons of the post-Arab Spring era.

One cannot be sure as to whether the kingdom will be able to absorb further upheavals or not but there are more reasons to speculate that there is actually a threat to the Saudi regime in future than to think there is not. Many have observed that the kingdom has been facing umpteen challenges internally after the 2011 uprisings.

> The rivalry between the disgruntled princes, the demographic youth bulge, the new class of educated women, the terrorists, the radical Wahhabi preachers, the aspiring middle classes, the marginalized poor, the unemployment crisis, the repressed minorities, and more recently the dramatic fall in oil prices are often among the list of potential structural problems that the kingdom will have to deal with sooner or later.[1]

The dissent in Saudi Arabia has escalated due to the spread and use of social media platforms like Facebook and Twitter. Political opposition is easily spread through internet forums, making it harder for Saudi authorities to address the issue. The assumption that the kingdom has a difficult future is based on the politico-socio-economic problems faced by the kingdom. "More active citizenry on the other hand is likely to produce serious upheaval in the future."[2]

The Saudi state is monarchial in nature, which makes it a traditional authority. It does, however, have religious elements. Saudi Arabia is a religious monarchy since religion and customs are combined, and the Saud family rules the country. According to Tim Niblock, the Saudi state derives its legitimacy from the following four sources; Ideological, traditional (inheritance of leadership role), personal (charismatic leadership) and eudeamonic (welfare and satisfaction of citizens).[3]

The traditional source of legitimacy and the personal source can both be clubbed in the form of monarchy prevalent in Saudi Arabia. Therefore, it can also be stated that there are only two real sources of the Saudi legitimacy: religious legitimacy and the eudeamonic legitimacy. It can be felt that both the sources of legitimacy, be it religious or eudeamonic, have been corroded in the case of Saudi state. The state ideology of Saudi Arabia is Wahhabism, which has generated much criticism and scrutiny since the attacks on Twin Towers in 9/11. As the attackers were Saudis, motivated by the ideology of Wahhabiya, it became important to conduct a thorough study on this ideology. The scrutiny of Wahhabism was given an impetus by the formation of the ISIS in 2014, which declared *Khilafah* who were also led by the ideology of Wahhabism. It was evident that Wahhabiya ushered in a radical ideology, which became an inspiration for many Jihadi groups. Thus, Wahhabism now is not only considered as a puritanical/conservative ideology propagated by its scholars, but also an ideology closely related to extremism and terrorism. As Saudi Arabia is the chief propagator of the ideology of Wahhabism, it is the most criticized state for propagating the aforementioned ideology also known for 'global jihad'.

RELIGIOUS CHALLENGES FROM WITHIN

The modern Saudi kingdom owes its political stability to Abd Al Aziz Al Saud. In fact, he was the chief architect in influencing and steering the political discourse by using religion. The Wahhabi ulama have had a major stake in the promotion of Abd Al Aziz's thought. The struggle has been to protect the monarchial system from the dissent using religion. In this context the scholars having the classical narrative are relied upon. The jurists and theologians of the past are also quoted for the purpose. The basic narrative of the Saudi rule is accordingly emphasized: as long as the rulers are implementing the Islamic laws, it is un-Islamic to revolt against them. It is also held by the Wahhabi ulama that even if the rulers are sinful, revolting against them is forbidden.

The promotion of the Saud regime by the ulama reflected the regime as the defenders of the Islamic faith. The Saudi government has since then made tireless efforts for spreading their religious ideology for which they have lent financial support also. It is well known that the situations in which the public deemed certain policies of the kingdom or the actions of its elite members questionable, the ulama would invoke the principles mentioned above to deflect any dissent.[4]

However, there have been some incidents that have predicted the religious dissent in the Saudi state. It is also worth mentioning that Wahhabism has actually backfired in many cases for the Saudi regime. The first dissent after the immediate creation of the Saudi state was the rebellion of the Ikhwan. The Ikhwan had played a very important role in the formation of the final Saudi state. The Ikhwan, which included the Bedouins, were excellent fighters and had the intention to continue fighting in the name of Islam in the British held territories also. Meanwhile, King Abd Al-Aziz saw Ikhwan's approach as a threat to his throne and decided to crush it. The Ikhwan wanted Abd Al-Aziz to go for *Khilafah* instead of the kingship, which the king would not have granted. Because the Khilafah would not have had international support, it became important to crush the Ikhwan, who was given to religious fanaticism on the matter.

The most significant internal difficulties occurred in 1979 when a Wahhabi organisation called for the end of the Al-Saud regime's reign. As a result, this mob went after the great mosque, resulting in a gun war that killed hundreds of people and injured many more. In the framework described above, there were striking similarities between the Ikhwan uprising and the one in Mecca in 1979. Both were targeted according to their ideologies against the unjust king who used Islam to his benefits. In the case of Ikhwan, however, the leader by the name of Faisal Al-Duwaysh fought against the king who had shunned Jihad and did not go for further expansions; rather the king followed a silent policy of appeasement for the outsiders and consolidated his own power in the land, which was made into a *Mulk* with well-defined boundaries.

The Ikhwan movement was revived by Juhayman Al-Utaybi in the form of the 1979 seizure, who revived the threat to the Saudi rule. As the religious authority in the Saudi state had become passive, there was great discontent with Al-Utaybi being no exception. As the Al-Saud family had taken the control of the overall wealth of the kingdom, it was evident that the attack had to come from the religious faction. Also, it was simple for the opposition to attack Saudi ideology based on religion as the other form of the political dissent media were absent.

Juhayman Al-Utaybi slammed the kingdom on the basis of Islam and demanded the political reformations. The clerical class was well-aware of his thoughts that he stood by for many years.[5] In 1979, Juhayman and his associates seized the grand mosque in Mecca that later resulted in a gun battle killing hundreds of people and leaving many wounded. The demands included severing diplomatic ties with the West, replacing the Saudi monarchy, ceasing oil exports to the United States, and withdrawing non-native military professionals. According to Al-Utaybi, the Ikhwan supported Ibn Saud on religious grounds. Utaybi saw Ibn Saud as someone who misused authority by submitting to the West, who were Christians and had also abandoned the goal of Jihad across the seas.

Utaybi also criticized the Saudi ulama for their silence, claiming that they would simply toe the line of the ruling elite so that their material rewards would not be compromised. It is worth mentioning that many individuals who took part in the seizure of the grand mosque were from the *Jajdi* tribes, who had a history of opposition to the Saud family.

In the post-gulf war era, there arose many young generation scholars, who overtly opposed the Saudi government for allowing the stationing of the US troops in the Saudi territories. Accordingly, it was for the first time that the ulama were involved in the political dissent. Previously, Saudi Arabia was considered as an Islamic government, and hence there was no dissent. As the Saudi government had a majority of scholars on their side, they captured those with different religious narratives and imprisoned them for many years. However, they were later released on the realization that the kingdom had made a mistake by not allowing the religious dissent according to traditions. Earlier, the anti-Saudi regime's religious ideology was brushed off by the kingdom as deviant ideas.

The divergence from Islam in the conduct of foreign affairs has immensely hit the Saudi foreign policy and often left criticized by many scholars. One such example can be quoted in case of Egypt after Muhammad Morsi rose to power in a democratically won election following the Mubarak regime. A coalition of Muslim Brotherhood party and Al-Noor party emerged and Morsi became the president in 2011. However, his term was short lived as there was a coup d'etat against a newly elected government to which Saudi Arabia was a party as well. The then King Abdullah declared the brotherhood party, of which Morsi was a member, to be terrorists and the Al-Noor party, which shares the same ideology as that of the Saudi Salafis, had to back withdraw from the coalition. The same concept utilised by Saudi Arabia for monarchy adherence was perceived as being ignored in the case of Egypt.

The obedience to any ruler, according to a saying of the prophet of Islam, will last till the time the ruler prays and does not open *kufr* (to reject) or goes against Islam. The Saudi monarchy is given obedience by its people through this hadith, yet the same hadith was undermined in case of Muhammad Morsi. Accordingly, people should not have protested against the Egyptian president rather should have been obedient. According to some reports, there were many religious scholars who criticized Saudi Arabia for its double standards in the case of Egypt, which later opted out of the Al-Noor party.

The Saudi state has been constantly criticized for marginalising women's rights within its territories. This has often been referred to as the segregation of sex and gender apartheid. Although for the state, the segregation of sex finds its credibility in Islam, yet, it does not mean that the women have no role to play in the society according to Islam. Islam recognizes that the women have an independent status from men and gives women equal (although not always identical) legal, political and social rights. The main obstacle that prevents women from fully participating in nation building is not Islam, but a "rigid clinging to the Saudi traditional way of life in the face of the pressures of the western challenge."[6]

Saudi Arabia has also been accused of oppressing the Shia minority within its borders. It does, however, have a history. In the recent decades, there have been many incidents that were influenced by the Shia militants. "In late 1970s, tensions between the regime and the marginalized Shitte population increased, culminating in the seven-day riots in the eastern province in November 1979, which left at least two dozen people dead and hundreds wounded."[7]

There have also been reports of the involvement of the Shias in the organization of the hajj riots in mecca in July 1987, which killed more than four hundred people and police later had to control the demonstrating Iranian hajj pilgrims. The late 1980s also saw the emergence of the smaller and radical organization like Hizbollah of Hijaz (Hizbollah Al-Hijaz).

> The Saudi Hizbollah is believed to have been responsible for a number of attacks in Saudi Arabia in the second half of 1980s, including the august 1987 bombing of an eastern province gas plant and the march 1988 bombing of oil installations at Ras Tanura and Jubayl, as well as a series of bombings in Riyadh in 1985 and 1989.[8]

With a history of Shia dissent and terrorism in the Saudi state, it is obvious that the regime's suppression of the Shia community becomes inevitable. According to Human Rights Watch of 2009, the Shia community as a whole faces systematic discrimination in some important areas like religion, education, justice and employment. There are many religious scholars from Sunni Islam who have the denounced the Shias as apostates and some even considered them as Kafir. Among the renowned scholars are Shah Walliullah Dehlvi, Ali Al-Khudair, Abd Al-Aziz Ibn Baaz, Manzur Numani (Deobandi). This is indicative of the fact that the Shias are considered as deviants even by the non-Salafi scholars.

This, however, does not mean that the discrimination on the basis of belief should be extended to other quarters of life like education and employment, as it is reported to be. The Shias make up to 10 per cent of the total Saudi population, with the highest concentration in the Al-Hasa region, where there is a good oil production.

> Shias also tend to be found at the lowest end of the economic scale, holding the poorer paid jobs. Until ARAMCO established their oil operations in the Al-Hasa and hired a large number of Shias, the disparity of income and influence between Shias and Sunnis was immense. Employment with Aramco and recent public sector commitments to Shia prosperity, but the relative disparities continue.[9]

Justice in Islam is of the highest priority, be it for a Muslim or a non-Muslim. If justice in the sense of accountability and transparency is not served in any case, the Saudi government will be judged to have committed an un-Islamic act.

It is worth noting that the most intense challenges to the Saudi regime have actually emanated from the ideology of Wahhabism in the form of Sahwa, Al-Qaeda and IS.

CHALLENGES POST-2011

In the context of legitimacy, there have been many challenges that the regime has been facing. The legitimacy to the Saudi regime is imparted by religion and rentier economy. "It is well known that Islam is deeply embedded in the legitimacy discourse of Saudi Arabia."[10] The ulama, who are linked with the Saudi regime by alliance of religio-politics, are seen supporting the regime. The rentier economy on the other side ensures the reallocation, culminating in stabilizing the country. The impact and the role of Islamic Republic of Iran in the region is seen as an alternate system of a progressive religio-democratic state that poses a threat to the Saudi regime with its contrasting ideology.

In the role of an Islamic government, the Saudi political culture is clubbed with effective Islamic denominations, which has shaped the mainstay of the social relations.

> Islam's influence on the political culture is traditionally interpreted in two general categories: religious and temporal. These categories seek to define the theological beliefs and transcendentally ordained ethical duties on one

hand and the interests of the ruling dynasties, military and financial affairs on the other.[11]

The politics of Saudi Arabia has in fact never detached itself from the religion because of the legitimacy attached to it. The Saud family and the ulama have worked hand in hand with each other to gain the legitimacy of the people by the religio-political knot. Abd Al-Aziz Al-Saud retained the patriarchal traditions after 1932 also and the consensus as the concept was put in to diffuse the internal rivalries. The concepts of Ibn Khaldun like 'royal authority' and *assabiyah* (group solidarity) also found their application for the simple reason to make the governance of the king sound over the people.[12] The position of the Saudi king is of the protector of Islam and the custodian of the two holy mosques. This also garners him the support of the ulama.

Although the ulama provided critical support to the regime to date, there have been differences of opinion, which led to the formation of the ulama that opposed the regime on the basis of their policies in the region. According to Leigh Noran:

> The ulama are not a monolithic body and have been divided on several occasions most notably during the 1979 siege of grand mosque of Mecca, after the first gulf war, and during protests against education reform in 2004 and gender mixing in 2009. The official or the establishment Ulama occupy positions of authority in the state-proscribed bodies such as the Senior Ulama Committee and enjoy a close relationship with them. This relationship has on several occasions led to changes of co-optation and inflamed popular support for dissident religious leaders.
>
> The most serious opposition to the regime in the 1990s came from young religious dissidents and university students; this became known as the *sahwa* (awakening) movement. This diffuse movement was critical of the establishment ulema's issuing of *fatwas* in support of U.S basing in the wake of Saddam Hussein's invasion of Kuwait. This relationship between the state sponsored ulema and dissident religious voices, such as the sahwa clerics and various islamist factions, is a complex one and an important factor in the push-pull dynamic between many reform efforts and the state.[13]

Many Sunni ulama have also criticized the Saudi regime for its policies and rule. The criticism has however been more vocal from some quarters of the ulama. “This radical group, the new guard is led by Salman Al Awda and Safr Al Hawali, both in jail for their involvement.”[14]

The Saudi legitimacy is also based on the rentier system which in turn is grounded on the principle of “no taxation, no representation.”[15] Rentierism gives legitimacy to the Saudi regime, which is bound to render services to the public. In return, the regime expects no proceeds from the citizens. The Saudi rentier economy has the features of legitimization and accumulation. These features in the contemporary era are witnessing significant changes that will alter the process of development in the economic context. The Saudi state on one side accumulates capital and gains legitimacy from the people, which can prove dangerous for the state. This view is also taken by James O' Conner, who opines:

> The state needs to devise a fiscal regime, which allows it to pursue either of the objectives because a state that openly uses its coercive force to help one class accumulate capital at the expense of the other classes loses its legitimacy and hence undermines support. However, a state that ignores the necessity of assisting the process of capital accumulation risks drying up the source of its own power, the economic surplus production capacity and the taxes drawn from the surplus.[16]

In case of a rentier economy, a state's expenditure is considered as contributing to the accumulation process, hence enhancing worker productivity. It is also perceived as funding industrial expansion, which harnesses social consumption and lowers manufacturing costs. The role of public finance in the rentier economy is significant. Rent is regarded as the most crucial component of revenue.

In the context of a rentier economy, state policy is perceived as being founded on particular concepts such as providing welfare services, state-sponsored bureaucracy and government dependent private sector that is also given an impetus to for its expansion. At last, it is made sure that the state is all-powerful, which influences every sector in the state. When all these functions are performed by the rentier state, it results in the consolidation of power by the state, thus giving legitimacy to the regime.

In the context of welfare in a rentier economy, the state has been in complete control of social distribution. However, there are drawbacks of a rentier economy also. There can be times where the rentier state can face crisis in fiscal terms. In a rentier state like Saudi Arabia, the state accumulates capital, which makes the state and many of its capitalist members to increase its expenditure in the market. This gives rise to market and industrial expansion, thereby increasing labor productivity. This in turn leads to the increased social consumption and decreases the total cost of production. Thus, it gives industries the advantage of 'economies of scale'.

As the Saudi state is a fiscal deficit economy, (expenditure exceeds the revenue) it is bound to reduce its expenditures. At the same time, if the expenditures are reduced, it can cause instability in the rentier economy. It also means that any alteration in the rentier system can lead to dissatisfaction and unemployment in the Saudi people. In this way, the Saudi regime's economic structure might be severely harmed, posing yet another danger to its legitimacy.

As a country deriving its legitimacy mainly from religion, the Saudi state ensures certain things within its boundaries that include morality enforcement, separation of gender, inviting people to Islam, etc. These traits of the state mute the Islamists who want to see these functions implemented. According to David Commins, Islamic dimensions can be comprehended primarily through the official clerics who protect the traditions of Wahhabism. The ulama also are the judges in the courts and the implementation on the ground is done by the religious police. It was observed that these clerics supported the kingdom's response to the challenges posed by the Arab Spring. The grand mufti of Saudi Arabia Abdul Aziz Al Shaykh held that the protests in the wake of Arab Spring were anti-Islamic. He did forbid the protests in Saudi Arabia but endorsed the 2013 coup of Egypt. The mufti also declared the Shia protest in Saudi Arabia as un-Islamic and supported the Saudi intervention in Yemen.

On the other hand, there are the Sahwa. These are the people responsible for the Islamic awakening, which started in 1990s. They were the people who had challenged the rule of the Saudi clan. "The Sahwa is an umbrella term for a group that was heavily influenced by the Muslim Brotherhood networks in the kingdom and fused Muslim Brotherhood ideology with the local Wahhabi tradition."[17] Although the formation of the political parties is banned in the kingdom, these groups work undercover.

The Muslim brotherhood sought refuge in the Saudi state after the crackdown on them by Nasser after 1950s. They were productive for the Saudi state in the sense that they also gave an impetus to the religious as well as the educational institutions initiated by the Saudi state. It more specifically was witnessed in 1970s oil boom when Saudi Arabia took to political Islam to counter the leftist ideologies and Arab nationalism as is supported by Stephane Lacroix in *Awakening Islam*.

It was, however, in the 1990s that the criticism of the Saudi regime by the Sahwa began in the lieu of liberating Kuwait. Kuwait was annexed by Saddam Hussein who claimed it to be a part of Basra. Saudi Arabia and the US both opposed Saddam, culminating in the Saudi regime allowing the US in 1991 to deploy its troops inside the kingdom for the liberation of Kuwait. The Sahwa were not in favor of allowing the American soldiers to step in the Saudi soil. As previously stated, the Sahwa in itself was composed of many Muslim brotherhood ideologues.

Overall, the Sahwa was an ideological mix of Wahhabism and the political principles of Muslim brotherhood. According to Lacroix, it is a mostly accepted narrative that this dissent exhibited by the Sahwa, which involved a heavy hand of the Muslim brotherhood, was the turning point in the opposition between the Saudi regime and the brotherhood. Hence, it won't be difficult to predict the Saudi regime's reaction to the Muslim brotherhood, especially since 2011, when the brotherhood showed vital signs of expansion in the Middle East.

The Sahwa and the others that were influenced by the Muslim Brotherhood were seen supporting the revolutions. They supported the Tunisian and Egyptian revolutions. When Muslim Brotherhood rose to power in Egypt after the Mubarak regime, it also got their support. "These people have connections to individual Saudi princes and may be employed by the state bureaucracy."[18] However, by and large, they criticized the Saudi state's reaction to the Arab uprisings. The most important cleric and critic of the Saudi rulers in the context above is Salman Al Awda.

Salman Al Awda is unlike the other Saudi religious scholars in the sense that he endorses the revolution within the Islamic premises. "He anchored peaceful collective revolutionary action in an Islamic framework and reached out for humanist interpretations that assimilate western intellectual positions with his own Salafi orientation."[19] He published his work *asilat al-thawra* (questions on revolution) in 2012 and left his followers surprised. It was obvious that the book would be banned in Saudi Arabia but Al-Awda ensured that it spreads on the Internet. "In this book, Al Awda's engagement with the question of revolution brought him back as a relevant figure at a critical moment in the Saudi and Arab public sphere."[20]

Al Awda provided the Islamic justifications and interpretations for the revolution. It once again gives us the idea of Islamic legitimacy prevalent in the Saudi state.

> Al-Awda fuses western political thinking on revolution by Marx, Popper and Fanon with his own Islamic Salafi heritage, producing a hybrid discourse that aims to reach beyond religious study circles. He defines revolution as building on the past, reform and reconstruction rather than destruction. It always starts peacefully but may later become militarized when confronted with oppression. Simply phrased, revolution is a fruit that may ripen, dry prematurely or be belatedly harvested.
>
> Al-Awdah proposes to go beyond the duality of total obedience to rulers or military revolt. His "third way" centers on "organized collective action that regulates political opposition and accountability". The social contract exemplified by the English Magna Carta, represents in Al Awdah's thinking an early example of limiting monarchial powers and asserting individual's rights. The strategy that collective action requires is not necessarily violent. Revolutionary attire, slogans and hunger strikes prove to be efficient and justified steps in a peaceful revolution. He acknowledges the diversity of al-jamahir, the critical Arab publics behind the revolutions.[21]

Salman Al Awda has risen to prominence as a Muslim revolutionary scholar in Saudi Arabia. Thus, his study of revolution and the opposition to the Saudi regime becomes important. Salman Al Awda sticks to his opinion that

Islam does not have any scope for theocracy. "The Islamic state is a contractual project between people on the basis of a civil contract (*madani*). The worst repression occurs when authoritarian rulers instrumentalize religion to cover or justify their oppression."[22]

Al Awda goes to the extent of preaching the distinction between the three organs of the government: legislature, executive and judiciary. He advocates for the separation of powers as the only way of solving the crisis. In this context, Al Awda goes much towards writing like a modern theorist as compared to a traditional Salafi cleric. He also favours democracy, believing that democracy has done better than monarchy in many countries, and also advocates the representation of the people and civil society. "Rhetorically, he asks why Muslims accept autocracy and reject democracy on the basis of latter being a western import, if it proves to be the best option available."[23]

In his approach of speaking about the revolution in a religious coating, Al Awda does not target Saudi Arabia specifically but rather takes a subtle way in criticizing the religious monarchies, which can immediately be understood in the Saudi Arabian context by the Saudi people.

Al Awda makes it easy for the readers to understand non-Muslim experiences and boosts their confidence to explore ideas within Salafism itself. According to Al Awda, Islam has not lost its relevance in finding a way out for the future states and societies. Despite this, Al Awda makes it evident that he is also open to the idea of learning from the non-Muslim societies that have experienced authoritarianism.

In order to usher in some reforms, there had to be coordination between many groups. "Indeed, in 2011 and 2012, there was some interaction between Sahwa Islamists, liberals and the political reformers of various persuasions."[24] An attempt was made by them to have some democratic reforms in Saudi Arabia in which they remained unsuccessful. The Saudi Civil and Political Rights Association (ACPRA), which is also known in Arabic as '*Jamiyyat al huquq al siyassa wa al madaniyya*' was an important group for consensus of the groups mentioned above whose leaders mostly were jailed owing to their activism.[25] A letter also followed from Al-Awda to the Saudi authorities in which he warned of dire consequences if the political prisoners were not set free and reforms were not implemented.[26] Accordingly, from 2011 till 2014, it was seen that the Sahwa scholars by and large did not subscribe to the Saudi state's reaction to the changes from within the state.

The Houthi rebels took over the capital of Yemen in 2014. On the other hand, the problem of IS also emerged. These two events posed a great challenge to the Saudi kingdom. It "caused a temporal realignment between these Sahwis and the Saudi regime, in particular since Salman took to the throne in early 2015."[27] In the course of political Islam in the Saudi state, the Jihadis were another group even though they did not sprout out of the traditions mostly followed in the Saudi state.[28] The Jihadis were mostly involved in Syria and Iraq. They were also supported by the Saudi state because they shared common interests, albeit for a short period. However, as the IS gained strength, they declared the caliphate. IS's growing anti-Saudi rhetoric strained their relationship with the kingdom.

In June 2014, ISIS as it was still called, declared the caliphate that immensely impacted Saudi Arabia.[29] It was due to this reason that Saudi Arabia was forced to reconsider the support they forwarded to the Syrian Alawite opposition. The IS also criticized the Saudi monarchy and expressed its expansion. Several attacks were also launched in Saudi Arabia by the IS, targeting Shias, border checkpoints, and other locations. The majority of those participating in the attacks were Saudis. The attacks were condemned by the official ulama of the Saudi state.

There is about 10 to 15 per cent of the Shia population in Saudi Arabia. Shias are mostly concentrated in Al Hasa and Qatif areas, which lie in the eastern province of the kingdom. In the context of the Islamist movements, there was a Shia uprising in 1979, which was put to rest by the authorities. Many leaders responsible for this were exiled that led to friction against the state with 1980s reaching its pinnacle. The most prominent Islamic Shia movement was the Shirazi movement. "An amnesty agreement in 1993 brought most exiles back, and led to an alliance of the state with the Shirazi movement, the most prominent of the Shiite Islamist movement."[30]

The Shirazi movement shares good relations with the government and they have also been pro-government. Although the Shirazi movement did not give a call to the protests openly during the Arab uprising, which many Shias saw as an opportunity, its splinter group, led by Nimr Al-Nimr did.

As a consequence, uprisings surfaced from February 2011. The protests were usually peaceful, with occasional clashes with the armed forces. This uprising was finally crushed by the end of 2013. It led to some killings and many imprisoned. Nimr Al-Nimr himself was sentenced to death.

There still exist some youth groups in coalition with the opposition groups who sometimes give a call for the protests. The number of people who join the protests has however shrunk. The coalition is given an Islamic outlook by the protestors who advocate revolutionary trends. There is also a Shia pro-Iranian movement namely *Khat al-Imam* who are the followers of Khoemeni. Since 2011, Khat Al-Imam has supported the protests and urged the government to release members of Hizbollah Al-Hijaz and those charged in the 1996 Khober tower attacks. There was a difference between Nimr Al-Nimr's group and Khat Al-Imam. A group influenced by Nimr Al-Nimr took a direct confrontation against the government, which Khat Al-Imam refrained from.

SAUDI ARABIA'S TRANSITION FROM ORTHODOX TO MODERATE ISLAM:

There has been a phase of reformations in the Saudi religious orthodoxy since 2011, especially after Salman Bin Abd Al-Aziz became the king. It has seen the moderation of Islam and expansion in the economic avenues. As the pressure mounted on the kingdom following the Tunisian revolution, it was expedient for the kingdom to widen the horizons of the religious interpretations that had been uncompromised in the past. Though the state did not understand for a long time how to strike a balance between the religion and the society, its need wasn't denied. A breakthrough in the reconciliation of religion and society was brought recently in the kingdom.

It was also observed that the religious orthodoxy was hurting the legitimacy of the Saudi state in the world outside, leading to its regime criticism. Some of its rules like banning women from driving was criticized in almost every article. It was observed that certain harsh rules the kingdom imposed were not because the religion demanded it, but because the orthodox clerics interpreted them that way.

After Salman Bin Abd Al-Aziz became the king in January 2015, there were many challenges that took place inside the kingdom. As mentioned earlier, the kingdom on a regular basis was hit on its legitimacy, it did make some efforts to make its governing style more acceptable inside out. With the result, initiatives like Saudi vision 2030, allowing the women to drive in 2017, and so on were seen as the major changes in the orthodox kingdom. The main reason behind these changes was the crown prince of Saudi Arabia, Muhammad Bin Salman. The Saudi war with Yemen is also seen as a strategy of the crown prince Muhammad. Many developments in the kingdom were attributed to Muhammad Bin Salman. He has often been described as a power behind the throne of his father (Salman). After the ageing king took to throne, Muhammad Bin Salman was seen taking hold of many aspects of power like economy, defense and the Saudi Arabian foreign policy.

> Now, he has set breathtaking targets to wean Saudis off what he calls an addiction to oil by replacing fast depleting hydrocarbon revenue with income from private investment, privatization and the creation of the world's biggest sovereign wealth fund.[31]

The reforms like allowing the women to drive and vision 2030 were directly seen related with the crown prince Muhammad. Apart from that, Muhammad was also responsible for regulating and restricting powers of the religious police. He is also the person, who under his name, has allowed concerts to take place. For the first time under the influence of the Saudi crown prince, the sports stadium allowed women to enter and more women were seen in the workforce.

Religion in Saudi Arabia has seen moderation ever since Muhammad became the crown prince. In fact, Muhammad Bin Salman strives for the moderate Islam of the kingdom. He has vowed to return the country to moderate Islam and asked for global support to transform the hardline kingdom into an open society that empowers citizens and lures investors. [32]

According to the crown prince, the kingdom had not been normal for the past thirty years. The rigidity of the religious doctrines was blamed for that. Earlier, the crown prince had said, we are simply reverting to what we followed—a moderate Islam open to the world and all religions.[33] In the moderation of Islam, he, for instance, curbed the powers of the religious police that previously arrested people on the basis of moral breach. He also intends to fight off the extremist tendencies without wasting any time further. It is, however, difficult to comprehend the moderate Islam that the prince seeks to introduce into the Saudi state. His remarks leave an imprint of his resistance to political Islam, which has generally been understood in the context of expansionist Islam. In this context, expansionist Islam refers to jihadi organisations that are seen as promoting extremism and are opposed by the kingdom.On the other hand, the ideology of the state remains that of Wahhabism. As long as Wahhabi ideology persists in the form of literature, there is every possibility that the extremism may keep coming back in the state. If we look back at the origin of the Saudi state, Wahhabism was used to give legitimacy to the cause for the establishment of the Saudi state. This in turn means that in the past also, there was the political Islam or expansionist Islam, which the prince has claimed to be a moderate Islam. It implies that in order to fight extremism, the literature that has the tendency to unleash the extremist forces has to be removed, which in the Saudi case is Wahhabism. Although it remains to be seen as to how the extremism in the state will be dealt. There is also a possibility of a backlash if Wahhabism as an ideology is taken out from the religious discourse of Saudi Arabia. As a result, there may be even more radical moves taking place inside the kingdom, which otherwise may have stuck to the state narrative.

The statement of the Islamic moderation by the prince creates confusion while understanding the religious ideology of the Saudi state. Thus, Islamic moderation cannot simply come by smaller peripheral issues like curbing the powers of the religious police. There is an ideological perspective that needs to be redefined in doing so.

Ever since Muhammad was made the crown prince, he has remained verbal about many issues.

> The crown prince's comments are the most emphatic he has made during a six-month reform program that has tabled cultural reforms and economic incentives unimaginable during recent decades, during which the kingdom has been accused of promoting a brand of Islam that underwrote extremism.[34]

It would not be an exaggeration to say that Muhammad Bin Salman is a well-known Saudi royal who advocates for reforms in the country. Having said that, he has made enemies with the organizations like IS and Al-Qaeda. There are also the Shia organizations like Hezbollah and Hamas along with the Houthi rebels who would love to see his downfall.

SAUDI FOREIGN POLICY AND THE NATIONAL INTEREST POST-2015

After Salman was appointed king in 2015, Muhammad Bin Salman was appointed as the crown prince shortly. It has ever since ushered in some unprecedented changes in Saudi Arabia. In order to understand the changes in the course of the Saudi Arabian foreign relations, Ali Al Shihabi gives an important account. "A careful reading suggests that the new Saudi doctrine is based on three strategies: strengthening its military, reevaluating its alliances and aggressively confronting the Iranian expansionism." For many years, the Saudi regime relied on the United States to pursue its foreign policy objectives. The Saudi government poured in millions of money for this reason and assisted their partners, who exploited the funding for their own purposes and did not deliver much for the purpose they were expected to deliver in. The negotiations with the enemies also failed, and the United States also provided less reliable guarantees. These problems were furthered by the 2003 invasion of Iraq that resulted in the Iranian expansionism. It was even furthered by the 2011 Arab Spring.

The United States administration under Obama decided for the withdrawal of their forces from Iraq.

> Unchallenged by the American might, Iran tightened its grip on Lebanon, took control of Iraq and Syria, infiltrated Yemen, backed insurgents in Bahrain, and trained and supplied terror cells in Kuwait and Saudi Arabia.[35]

Having witnessed the changes, Saudi kingdom understood that it was time to do away with the outdated policies if the challenges mentioned above were to be handled effectively.

> In this context, the military was the main priority for the kingdom, which needed to be strengthened. It was felt that there was a need to not rely solely on the United States for the objective. It meant expanding military forces that would be capable of dealing with both Iranian and terrorist threats. With some exceptions, today, Saudi military is, in many ways, a holdover from the parade ground army of the 1960s. In the aftermath of the midcentury Egyptian and Iraqi military coup d'etats, the kingdom designed its military to be predominantly symbolic force, incapable of mounting a takeover of the government.[36]

The power of the Saudi military was demonstrated during the first battle with the Houthis in 2009. The military responded poorly, and the Saudi government swiftly upgraded the training. Many reforms were proposed in the military bureaucracy also. Improvements in the relations with Russia widened the base of Saudi's arms purchase. After Sanaa was taken over by the Houthi rebels, the Saudi military was still reforming, and hence was actually not in a complete position to resist the threat. The Saudi military was seen lacking the precision to hit the targets although improvisation has started in the area.

The strategic aspect is being reevaluated in order to ensure that countries with bilateral or multilateral connections with the kingdom follow through on their commitments. To that end, the focus has been on the GCC in the context of economic alliance and security in the region. It has also resulted in improved relations between Saudi Arabia and the UAE, which culminated in the security cooperation. This cooperation was evident when action was taken against Yemen. The internal threats were also addressed by the empowerment of organization, which led to the boycott of Qatar that supported the Muslim brotherhood for many years. Qatar was also seen harboring the dissidents of the neighboring states and even intended to influence the military and religious officials of Saudi Arabia and UAE. All of Qatar's efforts have compromised the stability of Saudi Arabia and others.

The relations of Saudi Arabia apart from GCC with Egypt and Lebanon have also started to rebalance. In case of relations with Lebanon, King Abdullah sanctioned three billion dollars in aid to the Lebanese army in 2013. It was thought by many in Saudi Arabia that these funds went to

Hezbollah though. The new Saudi leadership consequently terminated the support in 2016.

With respect to Iran, the kingdom needed to resort to the proactive policy as the American presence in the region began to shrink. The kingdom now had to be in direct confrontation mode against the Iranian expansionism. The confrontation was intended after the Bahraini uprising of 2012 and was inevitable after the Houthis took over Sanaa in Yemen.

> But whereas Iran could rely on exploiting sectarian lines to create deadly proxies, the kingdom had no such capabilities (its one attempt to emulate the Iranian model in Syria was an unmitigated failure). Saudi Arabia therefore needed to turn to multilateral military force to complement its soft power capabilities.[37]

The intervention of the Saudi military operation in Bahrain was effective, but it presented significant issues in Yemen. The huge hilly terrain, combined with Iran-backed Houthi forces, is regarded as a major threat. Saudi Arabia went in believing that the Houthis would be defeated by air strikes, but this has not proven to be the case. In fact, it was discovered that the Houthis defended successfully during the initial clash despite receiving no support from Hezbollah and Iran. The kingdom also realized that the guerilla would be exhausting and a long process. On the other hand, Hezbollah along with the IRGC (Islamic revolutionary Guard Corps) have started to widen the Houthi capabilities by training and supporting them. That is when Saudi Arabia decided to rise to the occasion of zero tolerance towards the Houthi threat on its Southern borders.

The response of Saudi Arabia towards the Houthi threat came at a point in time when the American presence and credibility in the region was at its ebb. The United States sent clear signals that the Saudi's should take their regional responsibilities on their own shoulders and learn to deal with Iran in the regional politics. Although the United States ultimately provided some support to the Saudi's, the kingdom solely could not rely on them and had to garner the support of the other countries also with the most important being the UAE. The sole motive behind getting the support was to limit Iranian interference and expansion in Yemen.

The foreign policy with Israel is officially not established, but its importance can be felt by the Saudi regime. In an interview, Muhammad Bin Salman held that the Israelis had a right to their homeland, which is a very bold statement ever made by any Arab leader in the Israeli context. He also held "we have to have a peace agreement to assure the stability for everyone and to have normal relations."[38] This way of recognizing Israel, however, is not unprecedented. There are countries like Egypt and Jordan that have struck some peace with Israel.[39] This also brings us to the Saudi-sponsored peace effort, which began in 2002 as a regional peace plan providing full peace to Israel and resolving a number of concerns with them. According to several commentators, the Fahd plan granted partial recognition to Israel in 1981 as well. It was an eight-point plan to solve the Arab Israeli conflict after Camp David accords remained unsuccessful to solve the conflict. This plan offered recognition to Israel in return of surrendering the areas captured by Israel during 1967.

The statements regarding the recognition of Israel were however made by the crown prince only. This made the Saudi king reiterate his stand on the issue. In a phone call to the US president, he reaffirmed the kingdom's position on the Palestinian issue and the right of Palestinians to their own land. This however does not wash away the statements made by the crown prince. The reasons for the warming relations between the kingdom and Israel once again are not difficult to ascertain. Both the countries were in opposition to the Joint Comprehensive Plan of Action (JCPOA) or the Iran-US nuclear deal. Both countries oppose the Iranian expansionism in the region. It is yet to be seen as to how the kingdom can mold its foreign policy and reach an official cooperation with Israel. However, it is clear that Israel has been showing positive signs of establishing diplomatic relations with Saudi Arabia.

CONCLUSION

The contemporary Saudi state faces many challenges to its legitimacy. There is, however, a notion that there is no certainty to the instability of the Saudi state, but the instances taking place, especially in the post-2011 era, have tipped the scales slightly in favour of the idea that the Saudi regime will fall in future. The religious backlash against moderation or modernization, along with furthering the austerity drive for stabilizing the economy will be immensely challenging for the Saudi regime in future. This puts a serious strain on the legitimacy of contemporary Saudi Arabia. The image of Saudi Arabia has long been as the most important Islamic country in the Muslim world. This image has also started to corrode due to the liberal changes taking place domestically inside the kingdom. The Saudi foreign relations, with a tilt towards Israel, also convince many Muslims to raise their voices against the Saudi regime.

NOTES

1. Madawi Al-Rasheed, *Salman's Legacy: The Dilemmas of a New Era in Saudi Arabia* (Oxford & New York: Oxford University Press, 2018), 3.
2. Ibid., 4.
3. Madawi Al-Rasheed, "Review Article: Saudi Arabia Post 9/11: History, Religion and Security," *Middle Eastern Studies* 43, no. 1 (2007): 156.
4. Jajati K. Pattnaik, "Challenges to the Royal Legitimacy in Saudi Arabia," *Mainstream Weekly*, May 16, 2015, at http://www.mainstreamweekly.net/article5672 (accessed June 23, 2021).
5. Joseph A. Kechichian, Islamic Revivalism and change in Saudi Arabia: Juhayman Al-Utaybi's 'Letters' to the Saudi people," *The Muslim World* 80, no.1 (1990): 7.
6. Christine Eickelman, "Review Article: Women in Saudi Arabia Today," *Middle East Journal* 52, no. 2 (Spring 1998): 296.
7. Thomas Hegghammer, "Jihad Yes But Not Revolution: Explaining the Extraversion of Islamist Violence in Saudi Arabia," *British Journal of Middle Eastern Studies* 36, no. 3 (2009): 398.
8. Ibid.
9. T R McHale, "A prospect of Saudi Arabia," *International Affairs* 56, no. 4 (Autumn 1980): 635.
10. Pattnaik, n. 4.
11. Ibid.
12. Ibid.
13. Ibid.
14. Simon Henderson and Joshua Teitelbaum, *Saudi Arabia: Politics, Succession and Opposition*, The Washington Institute, Policy 228, December 1996.
15. Pattnaik, n. 11
16. Girjesh Pant, *The Arab Gulf Economies: From Crisis to Reform* (New Delhi: Har-Anand Publications, 1996), 91-92.
17. Toby Matthiesen, *The domestic sources of the Saudi foreign policy: Islamists and the state in the wake of the Arab Uprisings*, Working Paper (Washington DC: Brookings Institution), August 2015, 2, at https://www.brookings.edu/wp-content/uploads/2016/07/Saudi-Arabia_Matthiesen-FINALE.pdf (accessed July 5, 2021).

18. Ibid., 3.
19. Madawi Al-Rasheed, "Salman Al Awdah: In the Shadow of Revolutions," *Jadaliyya*, April 27, 2013, at https://www.jadaliyya.com/Details/28521 (accessed July 17, 2021).
20. Ibid.
21. Ibid.
22. Madawi al Rasheed, *Muted Modernists: The Struggle Over Divine Politics in Saudi Arabia* (London: Oxford University Press, 2015), 83.
23. Ibid., 84.
24. Matthiesen, n. 18.
25. Nora Abdulkarim, "Trial of Saudi Civil Rights Activists Mohammad Al Qahtani & Abdullah Al Hamid," September 2, 2012, at https://ana3rabeya.wordpress.com/2012/09/02/activiststrial/ (accessed August 1, 2021).
26. Toby Matthiesen, *Sectarian gulf: Bahrain, Saudi Arabia and the Arab Spring That Wasn't* (Stanford, California: Stanford Briefs, 2013), 85.
27. Matthiesen, n. 18.
28. Stephane Lacroix, "Osama Bin Laden and the Saudi Muslim Brotherhood", *Foreign Policy*, October 3, 2012, at http://foreignpolicy.com/2012/10/03/osama -bin-laden-and-the-saudi-muslim-brotherhood/ (accessed November 25, 2021).
29. Matthew Weaver, "Isis Declares Caliphate in Iraq and Syria," *The Guardian,* June 30, 2014, at https:// www.theguardian.com/world/middle-east-live/2014/jun/30/isis-declares-caliphate-in-iraq-and-syria-live-updates (accessed July 31, 2021).
30. Matthiesen, n. 18, 10.
31. David Gardner, "The religious compact that constrains Saudi economic reform," *Financial Times*, April 27, 2016, at https://www.ft.com/content/78294598-0bc9-11e6-9456-444ab5211a2f (accessed November 25, 2021).
32. Martin Chulov, "I will return Saudi Arabia to Moderate Islam, Says Crown Prince," *The Guardian* October 24, 2017, at https://www.theguardian.com/world/2017/oct/24/i-will-return-saudi-arabia-to-moderate-islam-crown-prince (accessed December 12, 2021).
33. Ibid.
34. Ibid.
35. Ali Al Shihabi, "Saudi Arabia new Foreign Policy Doctrine," *Al Arabiya English*, December 15, 2017, at https://english.arabiya.net/en/views/news/middle-east/2017/12/15/saudi-arabia-s-new-foreign-policy-doctrine (accessed December 18, 2021).
36. Ibid.
37. Ibid.
38. Jonathan Marcus, "Israel and Saudi Arabia: The Relationship emerging into open," *BBC News*, April 3, at 2018, https://www.bbc.com/news/world-middle-east-43632905 (accessed December 18, 2021).
39. Ibid.

9

PUBLIC SPACES AND THE ARAB UPRISINGS

SITES OF CONTENTION

Priya Singh

The Arab uprisings of 2011 are often depicted as synonymous with the occupation of squares and streets. Public space had occupied centrality in the events of the Arab Spring. Perhaps the most telling images of the Arab uprisings emanated from the Tahrir square in Cairo and the avenue Habib Bourguiba in Tunis. Squares and streets are public spaces, which are perceived as sites of confrontation and interaction, as well as locales of dissent, conversely, also depicting the notion of control and restraining rebellions and social revolts.[1] In other words, it can be both a hegemonic space and a flashpoint of resistance. However, though the centrality of these spaces to the narrative of the uprising in the Middle East has been explored and interpreted by academics, by and large, it has been sidelined to some extent by the emphasis on the role of social media or social networking sites in nurturing and inciting the rebellion. This in turn has elicited responses such as "the grey old spaces" where the youth revolutionaries congregated had been obliterated from the narrative. Nonetheless, the squares and streets that arose in the late 19th century, with no local historical background, replaced the "Market-Mosque Complex" which till then constituted what can be termed as public spaces. Gradually there was an emerging tendency towards the creation of newer nationalist spaces which had been constructed under European influence. In the 1950s, these spaces were increasingly utilized to protest against colonial rule, for demonstrations against ruling families, as emblems of colonial elites or the ruling elites as well as sites of dissent. Newer squares were constructed to constrain gatherings.

While protests were widespread in the older cities with a history of political upheavals, they were much less discernible in the Gulf nations. Cities, planning, and architecture were pushed to the margins under overly centralized regimes. At the same time, increasing privatization took place that resulted in benefiting the elites as was the case in Damascus. Most public friendly spaces had become reactionary sites laden with political connotations. These were the same spaces that were used for national celebrations but were now being appropriated for social or political agitations. Military rule resulted in increased surveillance and open spaces were converted into private expanses. The mosque (intrinsic to the space) and the plaza (appropriated from outside) could not perform any civic functions. The significance of the Arab revolutions of 2011 lay in the fact that it succeeded in re-utilizing both spaces in the form of a new variant of civil protests alongside with demands of material, and religious movements. Squares became both the resting room and windows to the revolution wherein the agitators slumbered, prayed, mingled, protested and these were the spaces that could mould their history. The spatiality of the Arab uprising appeared to facilitate a dialogue between spaces of tradition and modernity, and perhaps paving the way for an elusive synthesis that the modern Arab cities were in quest of, albeit for a short period of time.[2]

The article seeks to delve into the brief period in the modern history of the Arab world, which came to be known as the Arab uprising with a view to engage with the encounter between the physical public space and the revolutionary process and its subsequent repercussions. The article consists of three major sections. It begins with a brief exposition of the concept of public spaces, it then provides a concise overview of the Arab uprising via the lens of public space and finally concludes with reflections on this seemingly brief episode of public articulation in the Arab space.

DECONSTRUCTING THE PUBLIC SPACE

Public space is a copiously discussed term and as such is subject to multiple definitions. The notion of public space as a Western construct dates back to the times of the ancient Greek *agora*, which performed a dual function, acting both as a marketplace and as a forum for discussions pertaining to democracy and citizenship.[3] Though being multipurpose in terms of its functionality, the *agora*'s ability to facilitate political articulations, which was intrinsic to its character, made it stand apart from other open public spaces.[4] Lyn Lofland locates public space in "the city's streets, parks, its places of public accommodation," "the areas of the city to which …all persons have *legal access*."[5] Further, Iris Young contends that in utilising the explicitly available public space "one should expect to encounter and hear from people who are different (and have different) social perspectives, experiences and affiliations." [6] Loretta Lees, however, cautions that "these concepts are both slippery and interrelated" as they tend to confuse the meaning of public space and the role it is supposed to perform for the society.[7] Jurgen Habermas visualized the presence of a societal "public sphere" in which the public space is posited as the "material location" for social exchanges and political events and happenings to take place.[8] In other words, according to Stephen Michael Zigmund, "In essence, public space offers a physical space for democratic society."[9] In an article, "Neighbourhood Design: Public Spaces," Richard Sendi and Barbara Goličnik Marušić have pointed out that the "public space is an inseparable entity of a two-way process between both the components: public (people) and space (place). Public space is then not just a spatial frame, a waiting scene where an event will occur; it is more—it is *publicspace*."[10] Elaborating upon Don Mitchell and Lynn Staeheli's conceptualization, Damian Collins and Sophie L Stadler in "Public Spaces, Urban," explicate the character of public space as "First, it is space where "the public" is formed and where regulations governing public behaviour predominate. Second, it is conceptually separate from private space, although in practice this distinction is invariably blurred, due to ongoing legal negotiation and social struggle. Third, space can be envisioned on a continuum from mostly public to mostly private, but some overlap of interests is always present."[11]

Public spaces are used by myriad sections of the society to effect change, to safeguard rights, and to contest hegemonic perspectives and accounts. Although much political discussion and planning has shifted to the online platform, physical and tangible public spaces remain significant as sites for congregation, dissent and reinforcing association with a group. These functions may render the public space a character that is not necessarily serene and systematic, for example, in instances when agitators and their opponents gather at a locale, articulating amongst a fragmented multitude with contrary aims. Significantly, the gathered multitude harbour a common notion of the importance of taking over public space to further their demands and mould shared viewpoints and remembrances. However, public space in reality, has never quite acquired an egalitarian character. Considerations of ethical order, as well as the allures and perils linked with a public existence have from time immemorial encouraged non-inclusive tendencies.

Enforcing social and legal rules and regulations on this space has frequently resulted in the prohibition of groups considered to be possibly dismembering, consisting of women, minors, the impoverished, the proletariat and ethnic minorities. This non-inclusion has been defended on grounds of both safeguarding those who are marked to be persecuted and safeguarding the community from the chaos supposedly linked to their presence. Historically, public space was a philosophical and representative battlefield from which hegemonic clusters attempted to discount those they considered to be hazardous or unruly. One method of not including them was by way of enhanced private jurisdiction over spaces where the multitude congregated. Progressively a considerable part of public existence in the urban spaces was subsumed by private owners as shopping malls, markets and entertainment enclaves came under private ownership. Despite being accessible to public and performing a part in nurturing public sociability, these spaces were under private domination, with the management possessing the authority to exclude undesirable elements with no explanation.

Further, every day, routine accountability for conventional public spaces was gradually handed over to private players, in the process, substituting public methods of domination with privatized nature of regulations. With a predominant focus on strict vigil and fortressing, the private players aimed to offer neat, orderly, submissive public spaces appropriate for middle class consumption and the restructuring of nearby private owned spaces. Critics point out that the emergence of non-inclusive rationale and proclivity towards privatization, as well as the curtailing of divergences that complemented these tendencies represented "the end" or "the death" of public space.

Thus the core aspects of public space were intrinsically challenged: entry was progressively reliant on social and economic position and perceived reliability; proprietorship was under private control otherwise wherein public authorities were in charge at least formally, several related rights and duties could be handed over to private players; governance was not inclusive in nature and linked with the perception that the underprivileged urban inhabitants were fiscally and ethically perilous. This transmutation eroded the credibility of public space as a location of accommodation and divergences and restricted the notion of the public to discard those considered as unwanted. These transformations hinted at a kind of revenge or retaliation, alluding to a wider attempt by the affluent and the influential to reclaim urban space from the disadvantaged.[12]

In other words, there were critical transformations in the nature and performance of public space. However, in hindsight, the violation or incursion on public morality was limited and less potent, than frequently alluded to. Policies pertaining to urban spaces was seldom entirely antagonistic to peripheral clusters, and complimentary steps were often in force along with non-inclusive acts. Moreover, the restrictive measures were not essentially unalterable and committed as they appeared to be; the execution was generally limited; dissent and defiance was feasible. Even by the narrow yardsticks of its proprietors and controllers, a public space devoid of plurality and diversity, unconstrained, unplanned dialogues, would be regarded non-performing. As a result, the end of public space may be more aptly described as a deliberate transmutation, which was desired: an affluent, consumption-centric and order seeking public in place of the peripheral multitude. However, the patterns and methods of control and vigilance were definitely altered and the opportunity to partake in the shared existence of the urban space was surely constricted. Public space is a locale of reasonably high social, political and legal significance, at the same time, it is critical to the reading of the character or essence of the city as well as what it can constitute. It is true that publics also comprise digital spaces, yet, the online platform or the virtual world has as yet not uprooted the tangible, physical spaces of the city. On the contrary, the digital, social media and the tangible spaces coexist in a high-yielding, fruitful confluence. The digital media reacts to as well as performs an important part in moulding the happenings of what constitutes the conventional physical public space.[13]

SPATIAL CONNOTATIONS OF THE ARAB UPRISING

Between 2011 and 2014, global politics appeared to be taking place in the streets and squares, in other words, the public places. Perhaps the most well recognized of all the spatial occupation movements was the Arab spring, which saw the occupation of streets and squares in Tunisia, Egypt, Yemen and Bahrain.[14] The Arab uprising has by and large been interpreted as a set of predominantly "hard" revolutions which fall under the category of conventional uprisings associated with a degree of ferocity, clarion calls for change in the government, greater representation, civil rights, economic development and equal opportunities. However, the exemplary images and instances of the Arab uprising that went viral globally, were spatial in character like that of the "occupation" of the Tahrir square for example.[15] And political struggles are in essence about images, as Lina Khatib puts it,

> The image is at the heart of the political struggle, which has become an endless process of images battling, reversing, erasing and replacing other images........Political struggle, then, is an inherently visually productive process. It is also visual to a large degree: It is a struggle over presence and visibility.[16]

The occupation of a public space, as an act in itself, in contrast to the occupation of a private property, has to be read as symbolic of multiple demands, consciously initiated, with the goal of provoking reactions, rather than as an act in isolation or an end in itself. The occupation of the Tahrir square in Cairo and the avenue Habib Bourguiba in Tunis during the Arab uprising embodied the articulation of these demands, rendering an animated performative character to the hitherto silent public spaces. It did not merely connote the substitution of physical absence by physical presence but was a deliberate act, conscious of the fact that the space belonged to a hegemonic, police state with its concomitant implications of forcible ejection. The taking over of an empty space by the revolutionaries was an act of provocation with the view of eliciting a response. In the words of W. J. T. Mitchell:

> In the context of the rhetoric of public space *occupatio* is, as the original meaning of the word reveals, the seizure of an empty place, one that is supposed to be *res nullius*, not owned by anyone, not private property. It is a demand in its own right, a demand for *presence*, an insistence on being heard, before any specific political demands are made; a demand that the public be allowed to gather and remain in a public space. But the demand of *occupatio* is made in the full knowledge that public space is, in fact, *pre-occupied* by the state and the police, that it's *pacified* and democratic character, apparently open to all, is sustained by the ever-present possibility of violent eviction. *Occupatio* thus aims, not just at taking possession of an empty space in an argument, but of provoking a response and framing it in advance.[17]

Conversely, the occupation of the public space by the state with the aim of silencing the voices of dissent, characterized by vigil and surveillance, in other words, the creation of an empty space reflected in the post Arab uprising phase, is also laden with contradictory messages, of a silence pregnant with ideas and despair, as well as evocative of defiance and disapproval. This can be attributed to limitations within the space itself and of the articulators of resistance.

Meanwhile, the public space is no longer a static spatial category in the midst of a revolution wherein it absorbs the character of the uprising as it is permeated by the protestors from diverse backgrounds, encompassing multiple identities, and as a consequence assumes a dynamic, hybrid character and becomes a process in itself. In the context of the Arab uprising and Tahrir square in particular, Momen El-Husseiny contends:

> First "Tahrir" was more of a process than a fixed spatial signifier. The revolution reflected the spatial constituency of metropolitan Cairo, a city of mixed formal, informal, and peri-urban formations. Second, the social mix of people involved reflected a variety of identities. Protesters were associated with the Salafi, the Muslim Brotherhood, Copts, football fan groups (the Ahly and Zamalek Ultras), and ethnic groups from Lower and Upper Egypt, who were exposed to one another probably for the first time in their lives, producing Stuart Hill's "third space," or Nezar Al Sayyad's "hybrid urbanism."[18]

The participation of Arab streets and city squares in the uprisings of 2011 is the concrete manifestation of the criticality of public space in the political system. In other words, "Public space is not simply a metaphysical concept. Differing experiences of different spatial structures have directly political impacts."[19] However, the public spaces that encouraged dissent and anchored protestors in the Arab uprising were complemented by the articulation of resistance in the realm of digital, social media. Facebook, Twitter and the online editions of regional newspapers with global reach such as Al Jazeera, both intensified and amplified the agitation world-wide, highlighting the emergence of a public sphere of glocal resistance, necessitating an analysis of the same. "Public space can generate anxiety and resentment as easily as curiosity and diversity. That is why the inquiry into digital media is so important. A public sphere seems to be emerging in space, but it is also manifesting itself purely in time."[20]

Scholars have emphasised the potential of the public sphere in voicing dissent and its role in a democracy, political life and citizenship, frequently citing the Arab uprising as an example. Diana Boros and James M. Glass, therefore, remark:

> Public space, both literal and figurative, is foundationally important to democracy, to political life in general, and to individual citizenship, self- awareness, and emotional health. Recently, the diverse manifestations of the Arab Spring protests and their comprehensive seizing of public spaces ...remind us that both physical and abstract public space— what we often term the "public sphere"—is potentially

vastly underused, and not nearly inclusive enough in providing space for dissidence and dissidents.[21]

The politics of space, that is, the inherent ability of certain spaces to be sites of contentions has been explicated by Asef Bayat in his seminal works on "street politics" encompassing both its physical and social attributes. Bayat, in *Life as Politics: How Ordinary People Change the Middle East*,[22] elaborates upon the politics of the streets, arguing that there is a fundamental difference between passive use of public space, which is acceptable to authorities, and active use of such space, which invites stern response from the state in the name of public order. The Arab uprising constitutes an apt example of the active use of public space, wherein the Arab street connoting the public sphere, consisting of the both the spatial and the virtual, becoming locales of dissent. Bayat observes:

> When people are deprived of the electoral power to change things, they are likely to resort to their own institutional clout (as students or workers going on strike) to bring collective pressure to bear on authorities to undertake change. But for those urban subjects (such as the unemployed, housewives, and the "informal people") who structurally lack intuitional power of disruption (such as going on strike), the "street" becomes the ultimate arena to communicate discontent. This kind of *street politics* describes a set of conflicts, and the attendant implications, between an individual or a collective populace and the authorities, which are shaped and expressed in the physical and social space of the streets, from the back alleyways to the more visible streets and squares. Here conflict originates from the *active use* of public space by subjects who, in the modern states, are allowed to use it only *passively*—through walking, driving, watching—or in other ways that the state dictates. Any *active* or *participative* use infuriates officials, who see themselves as the sole authority to establish and control public order.[23]

Simultaneously, as Bayat points out the streets embodying public spaces at large are also sites of social solidarity founded on constructed identities, with the potential for inciting dissent at multiple levels and on varying scales, making them susceptible to repressive retaliation from the state. In Bayat's words:

> But "street politics" has another dimension, in that it is more than just about conflict between authorities and deinstitutionalized or informal groups over the control of public space and order. Streets, as spaces of flow and movement, are not only where people express grievances, but also where they forge identities, enlarge solidarities, and *extend* their protest beyond their immediate circles to include the unknown, the strangers. Here streets serve as a medium through which strangers or casual passersby are able to establish latent communication with one another by recognizing their mutual interests and shared sentiments. This is how a small demonstration may grow into a massive exhibition of solidarity; and that is why almost every contentious politics, major revolution, and protest movement finds expression in the urban streets. It is this epidemic potential of street politics that provokes authorities' severe surveillance and widespread repression.

According to Jillian Schwedler and Ryan King,[24] a reading of the Arab uprising from the lens of spatiality necessitates a systematic study. Both, the assembling of demonstrators and policing are almost always arranged according to spatial factors that comprise availability and conspicuousness of some sites, the layout of famous public squares and the prevalent utility of the expanses. The January 25 protests were initiated in the Tahrir square partially due to the fact that it was the site of previous demonstrations. At the same time, the Tahrir square was easy to locate and could accommodate large numbers. Adding the spatial dimension in the interpretation of the Arab uprisings demonstrates how large congregations of humans can reorganize the prevalent hegemonic "topographies" and abolish deeply ingrained emblems and means of oppression and obedience. Space has been predominantly analysed by academics even in the recent past as "the dead, the fixed, the undialectical, the immobile,"[25] while time has been interpreted as permeated by "richness, fecundity, life, dialectic."[26] This is despite the fact that philosophers such as Henri Lefebvre have shown that space is socially recreated via "'networks of flow among goods, information and bodies.'

Rather than being fixed in physicality, spatial characteristics are constituted by their social context."[27]

Spaces are never devoid of power. They have characteristics such as aggression, compliance, brutality, tenacity, inclusion or exclusivity. The populace becomes aware of these qualities and accordingly conducts itself within these spaces, at times contesting while at other times strengthening the power equations. In Tunisia, for instance, the spatial aspect and their representative control or authority was not restricted to urban centers, as such when protests spread to the marginal urban spaces, the police were unable to monitor and control dissent in myriad sites. The significance of the urban centres and peripheries in the analysis of protests need to be emphasized in a glocalized environment. Another important aspect of spatiality in protests is the class factor, for example, in wealthy localities with foreign embassies and foreign citizens, policing is severe as protestors are generally not tolerated. However, if demonstrations do occur in these spaces, as it did in the case of the Pearl Square in Bahrain in 2011 and 2012, the suppression, though swift, cannot overshadow the fact that the incident received significant global awareness and prompt condemnation. Moreover, the tangible public space was abetted by the networked space of digital media, thereby the local assumed a national character and found global visibility. This was particularly noticeable in the case of the Tahrir square where very little coverage was to be seen in the local media, but the intertwining of space and connectivity by way of technological revolution enabled the transgression of spatial or territorial boundaries. [28]

REFLECTIONS

A recap of the events between 2010 to 2012 would take us back to visuals depicting a sea of dissent spanning across the Arab space. Memories of the catchphrases of the protestors thronging Tahrir or Bourguiba avenue, and multiple other less-covered public spaces are difficult to erase. A mass of humanity had congregated to articulate in high pitch and intensity, the slogan, *ash-shab yurid isqat an-nizam*, or "the people want to topple the regime." The demands for a "social justice, effective citizenship, economic opportunities, more rights, less repression, and more political freedom"[29] were ubiquitous, be it in the form of newspaper headlines to social media platforms such as Twitter and Facebook; they surfaced on the banners that were displayed by the demonstrators in rallies or took the form of graffiti, the implication was plain and direct and the fight for dignified existence would remain. It appeared as though a deeply anticipated rupture was occurring in spite of the attempts of Arab autocrats and their benefactors to retain the existing state of affairs and prevent any critical transformation. As this chapter of contentious politics made its presence felt in the Arab expanse, it altered regional dynamics and confronted profoundly engrained presumptions pertaining to "Arab political culture," particularly the lacunae in terms of a representative ethos and the tendency of the populace to accept despotism. For the world at large, albeit for a short span of time, it was as if the Arabs eventually had reclaimed their empathy and ability to act independently.[30]

The Arab uprising epitomized contestations in the polity, which in terms of imagery predominantly played out in the public spaces of some of the urban and semi-urban expanses in the Arab world, highlighting the importance of political geography in dissent. The public space that provided a backdrop to the protests acquired a social and political character, which was in striking contrast to the hitherto prevailing sociopolitical identity. At the height of the uprising the squares and streets reflected a more egalitarian social character and a remarkably aggressive political behavior. The solitude symbolized by emptiness was replaced by a plethora of animated political performances, the desolate spaces, symbolic of a resigned attitude to fate, were replaced with uncommon vigour and determination to contest injustice. The social alienation, apathy and near despair reflected by the barren public spaces gave way to solidarity, a rare passion and hope for a fundamental transformation. The aesthetics of a spartan hegemonic public space controlled by the state of the pre-Arab uprising era was displaced by the aesthetics of a revolutionary expanse dripped in humanity, tumultuous, colorful and rebellious.

By way of conclusion, the spatial dynamics of the post Arab uprising period may be explicated along the trope of State Neoliberalism which can be contextualized in terms of a glocalized and post-truth world. Neo liberalization of public spaces may be explained as strategies aimed at procuring greater assets to compensate for a decrease in local funding. Therefore, ways and means to allure tourists and attract enterprise becomes the cornerstone of these policies, in the process abetting the market rationale, a corollary of which is social segregation as an intrinsic part of the spatial structuring of the urban expanse.

A crucial aspect of neoliberal urbanism is the ejection of the category of dispossessed or destitute. The objective is to permit public spaces to assume the form of lucrative locales for asset aggregation with the aim of reenergizing the urban centre. The concept that the individual is responsible for his condition and accomplishments, or lack thereof, is at the heart of the rationale to focus on the ejection of the destitute. In other words, the formal preference of a neoliberal dispensation is the reconfiguration of the spatial architecture to accommodate corporate concerns and maximize dividends. The aim is to draw the attention of a uniformly composed working class, who are acquiescent clients pitching in for the benefit of the local economy.

The creation of an enterprising character for the urban space necessitates absolving it of the homeless who occupy or clog the pavements. The Marxian philosopher, Henri Lefebvre[31] has dwelled upon the explicit connection between "urban planning and sociology," that is, the planning of the city performs the task of "social control" by way of separating or secluding its inhabitants, and in order to contend with the intertwined social and spatial seclusion, he conceptualized what was termed as the "Right to the City." The term, despite its lack of precision enables an understanding of the fact that though conceptualized as a public space, the street, contrary to the general perception, is not obtainable for all and this analogy could be extended to the city square as well. If citizenship is defined as connoting more than just enfranchisement, then streets and squares have a critical role to play in a democracy, and by that logic, a "common space" that is accessible for all is required.

While we live in a digital era, particularly in the times of a global pandemic, wherein virtual existence is the norm, the importance of the physical space does not recede as the very notion of a democracy necessitates the availability of a non-partisan, unhindered inclusive space for all, wherein any cluster or community can articulate its demands and opinions, which is crucial for a democracy. Under an autocratic dispensation, protests in public expanses, which have an emblematic significance are by and large denied. In actuality, public spaces can be regarded as the launchpads or initiators of democracy and should be analyzed from the perceptive of being platforms for civil articulations. The cultural geographer Don Mitchell contends, "the regulation of public space necessarily regulates the nature of public debate: the sorts of actions that can be considered legitimate, the role of various groups as members of the legitimate public and so forth."[32] Through the monitoring of conduct and framing "acceptable" conduct, the state decides upon who is granted access and who is not granted access to public spaces. By penalizing trivial misconduct that do not intend to harm others, "anti-homeless laws" threaten the fundamental ethics of empathy that is a prerequisite for democratic societies, in so far as they challenge the "individuals" and "groups" basic prerogative of survival.[33]

By the year 2013, the Arab uprising began to be labelled as a non-success, particularly in Egypt, where a military coup led to the culmination of the state's first democratically elected government. The subsequent military regime under President Abdel Fattah al-Sisi, who remains at the helm till this day, signified the end of the revolution and was regarded as the symbol of a "counter-revolution,"[34] because the military, "forge[d] alliances in order to restore the equilibrium and ensure the survival of its own apparatus"[35] The demands for restructuring that were raised during the revolution and the steps initiated towards it were stymied by the incumbent regime, which in fact, pursued the very policies that had compelled the populace to occupy public spaces in large numbers and protest, indulging in what has been termed as a "schizophrenic attempt to maintain" both a neo-liberal as well as a command economy, simultaneously.[36]

On the other hand, the economic policies consciously adopted by the post-revolutionary dispensation have been described as "statist neoliberalism," a hybrid. According to this perspective, the state is "the set of institutional forms through which a ruling class relates to the rest of society,"[37] thus the state and the ruling class are "mutually constitutive."[38] Most Arab states had followed the statist model of complete sway over the economy, polity and society. In the economic sense, it entailed that the state would regulate the "the antagonistic character of capitalist social relations'—in other words, it is the task of the state to contain social and class conflicts."[39]

Statism implied that the state had hegemony over means of production, engagement and articulation, and that there was in place a single political party and trade union under state control. The information and broadcasting system was completely under state control, so were professional groups, universities and corporations. The cardinal principles of statism were nationalisation of private enterprise, a rigorous system of subsidies encompassing education, healthcare, public education, essential domestic services, transportation and a centralized bureaucracy with unilateral authority to plan as well as execute policy decisions. The legitimacy of the state largely relied upon its system of subsidies, which enhanced the lifestyle of a burgeoning middle class. This variant of neoliberalism faced a major crisis due to regional factors like the war with Israel in 1967, for specific nations involved in it and global factors such as the oil crisis and the adoption of neoliberal policies in the 1980s. Thus, statism was replaced by neoliberalism, which called for severely restrained state participation and regulation, greater privatization with a partiality towards the entrepreneurial class.

The lacunae with the imposition of neoliberal policies in the Arab world was that it failed to satisfy both the global financial agencies and strategists for not being enough and the domestic populace for being excessive as it connoted minimal welfare provisions by the state, leading to mass discontentment. The neoliberal state, however, is not a homogenous construct in addition to being contradictory as it implies minimal state control in most spheres, barring popular discontent, which had to be suppressed with maximal state power. It also called for state intervention to facilitate an amicable investment ambience, protect entrepreneurship in crisis and proactively bring about legislative changes to benefit the entrepreneurs.[40] In other words, neoliberalism contains within it the seeds of authoritarianism. In the Arab world, state repression and police control were deliberate policies of the capitalist system in place.[41] The military regime's philosophy of "permanent state of emergency" has also been described as a deliberate plan, which has been "historically 'integral' to the capitalist state," along with the emergence of the " 'securocratic state', a neoliberal state working for the interests of the elite classes and utilizing policing strategically to reproduce capitalist relations and the neoliberal global order as a whole."[42] Similarly, the statism of post-2011 Egypt can be viewed as a deliberate plan to concomitantly regulate and accommodate the contrarian features of capitalism and preserve a dispensation that reflexively depletes and deprives the populace.[43] In the spatial sense, the post-revolutionary Arab states have invested in creating an architecture that is not amenable to resistance, that is, the public is not encouraged to dissent in public space.

Glocalization, signifies the concomitant existence of "universalizing and particularizing tendencies in contemporary social, political, and economic systems."[44] The implication is a mixture of *globalization* and *localization*, which contests the rather superficial understanding of globalization operations as unidimensional extension of spaces. Glocalization signifies that the increasing significance of transnational and global strata is taking place in tandem with the ever-growing criticality of the local and regional strata. It entails a cohabitation of homogenous, centralizing as well as heterogenous and decentralizing propensities. Most importantly the concept of glocalization focuses upon the intertwining of the global and the local and the resultant hybridity. As a result, global interactions, as well as local interactions, shape and produce local expanses and local individualities. Local environments and identities are changed and generated by globalised contacts as well as local events, so clarifying and reinstating that "globalization entails neither the end of geography nor declining heterogeneity." In fact, the concept glocal includes the subnational or local, national and supranational or global arenas.[45]

The post-revolutionary Arab world is an increasingly glocalized political, economical and cultural space. Be it the emergence of global cities such as Dubai, Abu Dhabi and Cairo, the multiple regional organizations such as the Arab League, Gulf Cooperation Council (GCC), educational spaces such as the American University of Cairo or local networks of artists and myriad civil society groups that cohabit the public space along with the national governments and agencies are an existential reality in the contemporary Arab world. Glocalization impacts the public space or rather the public sphere, which includes the digital space as evidenced by the year 2019, which was a year of global protests. The current protests in Israel-Palestine over an anticipated decision by the Supreme Court of Israel with regard to the eviction of Palestinian families living in east Jerusalem, and the global outcry even in the midst of a pandemic, reiterate the spatial dynamics of glocalization.

Post truth may be explicated as, "circumstances in which objective facts are less influential in shaping public opinion than appeals to emotion and personal belief."[46] Post truth politics, it is claimed, should be interpreted as a dilemma in which political articulation is progressively removed from the "factual" fabric. As a result, the capacity to respond to political happenings and to partake in an open process of opinion construction is undermined. The most powerful instances of post-truth politics as an approach open to political figures are situations wherein completely fabricated opinions or articulations that can be authenticated or proven otherwise, though not always done deliberately, are aimed either at opponents or advocates for multiple political reasons. It may be argued that these contentions are not, at first, attempts to win over or satisfy, but rather, the fundamental ramification is the production of confusion, outrage, and disarray. The basic objective is to attract attention.

Atrociously incorrect contentions strive to make regular political dialogue and critical analysis of actions unattainable. They efficiently deflect attention from the intricacies of the actions, and have the ability to mould public rhetoric even when repudiated. It can be contended that post truth is a process wherein both the "structures" and the "agents" are reciprocally reliant and augment each other. At the crux of the post-truth phenomena lies the concept of "careless speech," which is unperturbed by truth, as well as the understanding that the globe is a communal or shared expanse within which objects assume a public character. It connotes a disinclination to interact with other viewpoints and a refusal to believe that expression has ramifications and vocabulary has consequences. It entails a dilemma regarding whether what has been explicitly articulated was in reality intended, implying that everything that has been articulated can be denied. The growing insignificance of "factual truth" in public debates entails disintegration of a shared humanity and this phenomenon can be linked to transformations in the media, economy and politics. The appearance of "Lies, Inc." and the widespread use of public relations (PR) driven politics has to a considerable degree led to scepticism regarding facts. In the realm of politics, "appearances constitute reality."

The function of facts is to enlighten or educate assumptions, notions and they assume significance if there are interactions of assumptions with respect to them unless deconstructed from diverging viewpoints, facts have no value.[47] In a glocalised world dominated by neoliberal nations, the Arab public sphere is an intrinsic part of the post-truth rhetoric that has engulfed the global space. Authoritarian states, the rise of the right-wing with its concomitant national revivalist ideology, control over the media, both conventional and digital, which is the primary instrument of myth making, and the consequent counter-narratives are all tell-tale signs of a post truth era characterised by "performances" in the arena of "public discourse."[48]

NOTES

1. Majdi Faleh, "Places of protest or centres of state control," October 4, 2018, at https://theconversation.com/how-city-squares-can-be-public-places-of-protest-or-centres-of-state-control-102275 (accessed April 20, 2021).
2. Nasser Rabbat, "The Arab Revolution Takes Back the Public Space," *Critical Inquiry* 39, no. 1 (Autumn 2012): 198-208.
3. William Hollingsworth Whyte, *City: Rediscovering the Centre*, 1st ed (New York: Doubleday, 1988), 339.
4. Don Mitchell, *The Right to the City: Social Justice and the Fight for Public Space* (New York: Guilford Press, 2003), 130.
5. Lyn H. Lofland, *A World of Strangers: Order and Action in Urban Public Space* (Illinois: Waveland Press, 1985), 19.
6. Iris Marion Young, *Justice and the Politics of Difference* (Princeton, NJ: Princeton University Press, 1990), 119.
7. Loretta Lees, "Ageographia, Heterotopia, and Vancouver's New Public Library," *Journal of Environment and Planning D: Society and Space* 15 (1997): 322.
8. Don Mitchell, "The End of Public Space? People's Park, Definitions of the Public, and Democracy," *Annals of the Association of American Geographers* 85, no. 1 (March 1995): 116.
9. Stephen Michael Zigmund, "Ideologies of the Everyday: Public Space, New Urbanism, and The Political Unconscious of Bus Rapid Transit." (Thesis, University of Texas, 2012), 11.
10. Richard Sendi, and Barbara Goličnik Marušić, "Neighbourhood Design: Public Spaces," in *International Encyclopaedia of Housing and Home*, ed Susan J Smith (Amsterdam: Elsevier, 2012), 21.
11. Damian Collins, and Sophie L. Stadler, "Public Spaces, Urban," in *International Encyclopaedia of Human Geography,* edited by Audrey Kobayashi (2020), pp. 103-104. doi:10.1016/b978-0-08-102295-5.10212-4. (accessed on April 25, 2021)

12. Ibid., 104-105.
13. Ibid.
14. Wladimir Riphagen and Robbert A. F. L. Woltering, "Tales of a Square: The Production and Transformation of Political Space in the Egyptian (Counter)Revolution," *Arab Studies Quarterly* 40, no. 2 (Spring 2018): 117.
15. W. J. T. Mitchell, "Image, Space, Revolution: The Arts of Occupation," *Critical Inquiry* 39, no. 1 (Autumn 2012): 9.
16. Lina Khatib, *Image Politics in the Middle East: The Role of the Visual in Political Struggle* (London: I.B. Taurus, 2013), p. 1.
17. Ibid., 10.
18. Momen El-Husseiny, "Deconstructing the Myth of "Tahrir" and "the Facebook Revolution"", *Traditional Dwellings and Settlements Review* 24, no. 1 (Fall 2012): 78.
19. Diana Boros and James M. Glass, eds., *Re-imagining Public Space, The Frankfurt School in the 21st Century* (New York: Palgrave Macmillan, 2014), xi.
20. Ibid., xii.
21. Ibid., 3.
22. Asef Bayat, *Life as Politics: How Ordinary People Change the Middle East* (Amsterdam University Press, 2010).
23. Ibid., 11.
24. Jillian Schwedler and Ryan King, "Political Geography", in *The Arab Uprisings Explained: New Contentious Politics in the Middle East Explained,* edited by March Lynch (Columbia University Press, 2014), 160.
25. Ibid., 161.
26. Michael Foucault and Paul Rabinow, *The Foucault Reader* (New York: Pantheon 1984), 70. Cited in Schwedler and King, "Political Geography," 161.
27. Henri Lefebvre, *The Production of Space* (Oxford: Basic Blackwell, 1991). Cited in Schwedler and King, "Political Geography," 161.
28. Ibid., 164-168.
29. Fawaz A. Gerges, *Contentious Politics in the Middle East: Popular Resistance and Marginalized Activism Beyond the Arab Uprisings* (New York: Palgrave Macmillan, 2015), 1.
30. Ibid.
31. Lefebvre, *The Production of Space.* Cited in Marine Dassé, "The Neoliberalization of Public Spaces and the Infringement of Civil Liberties, The Case of the Safer Cities Initiative in Los Angeles," *Angles: New Perspectives on the Anglophone World [Online]* 8 (2019), at https://doi.org/10.4000/angles.595 (accessed May 2, 2021).
32. Donald Mitchell, *The Right to the City: Social Justice and the Fight for Public Space* (New York: The Guilford Press, 2003), 182. Cited in Dassé, "The Neoliberalization of Public Spaces and the Infringement of Civil Liberties."
33. Dassé, "The Neoliberalization of Public Spaces and the Infringement of Civil Liberties."

34. G. M. Selim, "Egypt under SCAF and the Muslim Brotherhood: The Triangle of Counterrevolution." *Arab Studies Quarterly* 37, no. 2 (2015), 177-199. Cited in Heba Khalil & Brian Dill, "Negotiating statist neoliberalism: the political economy of post-revolution Egypt", *Review of African Political Economy* 45 (2018): 574.
35. B. De Smet, *Gramsci on Tahrir: Revolution and Counter-revolution in Egypt* (London: Pluto Press, 2016), 97. Cited in Khalil & Dill, "Negotiating statist neoliberalism."
36. J. Stacher. "Egypt Running on Empty." *Middle East Report Online*, March 08, 2016, at https://merip.org/2016/03/egypt-running-on-empty/ (accessed on November 23, 2021), Cited in Khalil & Dill, "Negotiating statist neoliberalism".
37. A. Hanieh, *Lineages of Revolt: Issues of Contemporary Capitalism in the Middle East* (Chicago, IL: Haymarket Books, 2013). Cited in Khalil & Dill, "Negotiating statist neoliberalism."
38. Ibid.
39. R. Roccu, "Gramsci in Cairo: Neoliberal Authoritarianism, Passive Revolution and Failed Hegemony in Egypt under Mubarak, 1991-2010," (Doctoral dissertation, London School of Economics and Political Science, 2012), 72. Cited in Khalil & Dill, "Negotiating statist neoliberalism."
40. D. Harvey, *A Brief History of Neoliberalism* (Oxford: Oxford University Press, 2005), 64. Cited in Khalil & Dill, "Negotiating statist neoliberalism."
41. M. Abdelrahman, "Policing Neoliberalism in Egypt: The Continuing Rise of the 'Securocratic' State", *Third World Quarterly* 38, no. 1 (2017): 187. Cited in Khalil & Dill, "Negotiating statist neoliberalism."
42. Khalil & Dill, "Negotiating statist neoliberalism."
43. Ibid.
44. Joachim Blatter, "Glocalization," at https://www.britannica.com/topic/glocalization (accessed on May 21, 2021).
45. Ibid.
46. Ari-Elmeri Hyvönen, "Defining Post-truth: Structures, Agents, and Styles," E-International Relations, October 22, 2018, at https://www.e-ir.info/2018/10/22/defining-post-truth-structures-agents-and-styles/ (accessed May 21, 2021).
47. Ibid.
48. P. Fridlund, "Post-truth Politics, Performatives and the Force," *Jus Cogens* 2 (2020): 215-235, at https://doi.org/10.1007/s42439-020-00029-8 (accessed May 21, 2021). Fridland observes that "If one wants to *understand* post-truth political discourses and in so far as one wants to *change* the post-truth political climate, it is crucial to see political discourses as discourses that perform rather than report, that is, as being *performative*. .... the interesting aspect of understanding political discourses as performative is precisely the character of *doing*, *transforming* and *changing*, which also—and this is extremely important—must include the break with current structures, or, in other words, going *outside* and *beyond* established parameters and known patterns. That also means questioning ideas regarding the *types* of argument that are allowed or the *kind* of discourse that is appropriate in a given situation. Post-truth political discourses fundamentally function in the way political discourses

are supposed to function. Their task is to change and transform reality—or even create a new reality. In this particular sense, they *do* and they *perform*. A political discourse in general, and a post-truth political discourse in particular, cannot do and perform—cannot function—in a vacuum. A resonance and a response are required."

10

SPRING IN ARABIC LITERATURE AMID THE TURMOIL IN THE REGION

Md. Aftab Ahmad

The Arab Spring proved to be a significant event in contemporary Arab history, toppling many long-standing regimes, and sowing the seeds of democracy and social reform in several countries such as Egypt and Tunisia. Without a doubt, it occurred as a result of poverty, unemployment, and other local issues in the region, but it was fuelled and encouraged by the region's powerful Arab literature. The literature, both prose and poetry, gave ordinary Arabs the courage to express their outrage at the injustices perpetrated by the regimes.

The twentieth-century Egyptian writers like Tawfiq al-Hakim, Naguib Mahfouz and many others have written extensively on the issues of dire poverty, shattered dreams, despair, political oppression, torture in prisons and suppression. Egypt's Tahrir Square and other squares of the region had virtually turned into literary carnivals during the uprising. A large number of writers, academicians and artists have personally participated in the marches, and others have expressed their support for the uprisings. According to Egyptian novelist, Ibrahim Abdel Meguid '*the first days of the revolution were like an artistic or literary gathering and a cultural forum.*'

Literary figures in the Arab world are of the opinion that though the Arab Spring has not succeeded in bringing socio-political reforms in the region, but it has successfully changed the literary scenario in the region, where writers and poets are now feeling freer to express and literature has become sensitive towards socio-political issues of the region. The freedom of expression and the publication of prison literatures in post-Arab spring period is evidence of the spring in Arab literature. This article attempts to highlight the constructive role that the Arabic literature played in encouraging the common young Arabs and shaping their minds and hearts for these historical uprisings. The main focus will be on how the Arab Spring has provided an opportunity to the literature to flourish in terms of content and themes amid the turmoil in the region.

LITERATURE AND SOCIETY

It is said that the words are more powerful weapons than the weapons themselves. However, words in isolation have no meaning. It makes sense and becomes powerful only when they form part of literature of any society. The literature is truly regarded as the mirror of the society. It plays an important role in the socio-political formations of any society. It portrays the issues concerning the common men. It motivates people to stand up in the face of adversity and despondency and inspires them to face the challenges with fortitude and courage. Literature has the ability to inspire and shape the minds and hearts of the people by creating consciousness about the malaise which society is going through. It can become a powerful weapon to instigate the people to revolt against misgovernance, oppression, tyranny and injustices.

Arabic literature is regarded very rich and powerful in terms of content and heritage and its history goes back to the pre-Islamic Arabia. Despite severe censorships imposed by the despotic and authoritarian regimes in most of the Arab world, Arabic literature has made significant progress. Many important writers and poets had raised their voices through their pens (words) against the oppression and injustices perpetuated by most of the regimes in the Arab world. Thus, they have created the culture of resistance.

There is a close connection between Arabic literature and politics that represents the holistic character of Arab culture and attests the longstanding relationship between literature and socio-political life of the Arabs. Even in pre-Islamic Arab society, literature was used as a political tool and the tribes had a poet as their spokesperson.

LITERATURE AND ARAB SPRING

A series of popular marches in every capital of the Arab world had denounced and appealed for what these writers have already done in their writings throughout the last century. Literary critics believe that a true artist is prophetic and deeply intuitive. 'The true artist feels and hears sounds which alert him to dangers approaching. His or her natural antennae capture them, and he translates them into his writings in a constant effort to heighten people's awareness and sense of responsibility.'[1]

The Arab world is going through a lot of upheaval. It has witnessed a wave of popular uprisings and mass protest during the last decade that have swept across the Arab world. These uprisings were no doubt motivated by many important factors such as the tyranny, corruption, unemployment, sharp inequalities, denial of basic rights to the vast majority and disregard of the dignity and self-respect of the people. Apart from these factors, Arabic literature, both prose and poetry fuelled the young generation in the region to express their anger against the repressive and tyrant regimes. Khadija El Alaoui explains the reasons by saying:

> 'Poetry runs through the lives, the feelings and importantly, the politics of their world, a world that includes pride in Arab values and solidarity against the ongoing violence and injustices of authoritarianism and occupation.'[2]

Poetry is the most important genre of Arabic literature. Poetry's power and strength is not new in the Arab society. 'It has always played an important role in the society and it predates the arrival of Islam in Arabia that is known as pre-Islamic poetry (500-622 A.D). It is the poetry of a heroic tribal society revealing a heroic scheme of values.'[3] Poetry was rightly called the register of the Arabs, and it retains the same importance now. In the words of Muhsin Al-Musawi:

> 'The poetic and the spatial often converge and the selected text may well testify to the old saying of the Prophet's companion Ibn Abbas (d.687), made popular by Ibn Rashiq (d.1065) that "poetry is the register of the Arabs.'[4]

Arabic poetry has a very rich tradition and poets have always been considered as the nobles of the society.

> 'The Arabs used poetry as a weapon against their enemy tribes. They used it as a silent sword aimed at the hearts of the opposing camp, not with the purpose of drawing blood, but with the goal of insulting the pride of their enemies through words. The poet was expected to compose satires which would consequently provoke the poets of their enemy tribes to come up with retaliating satires.'[5]

Iraqi poet, Muzaffar al-Nawwab (b. 1934), is considered as the most influential contemporary writer and poet in this regard. He has left no Arab government unscathed by his bitter criticism.

> 'His poetry is full of Arab, Islamic and international leftist and revolutionary symbols and he tried to incite public emotions against political corruption, decadence, and injustice, in harsh and sometimes profane words.'[6]

On the importance of pre-Islamic poetry, Iraqi novelist, Ahmed Sarsawi points out that;

> 'Over the centuries, poetry was a source of revolutions and a tool for motivation and strength. Starting with the pride of *Antara bin Shaddad (525-608),* passing through the panegyric of *Hassan bin Thabit (d. 674)* (companion of Prophet Mohammed) and *Motanabbi (915-965)* and then the enthusiasms of *Baroudi (1839-1904),* the poetic contributions are clear and well established.'[7]

Poetry played a constitutive role in the current uprisings because of its well-established importance in Arab society. Explaining the importance of poetry in the Arab society, Khadija El Alaoui says:

> 'After all, 'poetry belongs to the streets, teahouses and living rooms rather than only lecture halls and libraries. Its beauty endlessly adorns our conversations and our political dissent and its ethical calls set the rhythm of our arguments. It is so common throughout the Arab world to hear people close their line of thought by stating: "as the poet says". Often the name of the quoted poet is not even mentioned, as the source of the

quote is not as important as the fact that the cited verses constitute moral references.'[8]

During the days of uprisings, people recited the verses from the collections of the Arab resistance poetry and the most popular slogan on every protest site and the street was the couplets of Tunisian poet, Abul Qasim al-Shabbi (1909-1934), who wrote these couplets against the French colonization of his country. People chanted couplets from his poem *'The Will of Life,'* which is one of the poems that bear evidence of people's determination and spirit to overcome the injustices heaped on them by France. The couplet reads:

'If, one day, the people desire to live
Then fate will answer their call.
And their night will then begin to fade
And their chains break and fall.'[9]

This couplet becomes the common slogan chanted by protestors all around the region. Tunisian novelist, Ibrahim Dargauthi says:

> This couplet proved to be a sharp weapon during the protest against Ben Ali in Tunisia and reached its echo to Tahrir Square in Egypt, Change Square in Sanaa, Pearl Square in Manama and the rest of the squares and streets in the region.[10]

Al-Shaabi's another poem titled *'To the tyrants of the world'* was also widely used as a slogan in Tunisia, Egypt and beyond. The poem reads:

'You the lovers of the darkness, you the enemies of life ...
Hey you, the unfair tyrants, you have made fun of innocent people's wounds,
and your palm covered with their blood
You kept walking while you were deforming the charm of existence
and growing seeds of sadness in their land.'[11]

Moroccan poet Youness Imghrane describes the love and application of poetry so eloquently even in modern times, particularly during the days of uprising by saying:

> 'It's true that poetry may not has a direct influence on change but one way or another it contributed to the success of the revolution in Egypt through strong poetic texts of *Salah Abdel Sabour, Amal Donqol, Ahmed Fouad Negm* and many others. Out of all the art genres, poetry has made room for change, reform and democracy. It is more potent and more able to influence and interact than novels and short stories.'[12]

LITERATURE FORECASTED ARAB SPRING

A thorough study of modern Arabic literature, reveals that the Egyptian literary works, including Tawfiq al-Hakim's '*The Return of the Spirit*', Naguib Mahfouz's *Cairo Trilogy* and Alaa Aswaani's '*The Yaqoobian Building,*' became the base of revolutions in the region. Al-Hakim and Mahfouz wrote their novels after the 1919 revolution in Egypt. Al-Hakim's 1933 novel tells the story of a patriotic young Egyptian and his extended family, ending with events surrounding the 1919 revolution that was according to the writer 'a literal awakening of the Egyptian spirit.' His novel with its strong expression of nationalist solidarity has particular resonance now. The 2011 Tahrir revolution has made it seem once again as fresh as today's news.

Exploring the importance of Arabic literature in the formation of popular uprisings around the world, the famous writer of Arab affairs, Peter Clark says;

> 'The anger that we have seen on the streets is basically the production of modern Arabic literature. A number of writers and poets were tortured and sent to jail to speak against the rulers. Many of them have to take refuge in foreign countries but their writings finally fuelled the anger among the Arabs. Themes of modern Arabic literature were limited and a huge part of literature was based on social realism. If there were historical novels, there were hidden contemporary messages. This reflected the influential 60s generation, when the Arab world was defensive and often confrontational (contradiction) towards the outside world. Writers who

> came of age in the 1960s often produced outstanding work and the emerging generation is fuelled by these writings.[13]

Iraqi novelist Ahmed Sarsawi (b.1973) explaining the close relationship between literature and current uprisings, wrote a detailed article on the current uprising and the literature in which he has outlined the importance of literature and how it has become a salient feature of the uprisings.

> 'His main assertion is that the current uprising in several Arab countries is the result of powerful Arabic literature whether in the form of prose or poetry. He said the diversified Arabic literature, produced by Egyptian society, has contributed a lot to the formation of consciousness for 25 January revolution. These literary works played a major role in guiding the Egyptians to overthrow Mubarak regime.'[14]

Dire political conditions, unemployment, lack of hope, taking refuge in religion, disillusionment, failed dreams and broken hearts were major themes of the modern literature. Wasini al-A'raj[15], the prominent Algerian novelist reminds us of the social importance of literature by saying:

> 'The political discourse is something ephemeral and goes with the wind, but the literary discourse, when genuine, will become a part of the individual memory, and eventually, the collective memory. According to him, the Tunisian revolution paved the way for other Arab revolutions and gave literature the opportunity to express itself.'[16]

Literature produced in Tunisia also forecasted the 2011 Arab uprisings. In this regard, the works of *Kamal Riyahi* (b. 1974) has played an important role in awakening the young minds of the Arab world. His novel *Al-Misrat* (Scalpel, 2006) falls in the category of revolutionary writing and predicted the uprising. Marek M. Dziekan writes:

> 'This novel is not political, at least on the surface—it refers more to social criticism, especially criticizing the attitudes of traditional Tunisian society to women. Despite that, the readers and critics concur that this work has

shed new light on phenomena silently omitted until then, and is therefore regarded as a voice calling for change.'[17]

Many other novels appeared soon after the revolution in Tunisia such as Kamal Riyahi's *Gurila* (Gorilla). This novel has many plots and contains several elements of criticism aimed at the socio-political situation in the country. Husain Al-Wad's novel *Saadatus Sayyed Al-Wazeer* (His Excellency the Minister) also criticises the prevailing corruption in the country and depicts the corruption in the regime.

'The protagonist is an ordinary man, a teacher, who to his own surprise suddenly becomes a minister and is drawn into the machinations of a system he cannot leave. His term of office is very short—once he completes the task the dictatorship has set for him, participating actively in all possible scandals, he faces up to what he has done. He attacks the president and his family, and ends up in a psychiatric hospital, where he is killed as a traitor and a plunderer of the country's wealth. The novel vividly depicts the corruption of those in power and their disdain towards society—the factors that became the key elements which contributed to the Jasmine Revolution.'[18]

In Syria, writers too forecasted the uprisings in many of their writings. Syrian female writer, Shahla Al-Ugayli published a historical novel *Saggad Agami* in which she described the historic incidents that resembled the current situation in Syria. Another famous novel *Al-Qawqa'a: Youmiyyat Mutalassis* (Shell: Memories of a Hidden Observer) of Mostofa Khalifa is considered as an important part of prison literature. The novel is partially autobiographical, with descriptions of the infamous Tadmor prison in Syria. Its protagonist, a graduate in film studies from Paris, was arrested at Damascus airport and jailed for 13 years without any charge.

Libyan writers have also criticized the regime of Muammar Qaddafi. Hisham Matar's 2006 novel, '*In the Country*' of Men, describes the terrible situation in Libya.

'In his novel, he describes the terror in Libya—the plot takes place in 1979, but one can easily compare it to more recent times. The novel in

> the view of the author of this paper, although generally praised, does not present any significant value as a source of information, but is rather a typical record of life and tragic events in a country ruled by a dictator, although one cannot deny the sheer artistic value of this work.'[19]

LITERARY GATHERINGS AT TAHRIR SQUARE

Literature has played an important role during the uprisings in the region, and with the presence of Egyptian poets, writers and artists the Tahrir Square in Cairo has virtually turned into a literary gathering. Khadija El Alaoui says:

> 'The main slogans on the streets were the couplets of Arabic poetry. One of the couplets which resonated throughout the mass marches at Tehrir Square was *I am the people, marching, and I know my way.*'[20]

Tahrir Square virtually turned into a cultural and literary gathering when a large number of cultural and literary figures joined the protestors at Tahrir Square. Participation of these contemporary Egyptian poets, writers and artists like *Ahmed Fouad Negm* (1929-2013), *Baha Taher*, *Nawal Al-Saadawi (1931-2021)*, *Alaa Al-Aswany*, *Burhan Ghalioun*, *Khaled Youssef*, *Alawiya Sobh* and many others in the mass gatherings was an extraordinary gesture from the literary fraternity. Egyptian poet Shaban Yusuf considers what is happening now in Egypt to be a major uprising conducted by the Egyptian people and youth and he stressed that no writer or poet can be content sitting alone in his house, separate from reality, when history is unfolding outside. He says, 'Writers and poets have strongly contributed to the Egyptian revolution, whether we are talking about their physical presence in Egypt's streets and squares or their literary output.' He further added:

> 'The Egyptian revolution served as an inspiration to many writers and poets, who decided they could not stand idly by and merely observe what was happening. A real writer is connected with the world around them, and the present period we are living in is more dramatic and inspirational than any other.'[21]

WRITERS AND ARTISTS AT TAHRIR SQUARE

Egyptian novelist Ibrahim Abdel Meguid,[22] who participated in the Egyptian revolution over 18 days, believes that 'a writer must not be isolated from what is going on around him. It had a profound influence on me that led me to write my book '*Every Land has a Birth: Days in Tahrir.*' He said 'this is because of Tahrir Square and the first days of the revolution were like an artistic or literary gathering and a cultural forum. It served as an inspiration to all artists.'[23]

The Egyptian writer Baha Taher[24] recounts the literary impact on these uprisings by saying:

> 'I was so incredibly happy when the revolution broke out, I have experienced enough joy over the past few weeks to last me 10 lifetimes. I am not exaggerating.' People recited his verses about freedom on Tahrir Square. Works of Al-Abnoudi and Sayed Hegab were also important, and of course Naghuib Mahfuz.'[25]

Egyptian poet Ahmed Fouad Negm, the poet of the people, who died in December 2013, had actively participated in the uprisings and joined his fellow protestors at Tahrir Square. The protestors were already chanting the couplets of his poetry. Khadija El Alaoui says:

> 'Ahmed's poetry had for decades not only tirelessly documented the obscenities of despotism, state violence and transnational relations of imperial power but also prophesied its inevitable failure. Indeed, the very multitude of protestors throughout Egypt embodied his poem '*I am the people*'.[26]

Arab poets and writers living abroad also extended their support to the uprisings through their writings and poems. Palestinian poet Tamim al-Barghouti, faxed a poem with the title "*O, Egypt, It is so Close*!" to an Egyptian newspaper.

> 'Inspired by the events in Egypt, the poem aimed to do what poetry always does in this world: insist on *sumud* and *muqawamah* (steadfastness and resistance). His poem immediately set to music and sung by artist Mustapha Said. The poem reads: *O Egypt, it's so close,*

Nothing remains of power but a few batons, If you don't believe it, come down to the square and see.'[27]

POST-ARAB SPRING LITERATURE

Arab writers are still busy in conceptualizing the most significant incident of the twenty-first-century Arab world, and they have yet to come out with their literary products on a large scale. But a considerable amount of literature in the form of poetry collections, memoirs, novels and other art forms are available in the public domain. In fact, the writers need more time to conceptualize and to come out with their productions because they often require time to contemplate and digest a subject or even, whilst it takes even longer to write a novel. However, there are other literary forms that allow a writer to immediately deal with such events including memoirs, commentaries, editorials and even poetry.[28]

No doubt, Arab Spring has created a positive environment for the literature to flourish, diminishing the fear which was among the writers and poets and liberating them from interrogation, torture, secret killing and forced exile. It has opened a broad horizon of freedom to the writers so that they can achieve their dreams. Arab Spring has offered writers to rediscover their courage, which was hidden due to the tight vigil imposed by the authoritarian regimes. A wave of prison writing has already started in Arab Spring countries. Several writers have started writing their bitter experiences of their stay in prisons and cells in several countries of the region.

Arab writers are finally feeling liberated and taking a fresh breath. They have started producing literary outputs in the form of memoirs, diaries and novels. A considerable amount of literature that is an eyewitness on the Arab spring is available. A significant amount of writing produced in Arab Spring countries describing popular uprising scenarios was discovered during the research for this article.

Egypt has produced a large amount of literature on the Arab uprisings. At the turn of the 21st century, Egypt witnessed prolific writings that warned of an upcoming political and social change. Such writings include the internationally acclaimed '*Emaret Ya'koubeyan*' (The Yacoubian Building), written by Alaa al-Aswany. The novel condemns the corrupt one-party state, whose citizens either abandon the country for promising careers abroad or show no loyalty to the government, and, in many cases, resort to extremism to counter the growing poverty, moral degradation and economic stagnation.

In 2009, the feminist, activist and writer Nawal al- Saadawi published '*Zeina*' where reality, dreams and fiction overlap to challenge the stigma of illegitimacy and confront the patriarchal oppression of the Egyptian society. Hamed Abd al-Sammad's novel '*Wada'an Ayotteha al-Sama*' (Farewell Sky) was written in 2010 that revolves around the Egyptians' lack of hope in the future in Egypt and their desperate attempts to emigrate. 'The novel that predicted the 25th January Revolution is what is written on the cover of '*Ajnihat al-Farash*' (Wings of the Butterfly). It was written by Mohamed Salmawy. It is considered as a foreshadow of the uprisings in both Tunisia and Egypt months before they actually took place.'[29]

Tahrir Square had a profound impact on the Egyptian writers and encouraged them to write novels/memoirs. Ibrahim Abdel Meguid (b.1946) wrote '*Every Land has a Birth: Days in Tahrir.*' He is the author of a number of critically acclaimed novels including '*No one sleeps in Alexandria*' and '*Birds of Amber.*' He was awarded the Naguib Mahfouz Medal for Literature for his novel '*The Other Place.*' He said, 'this is because of Tahrir Square and the first days of the revolution were like an artistic or literary gathering and a cultural forum. It served as an inspiration to all artists.'[30]

His memoir includes stories about the uprising, spanning the period from 1972 to the 25 January Revolution. 'It has 12 sections, each starts with a piece of poetry drawn from the likes of *Mahmoud Darwish, Ibrahim Abdel-Fattah* and *Pablo Neruda*. It also includes comments from his Facebook page, from the first day of the revolution until Mubarak stepped down. It gives readers a chance to go back to Tahrir Square, to the spirit of the Egyptian Revolution, through his unique expressive style, although the writer himself states that it is very difficult to capture, through writings or images or paintings, what really happened there. It had to be lived.'[31]

The role of women in Arab society has always been debated, but Egyptian women played an essential role during the Arab Spring. The participation of women in the current Arab upheavals in several Arab countries was a unique component of this revolution. This may invalidate the notion of Arab women's freedom in the region. Egyptian women authors and artists stayed at the forefront, not only actively participating in the revolutions but also documenting their experiences to inspire future generations. In this regard, the novels of Nawal El-Saadawi (1931-2021), Mona Prince and Ahdaf Soueif (b. 1950) are very important literary works. They wrote *Al-Thawrah Al-Arabiyah* (The Arab Revolutions)-2013, *Ismi Thawra* (Revolution is My Name)-2012 and Cairo: My City, My Revolution-2012 respectively. All the three novels depict the events of Tahrir Square since they were present in the protest marches.

Egyptian Journalist Ibrahim Eissa's 2012 novel '*Mawlana*' (Our Sheikh) reflects his political battles with authority. Eissa's work tackles the new phenomenon of the sheikhs who have become TV stars, as well as their shady, intertwined relationships with politicians, businessmen and security institutions.

> 'Although '*Ana Asheq*' (I Fell in Love) by Mohammed al-Mansi Kandeel does not directly discuss the revolution, its portrayal of the protagonist's journey from the slum areas to Cairo's posh neighborhood and from university to an over-crowded prison, sheds light on a city on the verge of a revolution. While, Ezzedine Shoukri Fishere's novel '*Bab al-Khuruj*' (The Exit) is not a testimony of the revolution as it happened but it is a struggle with the limitations faced by individuals and writers. In his novel he has unmasked the society and politics in Egypt and prophesized the future of Egyptian politics.'[32]

Literature in Tunisia, that was the birth place of the popular uprisings across the Arab world, was either banned or distributed in the black market before the Jasmine Revolution. Although the couplet of Abul Qasim al-Shaabi *'The Will of Life'* has become an important slogan on the streets of the Arab world, but the literature produced on Arab Spring was fairly less. Most of the available literature belongs to poetry. Fathi al-Nasri's *'The Tunisian Revolution'* and Al-Munsif al-Wahayabi's *'14 January 2011 and other collections'* are important ones. January 14 has become a historical day for Tunisians when their dictator, Ben Ali, fled the country. A number of collections, like Munsif al-Wahyabi's poem expresses happiness over the removal of former President

Ben Ali from power. It is worth mentioning here that most of the poetry collections are in free verses.

Like any other Arab Spring country, writers in Libya are busy documenting the prevailing socio-political situation and atrocities carried out by the Qaddafi regime. A number of publications are available in market that talk about the uprising in Libya and the police state of long-time dictator Muammar Qaddafi. Important among them are Libyan novelist, Ibrahim al-Koni's (1948) *Knights of Faded Dreams*, Faraj Ashsha's *'Regime of Our Leader'* and Hisham Matar's *'Anatomy of a Disappearance.'* Al-Koni's comic novel published in 2012 revolves around the prevailing situation in Libya. It narrates the story of Libya in a comic style starting with the fall of Qaddafi and reasons behind public opposition towards the regime. Faraj Ashsha's novel tells us about the current socio-political situation of the country, in which the political oppression and social injustices had reached new heights. The novel raises the question of identity and existence in the police state of Qaddafi. Hisham Matar's novel is one of the most important novels published shortly after the fall of Muammar Qaddafi. Matar's novel revolves around his parents, particularly his father, who was kidnapped by Muammar Qaddafi's agents in Cairo in 1990 and taken to Tripoli's notorious Abu Selim prison, where his fate remains unknown.

Syrian literary fraternity has always remained very vocal towards the wrong doings of its political masters. Syrian poets and writers like Nizar Qabbani, Sadullah Wannus, and many others have written against the wrong policies of the government and many of them were tortured and send to prison. Contemporary writers have expressed their feelings on the ongoing situation in Syria in the form of memoirs, poetry collections and novels. 'Khaled Khalifa's 'No Knives in the Kitchens of this City' is a beautiful account of the reasons behind the popular uprising in Syria. The novel uncovers the contradictions of the Syrian society.'[33] While 'Maha Hassan's (1966) 2012 novel *Tubulul Hubb* (Drums of Love) depicts the launch of pro-democracy revolution in Syria in 2011 and position of the Syrian intellectuals from the revolution and developments.'[34]

Syrian writer, Samar Yazbek (1970)'s memoir '*A Woman in the Crossfire: Diaries of the Syrian Revolution*' describes survival under the bombings and a crazy compulsion to fight this loathsome regime.

> 'Endangering not only herself but also her daughter, she follows the action, meets with fighters from the Free Syrian Army and records the government's atrocities. Samar confirms that the idea of a revolt against this regime had been brewing for years. She meets with Syrians from all walks of life and urgently records their witness to the regime's brutality.'[35]

Riyaz Mo'asas's 2012 novel '*Hammam Zunubia*' is a mixture of stories, thoughts and reflections on real events and ideas from the Syrian prisons. The writer says;

> 'The motivation to write this novel is just a feeling of deep concern and inclination to highlight the facts that the Syrian people suffered on daily basis under the unjust and oppressive regime.'[36]

Abdullah Maksoor's novel '*Days in Baba Amr*' tells the story of the Syrian city of Homs, which faced attacks by heavy weapons including guns, warplanes and tanks. Another novel '*Return to Aleppo*' documents the details of the prevailing situation in Syria. Omar Qaddur's novel (نوميس فـرعي ال نم) tells the story of the fear a man feels when he intends to return to Syria. The novel also explores the wrongdoings of a police state.

There is not much literary production in Tunisia but a few very important novels are in the public domain that are somehow related to the Arab spring because they deal with the police attitude of the Ben Ali regime. In this regard, Kemal Sharni's (1965) novel '*Friends of Allah*' is an important novel.

> 'It highlights his personal experiences of persecution, repression and torture meted out to him in jail for 5 years when he was a student under the regimes of president Habib Bourqeeba and ousted president Zain el Abdin Ben Ali. He was jailed due to his participation in a student protest march during his student days. His novel is a witness on the miserable history of Tunisia when the police state had put the students in the prisons and treated mercilessly due to their participation in anti state demonstrations.'[37]

It exposes the highest level of corruption and dictatorship prevailing in the country. Mohammad Chalabi's *'The Sons of Clouds,'* is another important novel dealing with the current socio-political situation under Ben Ali.

SPRING IN ARABIC LITERATURE

The literary fraternity in the Arab world is very optimistic about the upcoming literary prose and poetry because of many reasons. They now feel more confident after witnessing the influence of literature on the current uprisings and fall of corrupt dictators. They are also excited about the new available free and fair atmosphere to take breath. Arab writers like Ahmed Al-Sarsawi are ready to paint a new sketch of the region by saying:

> 'If literature has revolted against the tyranny of old cultural forces and announced its remorse from flattening extremism. A new era of intellectual and cultural freedom has started that has adopted the pen and paper as the sword of country and its shield.'[38]

Moroccan poet, Youness Imghrane is very confident about the role of literature, particularly poetry, in the future. He says:

> 'All poets' hearts and souls were affected by the Arab Spring and it gave us greater courage to express our demands and aspirations. We became more explicit in speaking about corruption, dictators and murderers. We believe the fundamental changes to which our Arab nations are heading, politically and socially, will provide our poetry with a sort of chemical power and effectiveness in terms of rebellion.'[39]

CENSORSHIP IN THE POST-ARAB SPRING ERA

Censorship has long been a big issue in the Arab literary community... Jordanian Poet, Amjad Nasser says:

> 'If you were to ask any Arab writer today about the main problem facing Arab culture, he or she would say without a second thought "Censorship".'[40]

Throughout history, intellectuals have thrived when freedom of expression is restricted. It's often because they felt challenged and provoked to express their views in unconventional ways, for example, through analogies or parodies.

> 'This was the case with all intellectual output in the Arab world, starting with Gamal Abdul Nasser's police state in Egypt in 1952. One needs to review Russian literature during the communist era, Iranian cinema under Ruhollah Khomeini, Egyptian plays under Gamal Abdel Nasser, or Iraqi poetry under Saddam Hussein, to see how creative writers, actors and poets were expressing themselves.'[41]

Taher Ben Jelloun talks about the censorship imposed by the authoritarian Arab regimes and the threat to the life of the poets and writers. He says:

> 'There was a lot of state censorship but there was also the powerful force of auto-censorship. Even those who lived in exile were very, very cautious. Exiled writers from Iraq and Syria, for example, could not talk or write freely out of fear for the safety of family members still in their home countries. For instance, Lebanese writers who criticized Syria and its role in Lebanon have received death threats. Samir Kassir, a Lebanese writer who published articles speaking out against the Syrian dictatorship, was assassinated in June 2005. It is widely thought that the Syrians killed him.'[42]

The writers always seek to be the voice of their people, reporting on their pain and suffering and working for a bright future. The writer is a reformer who leads his people through texts that he or she publishes on the pages of newspapers and magazines either in the form of prose or poetry. Sometimes they have to pay a huge price, perhaps death. Many writers have suffered the horrors of prison and exile because of their texts against the tyrants. The best part of the current Arab uprisings is that they included every people from all walks of life.

During the Arab Spring days, a court in Qatar sentenced a prominent Qatari poet, Mohammed bin Al-Dheeb, to life imprisonment on allegations of inciting against the state, defamation of the crown prince, Tamim bin Hamad al-Thani and attacking the constitution. 'His arrest followed the publication of the "Jasmine poem" which criticized governments across the gulf region, saying "we are all Tunisia in the face of the repressive elite.'[43] Ayat Al Qurmazi, a 20-year-old poet and a university student, was arrested in Bahrain when she joined the protesters in Pearl Square. 'Her mother said my daughter did nothing wrong. She added that "she didn't raise her hands in anger. She used words to express how they felt. She was only using her rights of free speech.'[44]

But soon after the fall of several dictators in the region, the shades of censorship started to fade in many of the Arab countries. Egypt tops the list of mitigating the burden of censorship in the region. Poets, writers and artists are now feeling more freedom Writers are enjoying a level of freedom unrivalled in their previous lives under authoritarianism. Around the region, writers are demanding greater independence. A group of Egyptian scholars raised their voices under the umbrella 'Protect the Egyptian Minds.' The tremors of the revolution has also shaken the giants of state publishing houses. In 2012, the staffs of a literary journal *Akhbar al Adab* went on strike demanding the removal of their regime-appointed editors.

Literary fraternity in the Arab world is very optimistic about the future of literary prose and poetry. Writers like Ahmed Al-Sarsawi are ready to paint a new sketch of the region by saying:

> 'If literature has revolted against the tyranny of old cultural forces and announced its remorse from flattening extremism. A new era of intellectual and cultural freedom has started that has adopted the pen and paper as the sword of country and its shield.'[45]

Books that were banned in earlier regimes are now available in book stores. Examining the status of censorship in Egypt, Peter Schwartzstein writes in one his articles:

> 'Books that were once banned, or atleast deeply frowned upon, such as George Orwell's *Animal Farm* and *1984*, are among the bestsellers at many bookstores in downtown Cairo.'[46]

Publishers are now more inclined to republish the books that were banned during the earlier regimes.

> 'Madarat Research and Publication, seized upon the power vacuum following Mubarak's toppling to print and distributed a nuanced take on the political theory of Hassan Al-Banna, the founder of the Muslim Brotherhood. Even the conservative Dar al-Shorouk, Egypt's largest privately owned publisher, produced a few critical takes on the previously untouchable former president, Gamal Abdel Nasser.'[47]

Peter Schwartzstein reiterates that 'the revolution appears to have roiled Egypt's censorship authorities, which previously presided over all cultural output with an iron fist. The censorship board is torn between liberal revolutionaries and Mubarak-era appointees, and Sefsafa, for one, has taken advantage of the impasse to sidestep the government requirement that it dispatch at least 10 copies of new publications for approval.'[48]

The sale of books is also showing a positive trend in post-Arab Spring period. On the basis of the interviews conducted with the publishers and book shop owners, Peter Schwartzstein says:

> 'Book sales have picked up substantially. General Egyptian Book Organization's takings were up 80% from 2014 at this year's (2015) Cairo book fair; small publishers report an expanding and diversifying readership as the economy shows signs of a recovery. And Aboul Naga remains cautiously optimistic that the book industry will fight to retain its relative freedom.'[49]

PRISON LITERATURE

The Arab Spring has allowed them to rediscover their courage, which had been hidden due to the authoritarian regimes' strict vigilance. In Arab Spring countries, A wave of prison writing has already begun. Several writers have begun to write about their traumatic experiences in prison and confinement. Hisham Matar's novel *'Anatomy of a Disappearance'* is one of the most important novels that fall into the category of prison literature, published shortly after the fall of Muammar Qaddafi. The novel revolves around his parents, particularly his father, who was kidnapped by Muammar Qaddafi's agents in Cairo in 1990 and taken to Tripoli's notorious Abu Selim prison, where his fate remains unknown.

Brahim El Guabli wrote an article that takes us into the history of prison literature in Arabic language and says:

> 'The prison writings are the crucible of Arab people's frustrations, hopes, broken promises and unflinching will to not turn a blind eye to crimes of dictatorship. The wave has already started in post-revolution Tunisia with the publication of a dozen prison literary works that would have been banned under Ben Ali's regime. The revolution has enlarged the potential of freedom of speech, and it is our hope that more and more victims of this period (and why not torturers too?) will share their insider's knowledge of these loci of shame.'[50]

TRANSLATION

The Arab world is a region where everyone has an interest because of many reasons, such as the birth place of Islam, Christianity and Judaism and the existence of natural resources and its strategic location on world map. After 9/11, there was an interest in Arabic literature due to the menace of terrorism originating from the region, but the interest in literature increased after its emphatic influence on Arabs. The Western world is now more interested in reading Arabic literature and a new era of translation is underway to make it available in English language. The famous Arab writer Sinan Antoon opines:

> 'There will be increased interest in the modern and contemporary culture and literature of the Arab world. These revolts have debunked the orientalist myth that portrayed these cultures and societies as static, despot loving, eternally fundamentalist. Now we know how vibrant and dynamic they are.'[51]

CONCLUSION

Arabic literature has always remained an important part of Arab society. In pre-Islamic Arabia, poets used to be role models and spokespersons of their societies. Every tribe used to have a poet to defend its honour and pride and to attack other tribes with their words. It is a well-recorded statement that *poetry is the register of Arabs* and that is true because if you want to know about pre-Islamic Arabia, poetry is the only source to know about them.

There is debate on the Arab Spring, whether it was successful in achieving its goals, but it is true that it brought spring in Arabic literature and Arab culture. Arab writers are of the view that the uprisings are an outcome of the literature that was produced by the Arab writers. Iraqi novelist Ahmed Sarsawi says, 'The current uprising in several Arab countries is the result of powerful Arabic literature whether in the form of prose or poetry.'[52]

The literary fraternity is very optimistic about the upcoming literary prose and poetry because of many reasons. They now feel more confident after witnessing the influence of literature on the current uprisings, and they are also excited about the new free and fair atmosphere in which they can breathe. There is a wave of publication of prison literature that was banned prior the Arab Spring period. There is an increased interest in Arab literature, particularly in the West, because of its emphatic influence on Arabs. The volume of translation of Arabic literature in many other world languages has increased manifold. We can say that there is spring in Arabic literature amid the turmoil in the region.

NOTES

1. Mona Takieddine Amyuni, "The Artist's Role in Society," *Arabic and Middle Eastern Literature* 2, no. 2 (1999): 219, at http://www.tandfonline.com/doi/pdf/10.1080/13666169908718225 (accessed March 14, 2013).
2. Khadija El Alaoui, "Chanting Tahreer and Compassion: People as Poetry," In *Tensions Journal* 5 (Fall/Winter 2011): 1, at http://www.yorku.ca/intent/issue5/articles/pdfs/khadijaelalaouiarticle.pdf (accessed April 15, 2013).
3. Muhammad Mustafa Badawi, *A Critical Introduction of Modern Arabic Poetry* (Cambridge: Cambridge University Press, 1975), 2.
4. Muhsin J Al-Musawi, *Arabic Poetry: Trajectories of Modernity and Tradition* (Oxon: Routledge, 2006), xiii.
5. Cle'ment Huart, *A History of Arabic Literature* (Lebanon: Khayat Book and Publishing Co, 1976), 7.
6. Edmund A. Ghareeb, *Historical Dictionary of Iraq* (UK: Scarecrow Press, 2004), 173.
7. Ahmed Sarsawi, "25 January Uprising and the Literary Discourse," *Diwan Al-Arab*, at http://www.diwanalarab.com/spip.php?article27653, (accessed March 14, 2011).
8. Alaoui, n. 2, 2.
9. Ibid., 12-13.

10. Ibrahim Dargauthi, "Tunisian revolution: The role of Literature in motivating and implanting of public awareness," *Haqqul Awda* (Right to Return) *Magazine*, no. 43.
11. Claire Chambers, "Cultural Production and the Arab Spring," at http://dawn.com/2013/01/27/column-cultural-production-and-the-arab-spring-by-claire-chambers/, (accessed February 22, 2013).
12. *Poetry Played a Part in the Arab Spring*, (Arabs Today, June 2012), a http://en.arabstoday.net/20120628156228/imghrane-poetry-played-a-part-in-the-arab-spring.html (accessed February 22, 2013).
13. Peter Clark, "The revolution in Arabic fiction prefigures the Arab spring," *The Guardian,* at http://www.guardian.co.uk/books/booksblog/2011/apr/18/arabic-fiction-revolution-spring (accessed April 18, 2011)
14. Ahmed Sarsawi, "25 January Uprising and the Literary Discourse," *Diwan Al-Arab,* at http://www.diwanalarab.com/spip.php?article27653 (accessed March 14, 2011).
15. Wasini al-A'raj (1954) is a famous novelist and university professor who is one of the most prolific writers and a prominent cultural activist and public intellectual in both France and Algeria. He is among the few Algerian writers who achieved fame around the Arab world.
16. For details, see a report of Ali Znaidi, *Al-Jadaliyya*, February 23, 2012, at http://www.jadaliyya.com/pages/index/4466/the-international-symposium-on-the-arab-spring-thr (accessed February 26, 2019).
17. Marek M. Dziekan, Writers and Poets as the Forecasters of the Arab Revolution of 2011, *Rocznik Orientalistyczny/Yearbook of Oriental Studies* LXIX, no. 2 (2016), at https://journals.pan.pl/Content/82364/mainfile.pdf (accessed February 26, 2019).
18. Ibid.
19. Ibid.
20. Alaoui, n. 2, 14-15.
21. Andy Morgan, "From fear to fury: how the Arab world found its voice," *The Observer*, at http://www.guardian.co.uk/music/2011/feb/27/egypt-tunisia-music-protests (accessed February 27, 2011)
22. Meguid (1946) is the author of a number of critically acclaimed books including *No one sleeps in Alexandria* and *Birds of Amber.* He was awarded the Naguib Mahfouz Medal for Literature for his novel *The Other Place.*
23. "The Arab Spring: Between the arts and political activism," *Al-Sharq Al-Awsat*, at http://www.asharq-e.com/news.asp?id=27709%20%20 (accessed December 15, 2011).
24. Born in 1935, he played a decisive role to topple the Mubarak regime. He has been involved in all major periods of upheaval in Egypt over the years, firstly as a journalist and later as a writer with political ambitions. He was a co-founder of the grassroots movement Kifaja which called for the end of the Mubarak regime and laid the foundation stone for the January revolution.
25. Ibid.
26. Alaoui, n. 2, 14-15.

27. Ibid., 18.
28. "The Arab Spring: Between the arts and political activism," *Al-Sharq Al-Awsat*, at http://www.asharq-e.com/news.asp?id=27709%20%20 (accessed December 15, 2011).
29. Nada Ramadan, "The Egyptian Contemporary Novel: A Survey of a Revolutionary Endeavour," *Al-Jadid Magazine* 17, no. 65, at http://www.aljadid.com/content/egyptian-contemporary-novel (accessed April 14, 2014).
30. "The Arab Spring: Between the arts and political activism," n. 28.
31. Marwa Mohie El-Din, *Al-Ahram Online*, 23/07/2011, at http://english.ahram.org.eg/NewsContent/18/0/17036/Books/Ibrahim-AbdelMeguids-new-book-brings-the-revolutio.aspx (accessed March 14, 2012).
32. Nada Ramadan, The Egyptian Contemporary Novel: A Survey of a Revolutionary Endeavour, *Al-Jadid Magazine*, vol. 17, no. 65, at http://www.aljadid.com/content/egyptian-contemporary-novel (accessed April 14, 2014).
33. Book Review in "Raya: The Agency of Arabic Literature," at http://www.rayaagency.org/clients-list/khalifa-khaled/there-are-no-knives-in-the-kitchens-of-the-city, (Accessed April 14, 2014).
34. Adib Abdulmajid, *First Book on Syrian Uprising* (ARA News, December 2013), at http://maha-hassan.blogspot.in/2013/12/first-book-on-syrian-uprising.html (Accessed on April 14, 2014).
35. Miriam Cooke, *Feminist Revolutionary Narratives from Egypt and Syria: Hopes and Disappointment*, at http://www.juancole.com/2013/07/revolutionary-narratives-disappointments.html (accessed on April 14, 2014).
36. Iman Adil, *New Novel of Syrian Novelist, Riyaz Mo'asas,* Al-youm al-Saabe, September 21, 2013, at http://www1.youm7.com/News.asp?NewsID=1259338&#.U2xaD4GSygQ (accessed April 14, 2014).
37. Iman Mohaddab, Al-Jazeera, February 23, 2012, at http://www.aljazeera.net/news/pages/b20a8553-bac1-4de9-ae68-74efa52753b7 (accessed March 14, 2013).
38. Ahmed Al-sarsawi, *25th January Uprising and the Literary Discourse,* Diwan Al- Arab, at http://www.diwanalarab.com/spip.php?article27653 (accessed March 14, 2013).
39. *Poetry played a part in the Arab Spring*, Arabs Today, June 2012, at http://en.arabstoday.net/20120628156228/imghrane-poetry-played-a-part-in-the-arab-spring.html (accessed March 22, 2013).
40. One Thousand and One Delights, *The Guardian*, April 12, 2008, at http://www.guardian.co.uk/books/2008/apr/12/publishing.society
41. Sami Moubayed, "Where are the poets of the Arab Spring?" Asia Times Online, December 9, 2011, at http://www.atimes.com/atimes/Middle_East/ML09Ak01.html (accessed 26/02/2013).
42. Interview with Taher Ben Jelloun, "Literature after the Revolt: Arab Writers 'Should Not Be Invisible Anymore," *SPIEGEL online*, September 15, 2011, at http://www.spiegel.de/international/world/literature-after-the-revolt-arab-writers-should-not-be-invisible-anymore-a-785689.html (accessed May 22, 2013).

43. "Poetic Injustice? Qatari poet gets life sentence for 'incitement against authorities," *Al Arabia News*, November 30, 2012, at https://english.alarabiya.net/News/2012/11/30/Poetic-injustice-Qatari-poet-gets-life-sentence-for-incitement-against-authorities.
44. Bahrain poet Ayat Al Qurmazi, 20, released from prison, *Open Salon*, July 15, 2011, at http://open.salon.com/blog/bellemeadebooks/2011/07/15/bahrain_poet_ayat_al_qurmazi_20_released_from_prison (accessed February 26, 2013)
45. Ahmed Al-sarsawi, *25th January Uprising and the Literary Discourse, (*Diwan Al-Arab, 14/03/2011), at http://www.diwanalarab.com/spip.php?article27653 (accessed on March 14, 2013)
46. Peter Schwartzstein, *The Arab Spring's best legacy: Egyptians are now reading once-banned books*, at https://qz.com/383385/the-arab-springs-best-legacy-egyptians-are-now-reading-once-banned-books/ (accessed December 12, 2020).
47. Ibid.
48. Ibid.
49. Ibid.
50. Brahim El Guabli, *A New Wave of Prison Writings After the Arab Uprisings?* at https://www.resetdoc.org/story/a-new-wave-of-prison-writings-after-the-arab-uprisings/ (accessed December 12, 2020).
51. This quotation is from an interview with Sinan Antoon, the Co-Editor of *Jadaliyya* on the relationship between the Arab uprisings and literature. You can see full interview on http://www.jadaliyya.com/pages/index/1680/kenyon-review-interview-with-sinan-antoon-on-liter
52. Ahmed Sarsawi, "25 January Uprising and the Literary Discourse, *Diwan Al-Arab*, at http://www.diwanalarab.com/spip.php?article27653 (accessed March 14, 2011).

11

HEZBOLLAH AND REGIONAL CONFRONTATION

THE ARAB SPRING CONTEXT

Sujata Ashwarya and Mohmad Saleem Sheikh

The Arab Uprisings caused socio-political turmoil in the West Asian region, allowing the Islamic Resistance Movement, also known as Hezbollah, to assert its regional presence. Hezbollah, based in Lebanon, is notorious for its terrorism and militancy, which have resulted in deaths and widespread violence. Hezbollah, Israel's sworn enemy, has a history of kidnapping Westerners in Lebanon in the 1980s and early 1990s, as well as fighting the Israeli army until it withdrew its forces in 2000. The United States, Israel, Canada, Australia, the Netherlands, the United Kingdom, and the EU and other Western countries have designated Hezbollah as a terrorist organisation. Hezbollah's position in Lebanon's society and politics has shifted dramatically over the last three and a half decades, as its ideology evolved from opposition to the Lebanese state in the 1980s to gradual integration into the political system today. Hezbollah has been able to carve out a political space for itself in Lebanon since 1990, when the Ta'if Agreement or National Reconciliation Accord ended the civil war and attempted to establish the principle of "mutual coexistence" among Lebanon's various sects.

Hezbollah's regional reputation is largely based on its resistance to Israel. Following the 2006 war with Israel, its prominence grew significantly, and it gained and it acquired internal as well as regional support from Iran and Syria. Iran has provided Hezbollah with a vast military arsenal to bolster its strategic deterrent in its conflict with Israel. However, Hezbollah's significance increased exponentially during the Syrian civil war, when its support for President Bashar al-Assad enabled him to avoid the fate of former Tunisian, Egyptian, and Yemeni presidents whose regimes collapsed following the Arab Spring uprisings.

Hezbollah initially celebrated the emergence of popular uprisings against the US and Western-aligned rulers. While Egyptian and Tunisian protesters called for the overthrow of authoritarian leaders, Hezbollah's al-Manar television channel was at the forefront of broadcasting images and reports in their support. Hezbollah has had a long-running feud with Egypt over Mubarak's alleged collaboration with Israel in containing Hamas. Muammar el-Qaddafi, the Libyan dictator suspected of ordering the assassination of Lebanese Shiite leader Imam Musa Sadr in 1978, was a particular target of Hezbollah's scorn. Hezbollah believed that as these dictators fell, the "resistance axis" against the West and Israel would be strengthened. It is unsurprising that al-Manar television, which used to receive substantial funding from Tunisia's Ben Ali regime, demanded an additional sum to boost Ben Ali's profile during the uprising, implying its disdain for the dictator.[1] This stance stemmed from Hezbollah's mistaken belief that the uprisings were fundamentally anti-Western. However, it quickly became clear that people desired good governance, freedom, democracy and social justice and were unmoved by Hezbollah's and its mentor Iran's anti-Western and anti-Israeli rhetoric.

When Syrians revolted against Syrian president Bashar al-Assad, the dynamics of Hezbollah's position changed dramatically. Hezbollah's feared that if Assad's regime fell, it would lose its ability to easily and quickly obtain arms from Iran, allowing Israel to launch another lethal offensive against it. As one of the few media outlets permitted inside Syria to cover the country's uprising, al-Manar framed events differently here, portraying the revolt as the work of a few troublemakers and coaxing people to speak in favour of the regime, while also alleging that Israel and US agents were attempting to incite violence.[2] Hezbollah eventually became deeply involved in the Syrian civil war on Assad's side, against the Sunni rebels backed by the Arab coalition led by Saudi Arabia, and faced Israeli bombings targeting its weapons caches.

The Syrian uprising, and Hezbollah's participation in it, marked a watershed moment in the organization's evolution as a regional force. The party portrayed itself as a protector of minorities, particularly Christians, while fighting alongside Syria's Alawi regime and providing logistical support to Yemeni Houthi militias, projecting its domestic agenda of reconciliation with other confessional groups onto the region. Thus, it appeared to veer between raison de la nation (pan-Islamism) and raison d'état (Lebanese national identity). Alternating between militancy and integration, with the former demonstrating the organization's hawkish stance in the aftermath of the Arab Uprisings. The latter demonstrates its dovish domestic face by virtue of being a constituent of the Lebanese state, from which it derives legitimacy.

The article analyses Hezbollah's rise and the growing power in the West Asian and North African (WANA) region following the Arab Spring. As the new 'Middle East' emerges, Hezbollah redefined its position and stake domestically and transformed from a moderate player to an active influencer in the regional context. The piece further argues that the geostrategic necessity trespassed the ideological commitment of fighting against "oppressor" while convincing Hezbollah to bandwagon behind the regional allies in averting any threat to the 'resistance axis.' Furthermore, the initial praise to the revolutions in Tunisia and Egypt proved to be transitory, and Hezbollah fell to the narrow sectarian narratives as the existential threat loomed over it and the resistance block.

HEZBOLLAH IN SYRIA

The Arab Spring protests in Syria in March 2011, as well as their brutal repression, sparked a horrific civil war that posed a threat to the Assad regime. Hezbollah jumped into the fray to support Assad's fight against Sunni-majority rebels and protesters, preventing his regime from collapsing. The initial Lebanese response to civil war came in the form of the 2012 Baabda declaration, which discouraged any kind of direct intervention and instead emphasised Lebanon's higher national interest, namely national unity.[3] However, Hezbollah distanced itself from the declaration by citing the survival of the Assad regime as a "strategic necessity," while injecting trainees and fighters into Syrian territory. The consequences of the involvement arose in the form of disagreements between political parties over Hezbollah's move, which resulted in the resignation of the cabinet in 2013 and a months-long political stalemate.[4]

Hezbollah's involvement jeopardised not only the delicate socio-political balance of Lebanon, but also its security. In response to Hezbollah's 2013 acknowledgement of its formal military involvement in Syria, Abu Muhammad al Jawlani, the leader of Syrian Sunni group, Al Nusra Front, a Salafist jihadist organization fighting against Syrian government forces in the Syrian Civil War, declared that "Hezbollah's actions will not go unpunished."[5] Several bombings and attacks have occurred inside Lebanon since then, primarily targeting Shia-populated areas and Hezbollah's operating sites.[6] As the Islamic State advanced from Iraq into Syria in 2015, it increasingly clashed with Hezbollah, bombing several Shia neighbourhoods in the country, including Beirut.[7] The attacks continued throughout 2016 and 2017, pitting Lebanese security forces against militia groups in border areas, particularly in Arsal, a town situated in the northeast of Beirut.[8]

While ensuring the Assad regime's survival, Hezbollah's power and influence grew in Syria and gradually spread to Yemen. So far, Hezbollah's role has been to balance the alliance against Israel, the US and other regional powers. However, its fight against the entrenchment and expansionism of jihadi groups in the region, while defending Shia communities, began with the uprisings and continues to this day in war-torn Syria, Yemen and Iraq. To avoid appearing antagonistic to its Sunni coreligionists, Hezbollah leader Hasan Nasrallah continued to justify his support for the al-Assad regime by blaming it on Israel. The group framed its role in Syria by claiming that the Syrian regime has always provided assistance in its fight against Israel. By doing so, Hezbollah drew a parallel between Sunni Jihadi groups, most notably the IS, Israel and the United States, and lumped them all together. Indeed Nasrullah commented that, "should Syria fall into the hands of the Americans, the Israelis, the takfiri groups and America's representatives in the region which call themselves regional states, the resistance will be besieged, and Israel would re-enter Lebanon."[9]

The fact that Syria has functioned as a transit site for Iranian weapons shipments to Heizbullah should not be obscured by off-track statements from its leaders. A regime change would imply the cessation of weapon supplies and restrictions on movement of its fighters throughout the region. One of the primary concerns prior to Hezbollah was that if the Assad regime were to be replaced by a Sunni-dominated regime, Saudi Arabia, the US and Israel would gain the upper hand, posing an existential threat. In 2018, Hassan Nasrallah stated that even if "the whole world comes together to force us to leave Syria, they will not be able to evict us," and that Hezbollah would leave Syria only "when the Syrian authorities demand it."[10]

Tehran has prioritised Hezbollah's Syria command, which has not only propped up Bashar al-Assad but also kept the Saudi-led coalition intervening in Syria on the side of Sunni jihadist groups at bay. In doing so, it was able to maintain supply lines and communication from Tehran to Beirut via Damascus. Hezbollah's involvement in Syria to defend Alawi Bashar al-Assad's Shia regime against Sunni claimants to power has fueled sectarian tensions in the region along confessional lines.

Since 2013, Hezbollah's direct involvement in Syria has changed the course of the civil war, and the experience has changed Hezbollah as well. The civil war put the fighting skills into practise and exposed its cadres to urban warfare utilising newly acquired sophisticated weaponry. Aside from improving its combat capabilities, the group's intervention has been successful in removing rebel groups from key strategic points, allowing the Assad regime to reclaim control of territories lost to jihadi groups. Above all, it enabled Iran to make significant inroads into Syria.

Despite Hezbollah's efforts to carefully craft its Syria policy in order to avoid a resurgence of domestic strife, the Syrian crises and Hezbollah's support for the Assad regime have had political ramifications on Lebanon's delicately balanced sectarian-confessional political arrangement. In addition to straining the economy, the massive refugee influx of approximately 1.5 million people exacerbated political instability, leading to a political impasse and instilling existential fear among Christians, Shias and Druze communities. Aside from the polarisation of support for and opposition to the Syrian revolution, clashes occurred between Syrian rebel militias and Lebanese security forces and Hezbollah. Furthermore, the group's intervention in Syria exacerbated sectarianism not only in Lebanon but also throughout the region.

Domestically, it has been accused of undermining Lebanese social unity and has been compared to Israel's occupation of Lebanon. In the regional context, Hezbollah contributes to the sectarian narrative by accusing Saudi Arabia and its allies of assisting rebel Sunni militants in Syria and thereby fueling sectarianism in the region.

HEZBOLLAH IN IRAQ

Iraq was ruled by Saddam Hussain's Ba'athist regime until 2003, when he was deposed by US intervention. Various groups and sectarian militias arose as a result of the long US intervention attempting to change the state structure. With the election of a new government, sectarianism unfolded in Iraq with all the parties functioning on a sectarian basis. Iraq's sectarianism paved the way for external actors to exploit sectarianism in the country to advance their interests.

Hezbollah is one such sectarian actor that has infiltrated the country. Its presence in Iraq dates back to the 1980s, as Al-Muhandis suggests, during Iran's conflict with Iraq, when Hezbollah's recognized commanders Imad Mughniyeh and Mustafa Badreddine trained Shias in Iraq to fight Saddam Hussain.[11] In the post-2003 period, Iran has asserted influence in Iraq through Hezbollah.

When Iraq's military disintegrated in the summer of 2014, former Prime Minister Nouri al-Maliki formed the Al-Hashid al-Sa'bi, or Popular Mobilization Front (PMF), to combat the Islamic State. Hezbollah's prominent role in Iraq in training the PMF's local Shi'a militias, which number around 100,000 volunteers, makes it a formidable force to be reckoned with. Hezbollah, helming the trained Shia forces, was successful in defeating Islamic State terrorists in Tikrit, Ramadi and Amerli, fighting at the front lines. The Shia militia Front is led by Abu Mahdi al-Muhandis, indicating that Iran has a strong presence in Iraq, ably aided by Hezbollah. Al-Muhandis, a former advisor to the late commander Qassem Soleimani, is the commander of the Quds Force, the Iranian Revolutionary Guards Corps' external operations wing.

Protest movements in Iraq that began in 2019 have crossed sectarian lines, providing a glimmer of hope that both countries are moving toward transcending sectarian divides and eroding the control of traditional confession-based leaderships. These demonstrations have also called into question the intentions of Hezbollah and Iran, where a sizable Shia population has sparked a wave of protests.[12] If Iraq succeeds in deposing the traditional sectarian leadership, Iran will be the most visible external loser. With the help of Hezbollah, Tehran has invested heavily in the formation of several Shia militias in Iraq that support Iranian hegemonic goals. If Hezbollah loses credibility among its Shia constituents in Iraq, Iran will lose a significant amount of influence in the country, which they both regard as critical for confronting Israel and supporting the Assad regime in Syria.[13] The status quoist Shia parties that support the Iraqi government see the protesters as an existential threat to their patronage system and their alliance with Iran.

Following the deaths of Qasim Soleimani and Abu Mahdi al-Muhandis in an airstrike by the US in January 3, 2020, Hezbollah's role in Iraq has grown. The task of Hezbollah is to unite Shia militias and demonstrate Shia unity against American forces in Iraq. Hezbollah stepped into the shoes of Soleimani, whose death left a leadership void. For Iran, the unity of these militias is critical to maintaining control over an unstable Iraq, where the government and its militia allies face public backlash over increasing Iranian influence. Sheikh Mohammad al-Kawtharani, the Hezbollah representative in Iraq, has been tasked with guiding and monitoring the operations of Shia militia groups backed by Tehran.[14] Hezbollah's involvement represents a significant expansion of its regional role. Hezbollah's primary objective is to consolidate support for the Iraqi government in the face of protestors demanding a systemic overhaul, economic transformation, anti-corruption measures and an end to Iranian influence.

HEZBOLLAH IN YEMEN

Hezbollah's presence in Yemen is more likely to be motivated by sectarianism, allowing Iran to consolidate its influence in the country. The connection between Hezbollah and the Houthi movement, officially known as Ansar Allah and colloquially referred to as the Houthis, is evident in the words of their leaders. According to a Houthi official in Beirut, "relations with the Lebanese movement span over a decade," while a Hezbollah commander stated that "Houthis and Hezbollah trained together for the past ten years in Iran, then in Lebanon and Yemen."[15] Hezbollah also assisted in the establishment of the Houthi Al-Masira television channel, which is based in Beirut's southern suburbs.

Hezbollah has influenced the Houthis in various ways. The use of militant *anashid* (jihadist anthems) in the group's videos further portrays it as more aligned with Hezbollah's models of'resistance.[16] Images of Houthi fighters with the sun in the background draw further parallels to other Shiite jihadist groups, giving the Houthis spiritual legitimacy in the Shia world.[17] The current Houthi leader, Abdul-Malik al-Houthi, is known for delivering speeches in the style of Hezbollah's Nasrallah.[18] These facts demonstrate Hezbollah's proximity to the Houthis and stranglehold in Yemen.

Furthermore, the Houthi takeover of Yemen's capital, Sana'a, in the aftermath of protests in September 2014 increased Shia Iran's influence in the country. Houthi leaders also named a prominent Iranian-educated religious figure with close ties to Tehran as Sana'a's top Islamic authority.[19] The 2015 nuclear deal empowered Iran to use Hezbollah to expand its sphere of influence and change the situation in Yemen by making the war costly for the Saudi Arabia and its allies, both in terms of material and human casualties. Hezbollah has been arming the Houthi Anasar Allah movement through logistical support and training, as well as coordinating the flow of Iranian weapons, particularly tactical missiles, across Yemen's long porous coastline.

Hezbollah's role enabled the Houthi militias to absorb the Saudi-led massive bombardment and superior air power. Saudi Arabia led a coalition of nine countries from the region intervening in Yemen beginning March 2015, in response to President Abdrabbuh Mansur Hadi's request for military assistance following his ouster by the Houthi movement. In some areas, Houthi forces also took the initiative to target Saudi Arabia's ground forces, inflicting severe casualties on them. Iran aided the Houtis through the Hezbollah. According to reports, the slain commander of the Islamic Revolutionary Guard Corps, Qassim Suleimani, visited Yemen in March 2015, indicating Iran's 'interests' in the war-torn country. This was followed by a high-level meeting between Hezbollah leader Hassan Nasrallah and Iran's First Deputy Foreign Minister Morteza Sarmadi to discuss the Yemen crisis in April 2015.

While the Iranian-backed Hezbollah has previously criticised Saudi Arabia, the tone was milder, owing to the Kingdom's popularity among Lebanese Sunnis and the Saudi King's custody of Islam's two holiest shrines in Mecca and Medina. This self-censorship is becoming less visible as Hezbollah leaders 'condemn' and 'reject' Saudi-led intervention in Yemen. Yemen is the first news item on Hezbollah's al-Manar TV since the Saudi Operation began. The logistics expertise of Hezbollah has been transferred to the Yemini militias in order to make the war costly, protracted, and a war of attrition.

In November 2017, Saudi Arabia accused Hezbollah of launching a ballistic missile from Yemen towards its international airport in Riyadh. Iran denied the Saudi charge and downplayed its ties to the Houthis. Nonetheless, the denial contradicts mounting evidence of an important Hezbollah and Iranian role in assisting the Houthi movement. In Yemen, "Hezbollah has become a direct partner in strengthening the military capabilities of the Houthi Ansar Allah, who consider Hezbollah to be their truthful ally," boasted Ibrahim al-Amin, the editor of *Al-Akhbar* newspaper, the unofficial mouthpiece of Hezbollah, in July 2017.[20]

Since then, there have been a number of attacks on Saudi targets claimed or blamed on the Houthis, including airports, air bases and energy infrastructure. Nasrullah, Hezbollah's leader, has chastised Saudi Arabia for its harsh war on the Houthis in Yemen, and has issued a clear call to end the conflict or face the consequences. While referring to September 2019 drone-and-cruise-missile attacks that knocked out more than half of Saudi Arabia's daily crude oil production, Nasrullah stated, "One strike knocked out half the oil production, and another strike, you can imagine what it will do."[21] Nasrallah linked the Houthis' struggle to the narrative of 'axis resistance,' saying, "This attack shows the strength of the axis of resistance."[22]

THE SECTARIAN FACTOR

One of the most notable aspects of Hezbollah's evolution as a political force has been its early condemnation of sectarianism in the domestic political sphere. However, its position gradually shifted following the Ti'af Accord. Hezbollah's active participation in the political process since 1992 has led to its acceptance of the sectarian political system of Lebanon.

Hezbollah stated in its 2009 manifesto that the sectarian system would continue to be "the fundamental basis for governance in Lebanon because it is the actual quintessence of the spirit of the constitution and the core of the Charter of coexistence."[23]

Despite this domestic opening, Hezbollah's regional policy is still dominated by sectarian affiliations. In the aftermath of the Arab Spring, Syria and Yemen fell to narrow sectarian politics. Hezbollah's long-term political goal since its inception has been the protection of Shia Islam, spread revolutionary activism, strengthen the resistance axis and expand its influence in the region.[24] In Syria, Hezbollah's pro-regime stance exacerbated sectarianism. It was chastised for its status quo stance, and was blamed for bringing instability home and jeopardising Lebanon's internal security. Its actions amounted to ignoring popular calls for change and freedom under the guise of fighting takfirists and jihadis.

Hezbollah's appeal to its Shia constituency allowed it to justify its actions and military operations across the region. Thus, Shiite allegiance has supplanted the discourse of existential threats used by the Sunni alliances, Israel and expansionist Sunni Islamist groups. Following the Arab Spring, Hezbollah's strategic focus has shifted from confrontation with Israel to regional intervention. Despite the fact that Hezbollah sent a military contingent to train Iraqi Shias during the Iraq War, where it worked under Iranian command, the party's commitment to Syria demonstrates the party's pan-Shia focus. Hezbollah's Yemen operation demonstrates its commitment to winning the Shia constituency in the Gulf. Hezbollah operations and support for Shia groups in the Gulf region continue outside of Yemen.

Saudi Arabia and its allies have long accused Hezbollah of inciting Shia minorities within their borders. However, in the aftermath of the Arab Spring, the rhetoric of accusations has taken on a more aggressive tone, with Hezbollah, through pan-Shiaism, openly challenging Saudi Arabia not only in the domestic sphere but also in the wider region. During the 2006 Lebanon war, Hezbollah established a reputation and gained widespread support throughout the region. It stated that this is a victory for all Muslims and that Hezbollah will continue to fight for the interests of the Muslim Ummah.[25] However, Hezbollah's post-Arab Spring role reduced it to nothing more than a 'sectarian entrepreneur' willing to engage in divisive politics.

Hezbollah's gains

So far, Hezbollah's involvement in Syria appears to have achieved its immediate goal. The war experience has bolstered Hezbollah's military capabilities and potential, which could be used in the event of another conflict with Israel or another adversary. Furthermore, the Syrian conflict provided an opportunity for the organisation to broaden its influence and footprints not only in the region but also globally. The Syrian conflict improved not only its urban warfare capabilities, but also its battlefield coordination while fighting alongside Iranian and Russian forces.

Furthermore, the battlefield has increased collaboration with less sophisticated irregular Iranian proxy militias from Iraq, Afghanistan and other countries. Aside from that, Hezbollah has gained access to a variety of weapons, ranging from short-range ballistic missiles to rockets. Hezbollah could amass a range of weapons systems in Syria, such as the Fateh-110/M-600 short-range ballistic missile, Shahab-1 and Shahab-2 short-range ballistic missiles, Toophan anti-tank guided missiles, Kornet man-portable anti-tank guided missiles, M113 armoured personnel carriers, T-72 main battle tanks, Karrar unmanned combat aerial vehicles, and Katyusha rockets.[26]

Despite significant losses of skilled fighters in the fight against the Free Syrian Army, the Islamic State and other militias, Hezbollah has recruited a large number of new members from across the region. Hezbollah's victories over ISIL, Al Qaeda and Jabhat al-Nusra have established it as the 'protector' of Lebanon's borders against terrorist attacks emanating from Syrian territory. In terms of security, Hezbollah's presence in Syria has alarmed Israel, as its proximity to the Jewish state's northern border confers strategic and military leverage on the group. Saudi Arabia is also concerned about Hezbollah's activities in neighbouring Yemen, Syria and Iraq, which aid Iran's regional ambitions for pre-eminence and hegemony. Simultaneously, with Shia minorities present in all Gulf states, Hezbollah's military-political capabilities are equally concerning.

Hezbollah's rise from a militant group to a political stakeholder in Lebanon's domestic politics, and then to regional player status, has been phenomenal over the last 30 years. Despite being labelled a terrorist organisation by the GCC, the Arab League, the OIC, and other international players, Hezbollah justifies its operations as a 'divine duty' to fight against 'aggressors' and their regional or extra-regional patrons.

It is also speculated that Hezbollah aspires to play a more significant role in the Syrian settlement process as a stakeholder, which would entitle it to the status of a regional player. The agreement would strengthen Hezbollah's role in Syria's future restoration. Aside from restoring political authoritarianism, a Syrian settlement would allow Hezbollah to maintain its domestic political and military influence, as well as its strategic ascendency in the border region. If the war ends and reconstruction begins, Hezbollah hopes to be useful in training and restructuring Syrian military forces. Furthermore, Hezbollah seeks to maintain military gains and dominance over extremist groups, so that it is "able to maintain a share in any peace settlement in Syria."[27] As a result, Hezbollah's participation in sectarian conflicts beyond Lebanon's borders is a strategic and politically vested struggle for sectarian survival and the resistance alliance, including in the domestic sphere alongside allies.

HEZBOLLAH AND THE REGIONAL SECURITY COMPLEXITIES: POST-2011

The turmoil caused by the Arab Spring resulted in the emergence of several armed entities, further complicating the regional security order. Hezbollah, a key player in regional security, arose from regional structural changes at the end of the 1970s and early 1980s, most notably the Iranian revolution (1979) and Israel's invasion of Lebanon (1982).[28] Following the 2011 destabilisation, Hezbollah faced both challenges and opportunities to expand its regional interests. Apart from spreading its 'Islamization' rhetoric in Arab countries and instilling revolutionary activism in the oppressed, Hezbollah aided in the propagation of sectarianism and security complexities.

Hezbollah's involvement in Syria, as well as its long-standing political and military support for Yemen's Houthi rebels, exemplify its strategic intent and security concerns. The survival of the resistance alliance (Iran-Syria-Hezbollah) is a strategic and survival necessity for Hezbollah, and its presence in Yemen and Iraq demonstrates a policy shift away from "Lebanese National Resistance" and towards regional influence. Hezbollah's interventionist approach along sectarian lines has signalled the strengthening of the Shia axis and shifted the balance in favour of its regional patron, Iran, in the post-2011 regional order. As a result, the region has witnessed the strengthening and proliferation of non-state actors, which has weakened the state.[29]

Hezbollah has emerged as a prominent sub-state actor, fueling sectarianism, assisting in the maintenance of authoritarianism, and encouraging and training transnational sectarian militias in troubled and weak states. The determination of Hezbollah to remain armed, antagonistic and committed to expansionism jeopardises regional security. Regular acquisition of weapons and missile systems, which Hezbollah transports to war-torn states, has emerged as one of the region's most pressing concerns. As previously reported, it has conducted many missile attacks on neighbouring nations such as Saudi Arabia and Israel from military sites in Yemen and Syria.

PROTESTS IN IRAQ AND LEBANON: HEZBOLLAH'S INVOLVEMENT

Iraq and Lebanon have been the sites of renewed political uprisings in the region dubbed 'Arab Spring 2.0' since 2019. The lack of economic reforms, as well as the continuation of corruption, have increased public distrust in the respective governments. The fact that Shia populations are protesting against the government, which is putting pressure on Hezbollah and Iran, is a recurring theme in these demonstrations. The growing protests indicate that Iran's influence in these countries may be fading. Tehran accuses Western and regional foes of fomenting unrest in order to create a schism between Shia power centres, namely Tehran and Bagdad.[30]

Iraqi public opinion appears to be shifting in favour of Iran and its clients. Iran and its allies were heralded as saviours and protectors during the fight against ISIS. Nonetheless, a common refrain among Iraqi protesters has been that the influence of Iran and its allies, specifically Hezbollah and Shia militias, is detrimental to Iraqi interests and should be limited. In Lebanon, recent protests have put Hezbollah on the defensive for its pro-government stance, so much so that "in terms of the public perception of its political role, Hezbollah is now relegated to the same rubbish heap as the other discredited Lebanese parties."[31]

CONCLUSIONS

Hezbollah has grown into a powerful military and political force in the region as a result of Iran's support and interventions in domestic conflicts in Syria, Yemen and Iraq. The militant ideology and sectarian outlook of the group have spread beyond Lebanon into the regional arena. Its growing military capabilities are causing concern in the region among Sunni regimes seeking to limit Iran's influence. Protests in Iraq and Lebanon have put to the test its professed ideological commitment to supporting the 'oppressed.' Its support for the Iraqi and Lebanese governments against the protestors reveals its weak ideology and reinforces the notion that it is an opportunistic actor pursuing its own geostrategic and political goals.

NOTES

1. "Lebanon: Did Tunisia's tyrant buy off Hezbollah TV?" *Los Angeles Times*, May 24, 2011, at https://latimesblogs.latimes.com/babylonbeyond/2011/05/lebanon-did-tunisian-tyrant-give-hezbollah-one-hundred-thousand-dollars-to-clean-up-his-image.html (accessed on December 9, 2021).
2. Margaret Besheer, "Hezbollah Supportive of Egyptian, Tunisian Uprisings But Not Syria's," *Voice of America (VOA)*, May 19, 2011, at https://www.voanews.com/a/hezbollah-supportive-of-egyptian-tunisian-uprisings-but-not-syrias-122348949/172965.html (accessed on December 9, 2021).
3. "Baabda Declaration," *Voltaire Network* (Beirut, Lebanon), June 11, 2012.
4. Ibid., p. 7.
5. Carla E. Humud, Lebanon, *Congressional Research Service*, October 5, 2018, p. 8.
6. "Jabhat al-Nusra claims deadly Lebanon bombing," *Al Jazeera*, February 1, 2014.
7. "ISIS claims responsibility for blasts that killed dozens in Beirut," *New York Times*, November 12, 2015.
8 Lebanon refugee camps hit by five suicide bombers, *BBC*, June 30, 2017, at https://www.bbc.com/news/world-middle-east-40454323 (accessed on April 25, 2021).
9. Seth G. Jones and Maxwell B. Markusen. "The Escalating Conflict with Hezbollah in Syria." *Center for Strategic & International Studies*, 2018.
10. Ibid.
11. David Daoud, "PMF deputy commander Muhandis details Hezbollah ops in Iraq." *FDD's Long War Journal* (2017), at http://www.longwarjournal.org/archives/2017/01/

pmf-deputy-commander-muhandis-details-hezbollah-ops-in-iraq.php (accessed on April 27, 2021).

12. Mohammed Ayoob. "Is the Middle East entering a post-sectarian phase?", *The Strategist*, November 7, 2019, at https://www.aspistrategist.org.au/is-the-middle-east-entering-a-post-sectarian-phase/ (accessed on May 2, 2021).
13. Ibid.
14. Tehran-backed Hezbollah steps in to guide Iraqi militias in Soleimani's wake, *Reuters*, FEBRUARY 11, 2020, at https://www.reuters.com/article/us-iran-iraq-hezbollah-insight/tehran-backed-hezbollah-steps-in-to-guide-iraqi-militias-in-soleimanis-wake-idUSKBN20520Y (accessed on May 7, 2021).
15. Yaakov Lappin, "Hezbollah's Firm Grip on Lebanon Fuels Region's Sectarian Strife," BESA Center Perspectives Paper No. 663, November 29, 2017, at https://besacenter.org/hezbollah-lebanon-sectarian-strife/ (accessed on December 12, 2021); "Lebanon's Hizbollah and Yemen's Houthis open up on links," *Financial Times*, May 8, 2015, at https://www.ft.com/content/e1e6f750-f49b-11e4-9a58-00144feab7de (accessed on March 1, 2022).
16. Barak A. Salmoni, Bryce Loidolt and Madeleine Wells, Regime and Periphery in Northern Yemen Book Subtitle: The Huthi Phenomenon Book, Santa Monica, CA: RAND Corporation, 2010, p. 225.
17. Ely Karmon, "Yemen's Houthis: New Members of Iran's Anti-Israeli/Anti-American Axis," *Jerusalem Post*, May 18, 2017, https://www.jpost.com/Opinion/Yemens-Houthis-New-members-of-Irans-anti-Israelianti-American-axis-494170 (accessed on March 21, 2022).
18. Ibid.
19. Lappin, n. 15.
20. Ibid.
21. "Hezbollah tells Saudi Arabia to stop Yemen war," ABC News, September 20, 2019, at https://abcnews.go.com/International/wireStory/hezbollah-tells-saudi-arabia-stop-yemen-war-65752067 (accessed on January 4, 2022).
22. "Hezbollah tells Saudi Arabia to stop Yemen war," *AP NEWS* September 20, 2019, at https://apnews.com/32ba67f739954cdf957bae3d109e2205 (accessed on March 3, 2022).
23. Joseph Daher, "Hezbollah, the Lebanese Sectarian State, and Sectarianism," *Middle East Institute* (2017).
24. Seth G.Jones, and Maxwell B. Markusen. The Escalating Conflict with Hezbollah in Syria. *Center for Strategic & International Studies*, 2018, at https://www.csis.org/analysis/escalating-conflict-hezbollah-syria (accessed on September 11, 2021).
25. Faiza Saleh Ambah, "Arab Leaders Unlike Much of Public: Uneasy About Hezbollah," *Washing Post*, July 24, 2006.
26. CSIS Transnational Threats Project estimates; David Daoud, "Hezbollah Is Preparing Syria as Second Battlefield against Israel," *Long War Journal*, March 16, 2017, at https://www.longwarjournal.org/archives/2017/03/hezbollah-is-preparing-syria-as-second-battlefield-against-israel.php (accessed on September 30, 2021).

27. Chafic Choucair, "Hezbollah in Syria: Gains, Losses and Changes," *Al Jazeera Center for Studies*, 2016., p. 7.
28. Kota Suechika, Strategies, Dynamics, and Outcomes of Hezbollah's Military Intervention in the Syrian Conflict, *Asian Journal of Middle Eastern and Islamic Studies*, 12:1, (2018): 90, DOI: 10.1080/25765949.2018.1436131.
29. Raffaella A. Del Sarto, Helle Malmvig and Eduard Soler i Lecha. "Interregnum: the regional order in the Middle East and North Africa after 2011." *MENARA Final Reports* 1 (2019): 12.
30. Sina Azodi and Giorgio Cafiero, Why Iran wants the Lebanon and Iraq uprisings to fade, *The Atlantic Council*, 7, November 2019, at https://atlanticcouncil.org/blogs/iransource/why-iran-wants-the-lebanon-and-iraq-uprisings-to-fade/ (accessed on March 9, 2022).
31. Jeffrey Feltman, What's next for Lebanon? Examining the implications of current protests, *Brookings*, November 19, 2019, at https://www.brookings.edu/testimonies/whats-next-for-lebanon-examining-the-implications-of-current-protests/ (accessed on September 30, 2021).

12

ARAB SPRING AND THE FRENCH REVOLUTION

THE LONGUE DURÉE OF TRANSFORMATION

Adil Rasheed

The season of spring does not last long in the arid, tropical climate of West Asia. It soon gives way to soaring temperatures and violent sandstorms. A similar unpleasant fate awaited the popular political uprising commonly known as the 'Arab Spring', which spread almost simultaneously across many countries of the region over a decade ago. Even among the more educated detractors of this unrest, the coinage "Arab Spring" was thus never a misnomer, as it refers to the Prague Spring—a short-lived democratization process in former Czechoslovakia under the leadership of Alexander Dubcek in 1968 that was soon crushed by the Soviet forces.[1]

Likewise, the crackdown against this widespread and mostly non-violent, civil uprising by the several entrenched authoritarian states in West Asia was swift and brutal, which in turn whipped up a perfect storm of self-righteous rage and violent religious extremism, leaving in its train a bevy of weak, failing, and failed states. Thus, the simple aspirations of the early protestors—who desired relief from poverty, unemployment as well as greater freedom and political rights—withered away in the heat of sectarian conflict and civil wars.

The banner of popular revolt—which once emblazoned individual liberty, human rights and democratic reform—was replaced by firebrand jihadist slogans, causing widespread death and havoc and the wholesale annihilation of state institutions and even ancient, pre-Islamic heritage.[2]

However, the disappointment caused by the Arab Spring in immediately delivering the desired outcomes for its early supporters does not imply that the revolutionary process for a democratic transformation has already run its course. The transition from authoritarian dispensation to a more representative polity is often an overlong, tortuous and complex process, riddled with many setbacks and reversals. For instance, Europe's most defining democratic uprising, namely the French Revolution, set off a chain of events in the pursuit of its political ideals that are considered fundamental to liberal democracy, which only fructified in the Constitution of 1875, almost a century after the Fall of Bastille in 1789.[3]

ANALOGOUS POLITICAL CONVULSIONS

There is no denying that any kind of analogy of different revolutions would never be entirely congruent, but there are striking similarities between the outbreak of popular discontent in the French Revolution that led to the removal of King Louis XVI and the successful overthrow by Arab masses of four Arab potentates—Zine Al Abidine Ben Ali of Tunisia, Hosni Mubarak of Egypt, Muammar Gaddafi of Libya and Ali Abdullah Saleh of Yemen. The fact that the Arab Spring did not produce liberal democratic governments in the immediate aftermath of these popular revolts sweeping across the region should not be considered a failed attempt as a revolution on its tenth anniversary, because it may be "too early to tell," as Zhou Enlai once purportedly claimed.[4]

The series of anti-government protests, uprisings, and armed rebellions that spread across much of the Arab world in the early 2010s, not unlike the French Revolution, came in response to the entrenched nepotism, rampant corruption and economic stagnation in several countries of the region. A major slogan of the demonstrators across the Arab world was '*ash-shab yurid isqat an-nizam*' ("the people want to bring down the regime"), which seems in sync with the revolutionary refrain of '*Liberté, égalité, fraternité*' (Liberty, Equality, Fraternity) against the feudal and monarchical order of France in the late eighteenth century.[5]

Despite their mass appeal, both movements were too spontaneous to sustain themselves for long because it is quite difficult for leaderless revolts to stage a systemic socio-political overhaul within a few years. Just as it took several decades for the French Revolution to bring about a full social and political transformation to realise its ideological goals, forces of change unleashed by the Arab Spring continue to operate at subterranean levels and make surface manifestations with visible changes only sporadically.

Notwithstanding Islamist co-option, old guard crackdowns and counter-revolutions, the rise in collective consciousness has since alerted even the kingdoms and monarchies of West Asia to be more responsive towards the aspirations of their populations in order to survive an increasingly integrated and globalised order of the future.

Revolutions are often followed by opposing forces staging their counter-revolutions. In fact, Crane Brinton's celebrated 1965 book titled *The Anatomy of Revolution*,[6] claims major revolutions often pass through four phases before successfully achieving their goals, namely the initial phase of moderate leadership; the reign of terror and virtue (or the rule of radical and violent extremists); Thermidorian reaction (or counter-revolution by the opponents); and the end of the revolution (which brings about the final adoption of revolutionary ideals). Therefore, one needs to take a longue durée approach while studying the still unfolding impact of a revolution in bringing about lasting socio-political change in its region.

There are many interesting parallels in the French Revolution and Arab Spring that conform to the stages suggested by Brinton. After the ouster of Louis XVI, France was ruled by the moderate group of Girondins. Similarly, Egypt's Supreme Council of Armed Forces (SCAF)—the statutory body of senior Egyptian military officers—followed the demands of protestors and deposed Hosni Mubarak from power on February 11, 2011, paving the way for elections.

The actions of SCAF at this point can be equated to the "Rule of the Moderates." It carried out the transition until the general elections of 2011 and 2012 were conducted without much political upheaval. The same phase was evident in Tunisia when the Army asked the prime minister Mohamad Ghannouchi to form a caretaker government.

The Islamist governments under the Ennahda party in Tunisia and President Mohamad Morsi in Egypt, who won elections on the ticket of the

Muslim Brotherhood-backed Freedom and Justice Party (FJP), ushered in the Islamist 'Reign of Purity', which was not accepted by the liberals and minority communities in Egypt.

THE REIGN OF TERROR

The French Revolution also saw a phase of terrorism under the reign of the Jacobin politician Maximillien Robespierre, who took power on August 10, 1793, and installed a "Reign of Terror and Virtue," which has been mentioned by Brinton as the second phase of revolution. Under "The Incorruptible" Robespierre, every violator of revolutionary principles was supposed to be guillotined. Around 19,000 people were eventually executed. Alongside the "Reign of Terror," there was also the "Reign of Virtue." Members of the Jacobin presented themselves as highly religious and held ceremonies dedicated to the "Supreme Being." They repressed individuals who engaged in gambling, drunkenness, sexual promiscuity and even "ostentatious displays" of wealth. Robespierre's revolutionary forces waged a war against royalist forces in the Vendée, west-central France, a civil war which caused 2,00,000 deaths.

Not surprisingly, we find an even gruesome parallel in the violent extremism of the terror group like ISIS, which like Robespierre, installed a "Reign of Terror and Virtue" in Syria, Iraq, Libya, Yemen and other parts of the world. It conducted ethnic cleansing of Shiite, Christians and Yazidis as well as killed many of their Sunni adversaries by claiming them to be apostates.[7]

However, the "reign of terror" following the Arab Spring is in relative decline, following the decimation of territories held by ISIS and Al-Qaeda from much of West Asia in recent years. It seems the second phase of the prolonged revolutionary journey is gradually petering out, much like the first decade following the fall of Bastille,.

Statistics from the recently published Global Terrorism Index (2020) provide us with evidence on this major shift. Figures show that terrorism-related fatalities fell for the fifth consecutive year in 2019 to 13,826 deaths. This represents a 15 per cent decline from the prior year and a 59 per cent fall from 2014 till the end of 2019.[8] The Middle East and North Africa (MENA),

Russia and Eurasia, South America and South Asia regions all recorded falls in deaths from terrorism of at least 20 per cent. In fact, seven of the ten countries with the largest increase in terrorism were in sub-Saharan Africa and not West Asia. Although the Taliban remained the world's deadliest terrorist group in 2019, deaths attributed to the group declined by 18 per cent to 4,990, which some experts attribute to the role of peace talks in Afghanistan.

A decline in jihadist violence was also registered in Europe for three years until 2018, which may continue in spite of periodic spikes in terror attacks over political controversies like cartoon publications, etc. The still unconfirmed death of Al-Qaeda supremo Ayman Al-Zawahiri and the gunning down of Abu Muhammad al-Masri, Al-Qaeda's second-in-command in Iran, are recent examples accentuating the serious leadership crisis facing the global jihadist movement. However, the return of Taliban to power, infighting within its ranks, the growing strength of ISIS in Afghanistan, etc., may register a spike in terrorist incidents in the Af-Pak region, still the FATF's increasing economic squeeze on Pakistan could inhibit its support for proxy terrorist groups.

Thus, almost two decades after the 9/11 attacks, Al Qaeda and ISIS appear to stripped off their erstwhile resources or militants, to disrupt international peace and security in major way, in spite of the few surprises they might spring like the 2019 Easter bombings in Sri Lanka or a major lone-wolf attack in the West.

In fact, from September 2019 to August 2020, the United States and its allies have also successful in taking out some of the key henchmen of global jihadist groups. These include:[9]

- Abu Bakr Al Baghdadi, the self-styled caliph of ISIS, was killed by the US Special Operations Forces during a raid in Syria on October 26, 2019.
- Abdelmalek Droukdal, head of Al Qaeda in the Islamic Maghreb, was eliminated by French Special Forces in Mali on June 3, 2020.
- Abdullah Orakzai, the supposed founder of ISIS in Afghanistan, was arrested by Afghan intelligence officials on April 4, 2020.
- Khalid al Aruri, de facto leader of al Qaeda's Syrian affiliate Guardians of the Religion Organization, was killed by a US drone strike in Syria on June 14, 2020.[10]

- Earlier Qassim al Rimi, founder al Qaeda's Yemen affiliate was killed in a US airstrike in Al Bayda Governorate of Yemen on January 29, 2020.
- Again in November 2020, *The New York Times* reported the gunning down of Abu Muhammad al-Masri, Al-Qaeda's second-in-command, by two Israeli operatives in Tehran.
- Unconfirmed reports of Al-Qaeda supremo Ayman Al-Zawahiri's death from natural causes appeared in noted Saudi daily *Arab News* on November 20, 2020.

There is no denying that jihadist non-state groups remain a serious threat as they try to re-assert their global presence. The coming of Taliban to power in Afghanistan in August 2020, following the complete meltdown of the Ghani government and its military even before the US forces could withdraw its forces from that country, has revived fears that Islamist forces may feel encouraged in reviving their militancy around the world.[11]

However, there are some political observers who believe that it is possible that Taliban distances itself from global jihadist groups in future in order to gain international legitimacy for its government and much needed economic aid for the Afghan people, who expect the so-called Islamic emirate to provide them a good administration.

THE THERMIDORIAN PUSHBACK

One of Brinton's contemporaries to have studied the causes and course of revolutions was Pitirim Sorokin, known for his seminal work *Sociology of Revolutions* (1925).[12] According to him revolutions pass through two stages. In the first stage, there is a lot of pent-up energy of public discontent that expresses itself vehemently and often brings about the downfall of the existing leadership.

However, the general chaos and anarchy that follows sobers the masses, and public apathy and fatigue soon sets in. This sense of exhaustion soon allows the old guard or a new tyrant to re-establish its tyranny. This counter-revolution is accepted by the masses if they have been subjected to a lot of violence and instability during the initial stages of the revolution. The new tyrants come in the name of establishing a new order of security through their oppressive ways.

In line with Sorokin's second stage, Brinton also speaks about the coming of counter-revolutions by the old order or new tyrants who seek to avenge revolutionary wrongs and to re-establish the old oppressive order. Thus, we find the rise of Napoleon Bonaparte as a new totalitarian Emperor, a little over a decade after the French Revolution.

The return to power of the deposed regime, following the moderate and terror phase of the revolution was known as the Thermidorian Reaction, in the French Revolution, when a parliamentary revolt initiated on 9 Thermidor, year II (July 27, 1794), resulted in the fall of Maximilien Robespierre and the collapse of revolutionary fervour and the Reign of Terror in France. However, the new regime soon started its own "White Terror" and executed hundreds of Robespierre's sympathizers. Brinton naturally calls this phase of counter-revolution as the Thermidor stage of the revolution.

The same pattern finds its refrain in the Arab Spring uprisings. After about a year of Adly Mansour's interim-presidency and the Egyptian government's allegedly brutal crackdown (which included the 2013 Rabaa massacre) against the Muslim Brotherhood and other revolutionary activists, Field Marshall Abdel Fattah al-Sisi won the presidential elections with 96.1 per cent of the votes.

Another major Thermidor moment in the Arab Spring happened in Bahrain. On February 14, 2011, tens of thousands of people took to the streets and called for an elected government. However, the Sunni monarch of a predominantly Shi'ite country brought troops from the GCC countries, the army of the Peninsula Shield. The uprising was brutally crushed within weeks and the iconic Pearl Roundabout in Manama, which had become the hub of the movement was demolished.

The Thermidorian reaction also becomes evident in the Saudi-Qatar conflict, wherein Saudi Arabia resorted to taking tough action against Qatar because of the latter's alleged support for the forces of change unleashed during the Arab Spring. On June 5, 2017, Saudi Arabia, the United Arab Emirates, Bahrain and Egypt broke their diplomatic ties with Qatar and banned its airlines and ships from crossing their airspace and sea routes. A trade ban of Qatar soon followed. The above mentioned quartet of Arab states then rallied other Muslim states around the world to join in their campaign against the tiny Gulf emirate and soon Jordan, the Comoros, Djibouti, the Maldives, Mauritania and Senegal joined the coalition.

These countries charged Qatar with harbouring "wanted terrorists" (mainly Arab Spring Islamist as well as liberal activists)[13] and for providing them financial and logistical aid. The Saudi-led coalition then issued a sweeping 13-point ultimatum[14] to Qatar, which included demands as the closing of Al Jazeera television channel (for its alleged support of revolutionary ideology), reduced cooperation with Iran (whose Islamist brand of democracy seeks the removal of monarchies in the Gulf region), shutting down of revisionist Turkey's military base in Qatar and severing of ties with the Muslim Brotherhood. However, Qatar did not accept the ultimatum and managed to withstand a 43-month blockade, largely because of its global pre-eminence as a natural gas exporter.

However, it is the Kingdom, and not the Emirate, which eventually initiated the process of rapprochement, a climb down attributed to changed regional circumstances.[15] Saudi Arabia regards its conflict with Qatar as a subset of Saudi-Iran proxy conflict. When the Trump administration's so-called "maximum pressure" policy against Iran failed to take punitive action against the 2019 drone attacks on key Saudi oil facilities, the Kingdom started doubting US security guarantees and initiated indirect and now direct talks (held on October 3, 2021) with Iran.[16] With the Biden administration planning to further drawdown its forces from West Asia and seeking a new Iran nuclear deal, Saudi Arabia led the GCC in restoring ties with Qatar, reflecting its revamped policy of building bridges even with arch-enemies, as it can no longer depend on distant friends to settle its feuds with permanent neighbours. Thus, the Thermidorian reaction has started to gradually give way to forces more amenable to Arab Spring revolutionaries.

INTERVENTION OF EXTRA-REGIONAL POWERS

The chaos ensuing in France following the beheading of Louis XVI in 1793 by the revolutionary forces alarmed the monarchist states around Europe. It also allowed Austria and Prussia to take advantage of the anarchy in France and send their forces into the country to grab territory.

We find similar military interventions by Turkey and Iran, two non-Arab Muslim states, into the Arab theatre following the outbreak and chaos caused by the Arab Spring. In fact, the excuse of religious affiliation has been exploited by these two peripheral states of the Arab region to revive their primeval geopolitical ambitions in West Asia. For the Arabs, the collective memory of Byzantine/Ottoman and Sassanid/Safavid oppression in history evokes a sense of existential threat to Arab identity, which was salvaged to a great extent by the people of the region through their independence movements in the 19th and 20th centuries. However, much like the invasion of Austria and Prussia into France following the revolution, the Arab world finds itself extremely vulnerable with military inroads made by neo-Islamist Turkey and Iran carving their spheres of influences in the Levant, Yemen and the Arab Maghreb (North Africa).

Since 2012, Iran is said to have sent in tens of thousands of its military personnel (particularly from its Quds Force) into the Levant on the pretext of clearing ISIS remnants in Syria and Iraq. Along with the Shi'ite fighters of Lebanese Hezbollah, these Iranian forces have taken direct combat roles in Syria. There are also US reports that Tehran is building a supposed 'land bridge' that links Tehran to the Mediterranean Sea, as it passes through the cities of Baghdad, Damascus and Beirut. "The regime continues to seek a corridor stretching from Iran's borders to the shores of the Mediterranean," claimed former US Secretary of State Mike Pompeo, "Iran wants this corridor to transport fighters and an advanced weapons system to Israel's doorsteps."[17] Former national security adviser, Ambassador John Bolton has also said on record: "Iran has established an arc of control from Iran through Iraq to Assad's regime in Syria to Hezbollah in Lebanon." This "invaluable geo-strategic position" he claimed enhances Tehran's ability to threaten Israel, Jordan, and US allies in the Persian Gulf.[18]

Initially dismissed as an implausible proposition, Western assessments began to change in the wake of increasing evidence to the contrary. By early 2018, there was a general consensus on the meaning of "land bridge," even though its significance was disputed. It was then understood as essentially three main road routes cutting through Iraq and Syria, ending at the Syrian coast, southern Lebanon and even Israel's border. However, since 2019, the 'land bridge' is being understood as a land corridor used for transporting people, resources and weaponry deep into Iranian-backed militias across various parts of the region.[19] In fact, the stretch of this corridor has extended further eastward with former Iranian foreign minister Mohammad Javad Zarif stating in December last year that the Iranian-trained militia Liwa Fatemiyoun, currently fighting in Syria, might be deployed to Afghanistan to help a future Afghan government with counter-terrorism operations.[20]

Many commentators liken Iran's 'land bridge' into the Levant and beyond,[21, 22] to the Achaemenid extension into the Mediterranean, as well as its growing sway over West Asia as reminiscent of Parthian and Sassanid hegemony over the region. But more than the 'land bridge' or 'corridor to the Mediterranean," Iran has developed over the decades a worldwide conglomeration of proxies, surrogates and partners, now known as the Iran Threat Network (ITN). The main posterchild of this enterprise is Lebanese Hezbollah, which by itself maintains a global outreach with operatives active in several countries across the globe, from Western countries, central Africa, Latin America and even Southeast Asian countries. The ITN also has groups trained and supported by the Islamic Revolutionary Guard Corps (IRGC) and the elite Quds Force and include the Houthis in Yemen, the Shi'ite militias (part of the Popular Mobilisation Forces) and the Afghan and Pakistan Shia militant groups—Liwa Fatemiyoun and Liwa Zainebiyoun battalions.[23]

Today, the ITN is said to be a key pillar of Iranian grand strategy, its most effective means of force projection. Thus, Iran is able to wield tremendous influence far from its borders to hurt the vital interests of its adversaries. Iran's revolutionary and revisionist outlook also gets a fillip from its version of Shiite Islamism—borne out of Ayatollah Khomeini's doctrine of *Vilayat-e-Faqih* (Guardianship of the Islamic Jurist) as well as Shi'ite millenarianism that envisions the coming of the Awaited Mahdi to liberate Jerusalem.

However, Iran's imperial revisionism in the region finds its match in the indomitable leadership of President Recep Tayyip Erdoğan of Turkey. In 1923, the fall of the Ottoman empire and the establishment of the modern Turkish state, came about with the signing of the Treaty of Lausanne. Following this treaty, Turkey oriented itself towards gaining a European identity. However, Turkey's failure in being accepted as member of the European Union brought in the rule of the Islamist AKP by the turn of the millennium. Over the last 15 years, Turkish government under Erdoğan has drifted away from the spirit of the Treaty of Lausanne in an attempt to revive a pre-Kemalist Ottoman outlook, showing greater interest in its Islamic identity and making more ingress in the affairs of West Asia and North Africa.[24]

For instance, in 2020 itself, the Turkish government converted the historic Hagia Sophia into a mosque, meddled with Greece in the Mediterranean waters, insulted the French president over his counter-terrorism policies, launched a military offensive in support of Azerbaijan in its war with Armenia over the Nagorno-Karabakh region. It also backed Islamist GNA coalition fighting Egypt-backed Haftar forces, continued its military incursions into Iraq and Syria, hobnobbed with Hamas and Islamic Jihad in Palestinian territories, backed Pakistan premier's vitriol against India, and spurred its business and media campaigns in countries of Central Asia and Central Africa.

Erdoğan's maverick policies seem to have antagonised not only its erstwhile allies, the US and Israel, as he seems to be foregoing its NATO commitments and pursuing his own plans at variance with Western interests, but it has also emerged as threat to Russia and Iran, following his support for Azerbaijan in the Nagorno Karabakh conflict.

Iran, in particular, has been incensed by Erdoğan's participation in the Azerbaijan victory celebrations over the 'liberation' of Nagorno Karabakh from Armenia, where he recited a line from the controversial Azeri poem 'Aras', thus "They tore the Aras [River] and filled it with rocks and sticks / I will not be separated from you. They have separated us forcibly."[25] Tehran took exception to Erdoğan's recitation with its foreign ministry issuing a harsh warning. Both the Iranian government and its media found the recitation an attempt to arouse Azeri-Turkish nationalist to foment separatism among the restive Azeri population of Iran. Interestingly, the editor-in-chief of Iranian daily *Sazandegi*, Mohammad Kuchani, reacted to Erdoğan's recitation thus: "As an Iranian, I believe that the only answer to neo-Ottomanism is 'neo-Safavism.' [I am not advocating] reviving the Safavi rule (which made many mistakes), but [reviving] a reformed [version of it] and reviving its heritage in the modern age, just as Erdogan shifted from Ottomanism to 'new' Ottomanism."[26]

It is noteworthy that throughout recorded history, Ionian and Persian rulers have fought legendary wars against each other to carve out their empires across much of West Asia—an archetypical rivalry which harks back to the Achaemenid conquests of Cyrus and Darius, followed by the Alexandrian victory over Persia, the Byzantine-Sassanid wars and the Ottoman-Safavid hostilities.

Therefore, the Russia-backed Turkey-Iran cooperation brought about by the Astana talks in 2017 is already starting to burst at the seams, with both countries objecting to each other's actions in Syria, Azerbaijan and other places. The rivalry is in fact quite old and bitter in that it is believed that Iran's conversion from majority Sunni Islam to Shi'ism was the result of the Safavid dynasty's (1507-1722) opposition to their Ottoman overlords, which led to such extreme animosity that Safavid Iran broke away and forged a different sectarian identity for itself.[27, 28]

NEW POPULAR REVOLTS AND REFORMS

Revolutions espousing major socio-political change initially face a strong resistance from the established power structures and may even go through severe setbacks like the French Revolution in the decades following its first outbreak. However, if there is continued resonance of their core messages among the masses and the major causes for the public unrest remain unaddressed for a long time, the resuscitation of the revolts becomes inevitable.

Therefore, it is simply too early to close the book on the Arab Spring. In the words of Nadim Shehadi,[29] the definition of the Arab Spring is not related to spring as a season, but to a metal coil. He writes, "The more pressure that is placed on a spring, the more tension is built up inside it and the higher it will jump when the pressure is released." In fact, it appears that the impact of jihadist terror (as mentioned above) and the 'Thermidors Reaction' are on the decline and popular revolts like those seen in the Arab Spring are making a comeback.

Over the last two years, popular revolts have erupted in Iraq, Lebanon, Sudan, Algeria and other countries. Most of these revolts have sought to rise above petty sectarian and ethnic divisions and seek systemic political changes in the interest of their countries. The youth seem to be more strategic in their methods of revolt than some of their radical predecessors. Meanwhile, the causes for a revolution are still to be found in demographics, social and economic injustice, and in the repression of free speech and political rights. In the words of Ellen Laipson and Mona Yacoubian: "...despite the setbacks, we may come to see the Arab Spring as a turning point of more strategic consequence than appreciated at the time."[30]

The Arab Spring may have deposed the long-time presidents of four states, but it barely touched the monarchs of West Asia. Through a variety of measures—including aid packages and development projects, brutal crackdowns and repression of civil liberties, support for counter-revolutions in neighbouring states and introduction of piecemeal social and political reforms (like allowing women to drive and opening up entertainment sectors in Saudi Arabia), the monarchies seem to have diffused public resentment against them thus far.

However, the growing aspirations of an increasingly youth bulge seeking better economic avenues and sociopolitical freedoms is putting pressure on many of these regimes as they face a post-oil future. The drawdown of Western forces from West Asia has put a greater strain on the security architecture for Gulf monarchies and the socio-economic disruptions caused by the ongoing COVID pandemic have come as an added burden. With the US administration engaging Iran in a bid to revive the erstwhile nuclear deal, the spilling over of violence from conflict-ridden failed states like Yemen, Syria and Iraq into Gulf states, the sense of insecurity among the monarchies is only increasing by the day.

Thus, the forces unleashed by the Arab Spring continue to be a clear and present danger for the stability of entrenched status quo states, as sympathies for the principles of the uprisings still resonate among large sections of restive populations as well as the international community. The analogy of the French Revolution running its full course over several decades before fully realising its democratic ideals may still come true for the Arab Spring uprisings as they have the potential of becoming full-fledged systemic revolutions. The sense of legitimacy even for Gulf monarchies and other status quo regimes in West Asia has significantly eroded following the Arab Spring revolts and the time for the revolution to manifest again seems more likely now than it did when it first erupted after the self-immolation of Tunisian street vendor Mohamed Bouazizi in Ben Arouz on 17 December 2010.

NOTES

1. Asher Susser, "The 'Arab Spring': Competing Analytical Paradigms," *Bustan: The Middle East Book Review* 3, no. 2, Penn State University Press, 2012, pp. 109-30, at https://doi.org/10.1163/18785328-00032002.
2. Jessica S Johnson et al. "The Nimrud Rescue Project," *Studies in Conservation* 65 (sup 1; 2020): pp. 160-65.
3. Rafe Blaufarb,"The French Revolution: The Birth of European Popular Democracy?" *Comparative Studies in Society and History* 37, no. 3, [Society for Comparative Studies in Society and History, Cambridge University Press], 1995, pp. 608-18, at http://www.jstor.org/stable/179222 (accessed on October 15, 2021).
4. Egas Moniz Bandeira, 'Between Chaos and Liberty: Chinese Uses of the French Revolution of 1789,' i*n book*: *Alternative Representations of the Past*: The *Politics of History in Modern China* (De Gruyter, Berlin, 2020): 119-148,
5. *Larbi Sadiki*, 'En passant in Jordan: The king's dilemma,' *Al Jazeera English, February 29, 2012, at* https://www.aljazeera.com/opinions/2012/2/29/en-passant-in-jordan-the-kings-dilemma/ (accessed on October 15, 2021).
6. Crane Brinton, *The Anatomy of Revolution* (New York: Random House Inc., 1965).
7. Kevin McDonald, "ISIS jihadis aren't medieval-They're shaped by modern western philosophy,' September 9, 2014, *The Guardian*, at https://www.theguardian.com/commentisfree/2014/sep/09/isis-jihadi-shaped-by-modern-western-philosophy (accessed on October 19, 2021).
8. Global Terrorism Index 2020, Measuring the Impact of Terrorism, Institute for Economics and Peace, November 2020, at https://www.visionofhumanity.org/wp-content/uploads/2020/11/GTI-2020-web-1.pdf (accessed on October 22, 2021).
9. Andrew Hanna and Garret Nada, 'Jihadism: A Generation After 9/11,' Wilson Center, September 10, 2020, https://www.wilsoncenter.org/article/jihadism-generation-after-911 (accessed on October 23, 2021).
10. Adam Goldman, Eric Schmitt, Farnaz Fassihi and Ronen Bergman, 'Al-Qaeda's Abu Muhammad Al Masri Secretly Killed in Iran,' *The New York Times*, November 27, 2020, https://www.nytimes.com/2020/11/13/world/middleeast/al-masri-abdullah-qaeda-dead.html (accessed on October 23, 2021).

11. Nabih Boulos, 'For the Taliban, A Victory. For Other Jihadis, An Inspiration,' *Los Angeles Times*, August 17, 2021, at https://www.latimes.com/world-nation/story/2021-08-17/jihadi-renaissance (accessed on October 26, 2021).
12. Pitirim Sorokin, *The Sociology Of Revolution* (Philadelphia : J.B. Lippincott, 1925).
13. 'Doha's Actions Might Destabilise the Region: Saudi Minister,' *Newsweek*, September 10, 2017, at Doha's Actions May Destabilize the Region: Saudi Minister—NewsWeek Me (accessed on November 2, 2021).
14. 'The Ultimatum Facing Qatar: What are the Demands?,' *Euronews*, August 4, 2017, at https://www.euronews.com/2017/07/04/the-ultimatum-facing-qatar-what-are-the-demands (accessed on November 7, 2021).
15. Kristian Coates Ulrichsen, 'Analysis: Has the Gulf reconciled after the Qatar Conflict?,' Al Jazeera, June 5, 2021, at https://www.aljazeera.com/features/2021/6/5/has-the-gulf-reconciled-after-the-end-of-the-qatar-blockade (accessed on November 8, 2021).
16. 'Saudi confirms first round of talks with Iran Government,' *Reuters*, October 3, 2021, at https://www.reuters.com/world/middle-east/saudi-confirms-first-round-talks-with-new-iranian-government-2021-10-03/ (accessed on November 11, 2021).
17. 'After the Deal, A New Iran Strategy,' May 21, 2018, The Heritage Foundation, at https://www.heritage.org/defense/event/after-the-deal-new-iran-strategy (accessed on November 11, 2021).
18. Paul Sonne and Missy Ryan, 'Bolton: U.S. forces will stay in Syria until Iran and its proxies depart,' *The Washington Post*, September 24, 2018, at https://www.washingtonpost.com/world/national-security/bolton-us-forces-will-stay-in-syria-until-iran-and-its-proxies-depart/2018/09/24/be389eb8-c020-11e8-92f2-ac26fda68341_story.html (accessed on November 14, 2021).
19. Tyler Kotler, 'How Iran's Land Bridge Threatens the Entire Middle East,' August 1, 2019, at https://honestreporting.com/iran-land-bridge-threat-israel-middle-east/ (accessed on November 14, 2021).
20. Colin P. Clarke, 'Trends in Terrorism: What's on the Horizon in 2021,' January 5, 2021, at https://www.fpri.org/article/2021/01/trends-in-terrorism-whats-on-the-horizon-in-2021/ (accessed on November 21, 2021).
21. Eliora Katz, 'The Old and New Persian Empires,' *Newsweek*, May 28, 2020, at https://www.newsweek.com/old-new-persian-empires-opinion-1507202 (accessed on November 21, 2021).
22. Emil Avdaliani, 'Iran and the New Land Corridor,' The Begin-Sadat Center for Strategic Studies, December 19, 2017, at https://besacenter.org/perspectives-papers/iran-land-corridor/#:~:text=This%20was%20a%20momentous%20event,Achaemenid%20Empire%20in%20330%20BC.&text=It%20means%20that%20at%20long,through%20to%20the%20Mediterranean%20coast (accessed on December 1, 2021).
23. Ariane M. Tabatabai, 'Iran Seeks to Cement Legitimacy of Shia Militias,' The Foreign Policy Research Institute, May 10, 2019, at https://www.fpri.org/article/2019/05/iran-seeks-to-cement-legitimacy-of-shia-militias/ (accessed on December 1, 2021).

24. Claude Salhani, 'Is Erdogan out to Undo the Treaty of Lausanne?,' *The Arab Weekly*, March 22, 2020, at https://thearabweekly.com/erdogan-out-undo-treaty-lausanne-0 (accessed on December 3, 2021).
25. A. Savyon and M. Manzour, 'Anti-Turkey Statements in Iran—Part III: Erdogan is Undermining Iran's Territorial Integrity,' MEMRI, January 11, 2021, at https://www.memri.org/reports/anti-turkey-statements-iran-%E2%80%93-part-iii-erdo%C4%9Fan-undermining-irans-territorial-integrity (accessed on December 3, 2021).
26. Ibid.
27. See Nikkie R Keddie, *Modern Iran: Roots and Results of Revolution* (Yale University Press, 2006).
28. Rula Abisaab, *Converting Persia: Religion and Power in the Safavid Empire* (IB Tauris, 2015).
29. Nadim Shehadi, 'Learning the Lessons of the Coiled Arab Spring,' *Arab News*, March 11, 2021, at https://www.arabnews.com/node/1823906 (accessed on December 7, 2021).
30. Ellen Lapison and Mana Yacoubian, 'The Living Legacy of the Arab Spring,' *DAWN (Democracy for the Arab World Now)*, July 26, 2021, at https://dawnmena.org/the-living-legacy-of-the-arab-spring/ (accessed on December 7, 2021).

SELECT FURTHER READINGS

Abdo, Geneive. *The New Sectarianism: The Arab Uprisings and the Rebirth of the Shi'a-Sunni Divide*. Oxford: Oxford University Press, 2017.

Al Rasheed, Madawi. *Muted Modernists: The Struggle Over Divine Politics in Saudi Arabia*. London: Oxford University Press, 2015.

Al-Musawi, Muhsin J. *Arabic Poetry: Trajectories of Modernity and Tradition*. Oxon: Routledge, 2006.

Alsaikhan, Abdullah. *Social Media During Arab Spring in Egypt and Tunisia*. Virginia, VA: Virginia State University, 2019.

Ashwarya, Sujata and Mujib Alam, eds. *The Arab Spring: Ten Years On*. Berlin, London: Gerlach Press, 2022.

Aspden, Rachel. *Generation Revolution: How the Arab Spring Has Changed the Lives of Ordinary People in Egypt*. New York: Other Press, 2016.

Baumann, Hannes. *Citizen Hariri: Lebanon's Neo-Liberal Reconstruction*. Oxford: Oxford University Press, 2016.

Bayat, Asef. *Revolutionary Life: The Everyday of the Arab Spring*. Cambridge: Harvard University Press, 2021.

Brancati, Dawn. *Democracy Protests: Origins, Features, and Significance*. Cambridge: Cambridge University Press, 2016.

Brandt, Marieke. *Tribes and Politics in Yemen: A History of the Houthi Conflict*. Hurst and Company: London, 2017.

Brinton, Crane. *The Anatomy of Revolution*. New York: Random House Inc., 1965.

Brownlee, Jason, Tarek Masoud, and Andrew Reynolds. *The Arab Spring: Pathways of Repression and Reform*. Oxford: Oxford University Press, 2015.

Burns, Sean. *Revolts and the Military in the Arab Spring: Popular Uprisings and the Politics of Repression*. London & New York: I.B. Tauris, 2018.

Byman, D. "Sectarianism Afflicts the New Middle East." *Survival* 56, no. 1, (2014).

Cerny, Karol. *Instability in the Middle East: Structural Changes and Uneven Modernisation 1950-2015*. Prague: Charles University in Prague, Karolinum Press, 2017.

Cockburn, Patrick. *The Rise of Islamic State: ISIS and the New Sunni Jihadism*. London: Verso, 2016.

Dabashi, Hamid. *The Arab Spring: The End of Postcolonialism*. London and New York: Zed Books, 2012.

Dacrema, Eugenio and Valeria Talbot. eds. *Rebuilding Syria: The Middle East's Next Power Game?* Milano: ISPI, 2019.

Davis, John, ed. *The Arab Spring and Arab Thaw: Unfinished Revolutions and the Quest for Democracy*. London & New York: Routledge, 2016.

De Smet, B. *Gramsci on Tahrir: Revolution and Counter-revolution in Egypt*. London: Pluto Press, 2016.

Dziekan, Marek M. "Writers and Poets as the Forecasters of the Arab Revolution of 2011." *Rocznik Orientalistyczny/Yearbook of Oriental Studies* LXIX, no. 2 (2016).

El Alaoui, Khadija. "Chanting Tahreer and Compassion: People as Poetry", In *Tensions Journal* 5 (Fall/Winter 2011).

El Issawi, Fatima, and Francesco Cavatorta, ed. *The Unfinished Arab Spring: Micro-Dynamics of Revolts Between Change and Continuity*. London: Gingko Library, 2020.

El-Hasan, Hasan Afif. *Killing the Arab Spring*. New York: Algora Publishing, 2019.

Erdogan, Ayfer. *Arab Spring-Arab Fall: Divergent Transitions in Post-2011 Tunisia and Egypt*. New York: Lexington Books, 2021.

Falk, Richard. "Rethinking the Arab Spring: uprisings, counterrevolution, chaos and global reverberations." *Third World Quarterly* 37, issue 12 (2016): 2322-2334.

Feldman, Noah. *The Arab Winter: A Tragedy*. Princeton & Oxford: Princeton University Press, 2021.

Feldman, Noah. *The Arab Winter: A Tragedy*. Princeton, NJ: Princeton University Press, 2020.

Fraihat, Ibrahim and Taha Yaseen. "Evolving Trends in the Post-Arab Spring Era: Implications for Peace and Stability in the MENA Region." *Journal of Peacebuilding & Development* 15, no. 03, (2020).

Freer, Courtney Jean. *Rentier Islamism: The Influence of the Muslim Brotherhood in the Gulf Monarchies*. Oxford: Oxford University Press, 2018.

Gelvin, James L. *The Arab Uprisings: What Everyone Needs to Know*. Oxford: Oxford University Press, 2015.

Gerges, Fawaz A. *Contentious Politics in the Middle East: Popular Resistance and Marginalized Activism Beyond the Arab Uprisings*. New York: Palgrave Macmillan, 2015.

Guzansky, Yoel. *The Arab Gulf States and Reform in the Middle East: Between Iran and the "Arab Spring"*. London: Palgrave Macmillan, 2015.

Haas, Mark L., and David W. Lesch, eds. *The Arab Spring: The Hope and Reality of the Uprisings*. New York & London: Routledge, 2018.

Hashemi, Nader. "The Arab Spring Two Years On: Reflections on Dignity, Democracy and Devotion." *Ethics and International Affairs* 27, issue 2 (May 2013).

Hassan, Farhad. *The Arab Spring in Egypt: The Role of Social Media*. Beau Bassin: Scholars' Press, 2020.

Heidarpour, Mashallah. "Syria Crisis and a New Political Agenda for China: Changes or Continuity?" *Middle East Political Review* 4, no. 1-2 (2015).

Heinze, Marie-Christine. *Yemen and the Search for Stability Power: Politics and Society after the Arab Spring*. I.B. Tauris: London, 2018.

Hinnebusch, Raymond and Özlem Tür, eds. *Turkey-Syria Relations: Between Enmity and Amity*. New York: Routledge, 2013.

Hinnebusch, Raymond and Tina Zintl. *Syria from Reform to Revolt: Political Economy and International Relation*, Vol. 1, New York: Syracuse University Press, 2015.

Houlden, Gordon and Noureddin M. Zaamout. *A New Great Power Engages with the Middle East: China's Middle East Balancing Approach*. Canada: China Institute, University of Alberta, 2019.

Hughes, Geraint Alun. "Syria and the perils of Proxy war." *Small Wars and Insurgencies* 25, No. 3, July 1, 2014.

Jumet, Kira D. *Contesting the Repressive State: Why Ordinary Egyptians Protested During the Arab Spring*. New York: Oxford University Press, 2018.

Karakoç, Jülide, ed. *Authoritarianism in the Middle East: Before and After the Arab Uprisings*. Palgrave Macmillan: London, 2015.

Ketchley, Neil. *Egypt in a Time of Revolution: Contentious Politics and the Arab Spring*. Cambridge: Cambridge University Press, 2017.

Khatib, Lina. *Image Politics in the Middle East: The Role of the Visual in Political Struggle*. London: I.B. Taurus, 2013.

Khosrokhavar, Farhad. *The New Arab Revolutions that Shook the World*. Boulder, CO and London; Paradigm Publishers, 2012.

Kiyici, Hakan. "Yemen in the International Security Agenda: The Context of Tribalism, Sectarianism, and Intervention." *Insight Turkey* 22, no. 1 (Winter 2020): 238-240.

Koch, Bettina, and Yannis A. Stivachtis, eds. *Regional Security in the Middle East*. E-International Relations Publishing, 2019.

Kücükasci, Ebrar Sahika. *Saudi Arabia Under Mohammed bin Salman: Crisis, Reform or Stagnation*, Discussion Paper, TRT World Research Center, 2019.

Lesch, David. *Syria: Fall of the House of Assad*. New Heaven: Yale University Press, 2012.

Lister, Charles. *The Syrian Jihad: Al-Qaeda, the Islamic State and the Evolution of an Insurgency*. Oxford: Oxford University Press, 2015.

Lynch, March, ed. *The Arab Uprisings Explained: New Contentious Politics in the Middle East Explained.* Columbia University Press, 2014.

Madawi Al-Rasheed, *Salman's Legacy: The Dilemmas of a New Era in Saudi Arabia.* Oxford & New York: Oxford University Press, 2018.

Makdisi, Ussama. "Understanding Sectarianism in the Middle East." *The Cairo Review of Global Affairs* (2017).

Mako, Shamiran, and Valentine M. Moghadam, *After the Arab Uprisings: Progress and Stagnation in the Middle East and North Africa*. Cambridge: Cambridge University Press, 2021.

Marcin Adamczyk, "The Islamic State as a Potential Threat to the National Security of the People's Republic of China." *Historia i Polityka* 37, no. 30 (2019).

Mason, Robert, ed. *The International Politics of the Arab Spring: Popular Unrest and Foreign Policy*. New York: Palgrave Macmillan, 2014.

Matthiesen, Toby. *Sectarian gulf: Bahrain, Saudi Arabia and the Arab Spring That Wasn't*. Stanford, California: Stanford Briefs, 2013.

Matthiesen, Toby. *The domestic sources of the Saudi foreign policy: Islamists and the state in the wake of the Arab Uprisings*, Working Paper (Washington DC: Brookings Institution), August 2015, 2.

Mohamed, Eid, and Ayman A. El-Desouky, eds. Cultural Production and Social Movements After the Arab Spring: Nationalism, Politics, and Transnational Identity. London: I.B. Tauris, 2021.

Mohamed, Eid, and Dalia Fahmy, Arab Spring: Modernity, Identity and Change. London: Palgrave Macmillan, 2020.

Napoleoni, Loretta. *The Islamist Phoenix: The Islamic State and the Redrawing of the Middle East*. New York: Seven Stories Press, 2014.

Oktav, Özden Zeynep, Emel Parlar Dal and Ali Murat Kurşun, eds. *Violent Non-State Actors and Syrian Civil War the ISIS and YPG Cases*. Zürich: Springer, 2018.

Ottaway, Marina, and David Ottaway. *A Tale of Four Worlds: The Arab Region After the Uprisings*. New York: Oxford University Press, 2019.

Rabbat, Nasser. "The Arab Revolution Takes Back the Public Space." *Critical Inquiry* 39, no. 1 (Autumn 2012): 198-208.

Rabi, Uzi. *The Return of the Past: State, Identity, and Society in the Post–Arab Spring Middle East*. Lexington Books: London, 2021.

Ramadan, Nada. "The Egyptian Contemporary Novel: A Survey of a Revolutionary Endeavour." *Al-Jadid Magazine* 17, no. 65.

Riphagen, Wladimir and Robbert A. F. L. Woltering. "Tales of a Square: The Production and Transformation of Political Space in the Egyptian (Counter) Revolution." *Arab Studies Quarterly* 40, no. 2 (Spring 2018).

Robinson, Heather M. *et al. Sectarianism in the Middle East: Implications for the United States*. Rand Arroyo Center Santa Monica Ca Santa Monica United States, 2018.

Sakr, Sherif. *The Arab "Spring" of Egypt*. Saarbrücken: Lap Lambert Academic Publishing, 2015.

Schulze, Reinhard. *A Modern History of the Islamic World*, translated by Azizeh Ozodi. London and New York: I.B. Tauris Publishers, 2002.

Sham, Naame. *Silent Sectarian Cleansing: The Iranian Role in Mass Demolitions and Population Transfers in Syria*. Naame Sham report, May 2015.

Stolleis, Friederike. *Playing the Sectarian Card Identities and Affiliations of Local Communities in Syria*, Friedrich-Ebert-Stiftung Beirut, 2015.

Suechika, Kota. "Strategies, Dynamics, and Outcomes of Hezbollah's Military Intervention in the Syrian Conflict." *Asian Journal of Middle Eastern and Islamic Studies* 12, no. 1 (2018).

Susser, Asher. "The 'Arab Spring': Competing Analytical Paradigms." *Bustan: The Middle East Book Review* 3, no. 2 (2012): 109-30.

Teti, Andrea, Pamela Abbott, and Francesco Cavatorta. *The Arab Uprisings in Egypt, Jordan and Tunisia: Social, Political and Economic Transformations*. London: Palgrave Macmillan, 2018.

Tragger, Eric. *Arab Fall: How the Muslim Brotherhood Won and Lost Egypt in 891 Days*. New York: Georgetown University Press, 2016.

Volpi, Frédéric, and James M. Jasper, ed. *Microfoundations of the Arab Uprisings: Mapping Interactions Between Regimes and Protesters*. Amsterdam: Amsterdam University Press, 2018.

Wahab, Hadi. "Syria's Sect-coded Conflict: From Hezbollah's Top-down Instrumentalization of Sectarian Identity to Its Candid Geopolitical Confrontation." *Contemporary Review of the Middle East* (2021).

Wilf, Einat. *The Battle for Hegemony in the Middle East*, ASIP Special Report. Barton: Australian Strategic Policy Institute, 2017.

Wolf, Anne. *Political Islam in Tunisia: The History of Ennahda*. Oxford and New York: Oxford University Press, 2017.

Yergin, Daniel. "The Oil Collapse: A Pandemic and a Price War Have Together Brought Energy Markets to a Crisis." *Foreign Affairs* (April 2, 2020).

Yeşiltaş, Murat, and Tuncay Kardaş, eds. *Non-state armed actors in the Middle East: Geopolitics, ideology, and strategy*. Springer, 2017.

Yildirim, A. Kadir. *Pluralism and Inclusion in post-2011 Kuwait*. Carnegie Corporation of New York and Rice University's Baker Institute for Public Policy, Houston, Texas, 2018.

Yossef, Amr, and Joseph Cerami. *The Arab Spring and the Geopolitics of the Middle East: Emerging Security Threats and Revolutionary Change*. London: Palgrave Macmillan, 2015.

INDEX